D1599335

What Is Constructionism?

Social Problems, Social Constructions

Joel Best and Scott R. Harris, series editors

What Is CONSTRUCTIONISM?

Navigating Its Use in Sociology

Scott R. Harris

LYNNE
RIENNER
PUBLISHERS

BOULDER
LONDON

Published in the United States of America in 2010 by
Lynne Rienner Publishers, Inc.
1800 30th Street, Boulder, Colorado 80301
www.rienner.com

and in the United Kingdom by
Lynne Rienner Publishers, Inc.
3 Henrietta Street, Covent Garden, London WC2E 8LU

Library of Congress Cataloging-in-Publication Data
Harris, Scott R., 1969 Sept. 16–
  What is constructionism? : navigating its use in sociology / Scott R. Harris.
     p.   cm. — (Social problems, social constructions)
  Includes bibliographical references and index.
  ISBN 978-1-58826-727-6 (alk. paper)
  1. Social constructionism. 2. Knowledge, Sociology of. I. Title.
  HM1093.H37 2010
  301.01—dc22
                                        2009031199

British Cataloguing in Publication Data
A Cataloguing in Publication record for this book
is available from the British Library.

Printed and bound in the United States of America

 The paper used in this publication meets the requirements
of the American National Standard for Permanence of
Paper for Printed Library Materials Z39.48-1992.

5 4 3 2 1

Contents

Preface   vii
Acknowledgments   xi

1 Introduction   1

2 Constructing Minds   27

3 Managing Emotions   47

4 Family Diversity   71

5 Creating Equal Marriages   87

6 Producing Social Inequality   107

7 Conclusion   131

Bibliography   143
Index   165
About the Book   169

Preface

Anyone who seeks a broad understanding of social constructionism has their work cut out for them. The constructionist perspective has been described, developed, and applied many thousands of times. There is a virtual ocean of publications to wade through, and the waters are muddy. This book provides one way to distinguish between the competing and often contradictory versions of "constructionism" that can be found in an ever-increasing number of books and articles. I hope to add a dose of clarity to the literature, but I do not intend to provide the only way to answer the question "What is constructionism?"

I used to say—in my classes or to anyone who would listen—that certain self-proclaimed "constructionist" authors were not *really* constructionists at all. In this book I present an argument that moves in what I think is a more helpful direction. I have resisted the urge to act as a "discourse cop" who tells others how they may or may not use particular analytical terms. Rather, my goal now is to understand how seemingly identical constructionist concepts can be put to divergent, yet justifiable, purposes.

The book's central thesis is that a rough distinction can be made between two forms of constructionist analysis—objective and interpretive. The difference hinges, as Ian Hacking (1999) might say, on what is being constructed. In objective analyses, what is constructed are real states of affairs; what is made or produced are actual behaviors, conditions, or entities. In more interpretive analyses, what is made or produced are meanings of those phenomena. Two scholars may study the same topics, using the same conceptual resources, citing identical theoretical foundations, and employing similar methodologies, yet compose reports that can vary dramatically along objective or interpretive lines.

Consider a simple piece of furniture: A chair can be said to be constructed in that it is a product of human labor. To exist as, when, and where it does, a chair must be designed, manufactured, marketed, sold, transported, and placed in its exact location of use. The presence and nature of the chair is not automatic but is the contingent outcome of numerous social processes. This is a very brief example of objective constructionism. An interpretive analysis would not necessarily disagree but would focus on the meaning of the "chair"—in quotation marks to highlight that the object's ontological status is no longer assumed. For an interpretive scholar, the meaning of a chair depends on the perspectives and purposes that people bring to it. A chair could be viewed or described as beautiful or ugly, expensive or cheap, cozy or uncomfortable—assuming it was defined as a place to sit. Alternatively, the "chair" could be viewed or described as a collection of atoms and molecules; as something to burn; as a commodity to sell; as something to climb on or (in some cases) to roll around on; as a defensive or offensive weapon; and so on. On many occasions, the chair might be barely noticed at all. Here the *meaning* of the chair is not automatic but is the contingent outcome of social processes.

At first glance the contrast between objective and interpretive constructionism is a simple one, but there are many complications. After all, the (objective) manufacturing of a chair does involve many matters of interpretation, such as how best to design and market it. And while a "chair" can be interpreted in many ways, its (objective) properties will likely resist being defined as nutritious food; moreover, some interpretive researchers might study the social factors that (objectively) influence why a chair is seen or described as "ugly" or as "a weapon." These sorts of complicated divergences and overlaps tend to recur in studies of crime, divorce, organizations, the self, and myriad other topics across the social sciences. This book will examine a sample of constructionist theory and research that emanates primarily, but not exclusively, from sociology.

The first chapter provides a general introduction and attempts to articulate the distinction between objective and interpretive constructionism. It takes practice to detect the subtle differences and similarities between the two camps, however. Exposure to a wide range of topics can help one identify the analytical tendencies and dilemmas that recur across disparate areas of inquiry. Thus, in Chapters 2–6, I attempt to demonstrate the use-

fulness of the objective/interpretive distinction by closely examining constructionist literature on five specific subjects: mind, emotions, family
diversity, marital equality, and social inequality. The seventh and final
chapter summarizes my argument and addresses questions that I anticipate
readers may have.

Acknowledgments

This book could not have been completed without the generous support I received from Saint Louis University in the form of a sabbatical leave, a provost leave, and a summer research award. I am also very grateful for the feedback and encouragement I received over the past few years from friends, relatives, colleagues, and reviewers, including (but not limited to) Gretchen Arnold, Mitch Berbrier, Joel Best, Ric Colignon, Jay Gubrium, Jenine Harris, Jim Holstein, and Dave Schweingruber. I also appreciate the library assistance provided by Sharilyn Bazile and Anastasia Kemp and the editorial guidance of Andrew Berzanskis.

1
Introduction

Social constructionism occupies a prominent place in sociology and the social sciences in general. Since the term was popularized by Peter Berger and Thomas Luckmann's 1966 book *The Social Construction of Reality,* a substantively, methodologically, and theoretically diverse array of scholars have conducted research under the general rubric of constructionism. These constructionists have made significant contributions to the study of deviance, social problems, social movements, the self, gender, race, education, health, emotions, family, and other areas. As a simple library search indicates, there is a large and growing number of sociological books and articles titled *The Social Construction of X* or simply *Constructing X* (see Best 2000; Hacking 1999; Spector and Kitsuse 1977). The list grows exponentially when one considers constructionist works that are not explicitly titled as such or that employ synonyms for constructing, such as assembling, building, crafting, fabricating, fashioning, forming, making, manufacturing, and producing. Terms that merely signal agency or creativity—accomplishing, becoming, discovering, doing, inventing, managing—are also popular concepts in constructionist titles and analyses. Constructionists enjoy gerunds. They use them to highlight the recurring processes (Prus 1996), strategies (Lofland 1976), and practices (Gubrium and Holstein 1997) through which people actively generate, maintain, and transform reality.

Not all commentators consider the proliferation of constructionist analyses to be an entirely positive development, however. Philosopher and social theorist Ian Hacking (1999) has suggested that there is a great deal of vague thinking and superficial "bandwagon jumping" in these ostensibly constructionist analyses (see also Hollander and Gordon 2006). David Maines (2001, 2003) has argued that the adjective

1

constructionist too often serves as an empty rhetorical device, as virtually all sociological analyses rest on the assumption that social life is somehow "constructed."

The concept of "constructing" is too entrenched and important to be dispensed with, however. What is needed is not the dismissal of that metaphor but more precise, careful, and self-conscious applications of it in authors' works. Constructionists need to specify their particular brands of constructionism. Readers, too, could bring more critical and discerning mind-sets to constructionist research.

Whereas others have dealt with the intellectual history and philosophical foundations of constructionism (Best 2008; Weinberg 2008), this book focuses on two general forms of constructionism that are most frequently confused in the literature: *objective social constructionism* (OSC) and *interpretive social constructionism* (ISC). These are not currently accepted terms, but I believe they are helpful in distinguishing two dominant and competing (if only implicit) uses of the constructionist perspective.

This distinction between OSC and ISC is at first glance relatively simple to understand. Yet its implications are broad, and many complexities appear upon closer inspection. Interpretive and objective constructionists may use almost identical language to advance very different arguments. At the same time, there are overlapping concerns between the two approaches, and there can be intricate connections between the processes and outcomes of the interpretive and objective construction of social life (see Gubrium and Holstein 1997; Hacking 1999; Loseke 1999).

Interpretive Social Constructionism

Interpretive social constructionism is frankly what I consider the more radical form of constructionism. It has roots in a number of diverse traditions, especially pragmatism, symbolic interactionism, phenomenology, and ethnomethodology.[1] Other orientations and developments, such as narrative analysis, cognitive sociology, semiotic sociology, and postmodernism also sometimes derive from and contribute to what might be called the interpretive constructionist movement.[2]

Although these approaches are sometimes difficult to define and compare, and are by no means equivalent, it is possible to identify some fairly common themes. I begin by focusing on one in particular. For many scholars, the core principle of ISC is the idea that "the meaning of things is not inherent." This assumption is reflected in Herbert Blumer's

(1969, pp. 2–6) fundamental premises of symbolic interactionism, in which he argues that meanings are created, learned, used, and revised in social interaction. All objects—"objects" being cows, chairs, actions, selves, social problems, decades, or anything else that can be referred to—derive their meaning from the purposes and perspectives that people bring to them (Blumer 1969; Mead 1934). Alfred Schutz's (1964, p. 227) phenomenological sociology also presumes the "ambivalence of the meaning of all social phenomena," as does the ethnomethodological argument that descriptions "reflexively" constitute the situations they appear to report about—even as those descriptions "indexically" derive their sense from the circumstances surrounding their use (Coulon 1995, p. 23; Heritage 1984, p. 140).

Similarly, when Berger and Luckmann (1966) initially formulated the social constructionist project, the issue of meaning was central to it. Their goal was to expand the sociology of knowledge—previously preoccupied with abstract ideas, philosophies, and the like—to the realm of everyday life:

> The sociology of knowledge must first of all concern itself with what people "know" as "reality" in their everyday, non- or pre-theoretical lives. In other words, commonsense "knowledge" . . . must be the central focus. . . . It is precisely this "knowledge" that constitutes the fabric of meanings without which no society could exist. The sociology of knowledge, therefore, must concern itself with the social construction of reality. (Berger and Luckmann 1966, p. 15)

Their frequent use (including scare quotes) of the terms "knowledge" and "reality" indicate that Berger and Luckmann were taking a highly relativistic stance toward issues of truth. What is "constructed," in their initial formulation of the constructionist perspective, was first and foremost the meaning of things.

For interpretive constructionists, the premise "meaning is not inherent" applies to everything. Although there may be some limits to what humans can get away with—for example, a chair usually cannot be eaten as food and others may sanction an individual for trying—there are always many purposes and perspectives that people can bring to things that interest them. What is taken to be a simple chair could be used as a strange weapon, as something to stand on, as something to burn or to sell, and so on (Blumer 1969, p. 69). It might be viewed or described as beautiful or ugly or plain, as cheap or expensive or moderately priced, as an ordinary seat or a place of honor. A chair might be vaguely noticed but deemed irrelevant. And what holds for such a relatively simple and non-

controversial item of experience also holds for more complex and contentious examples. A war, a political leader, tattoos, animal cruelty, home-
lessness—the meaning of these and everything else is contingent on the
actions of people, who must supply classifications, interpretations, and
narratives to make sense of them.

Whole schools of interpretive constructionist thought have been
founded on or at least inspired by the idea that meaning is not inherent. ISC studies of self-identity often hinge on the assumption that
"who we are" is a socially created idea, negotiated in interaction
(Gubrium and Holstein 2001; Vryan, Adler, and Adler 2003). ISC studies of deviance frequently assume that no behavior or personal attribute is inherently deviant, that people's actions and appearance must be
defined as deviant to be seen that way (Becker 1973, p. 9; Herman-
Kinney 2003; but see also Pollner's [1987] critique of Becker). ISC
studies of family are sometimes premised on the idea that "family" can
be defined in a number of different ways, that no set of social bonds
are inherently familial or nonfamilial, and that there are no incon-
testable versions of what is going on in any particular family relationship (Gubrium and Holstein 1990; Knapp 1999, 2002). ISC studies of
social problems regularly assume that no social issue is troubling
exactly as someone says it is, that interpretive claimsmaking gives
order to indeterminate states of affairs (Blumer 1971; Schneider 1985;
Spector and Kitsuse 1977).

Thus, ISC analyses tend to assume or argue that social phenomena
are *interpreted* entities whose existence and qualities are dependent in
large part on people's meaning-making practices. Human beings are
construction workers in the sense that they create (or assemble, build,
manufacture) meaning. Just as there is virtually always more than one
way to build something, there is virtually always more than one way to
define something. ISC scholars usually argue or assume that a particular
understanding of "X" is not the only understanding possible, that what is
taken as the "truth" of the matter depends on people's agendas and orientations. Everything can be seen or described or used in different ways.
Interpretation is not a completely spontaneous or random process, however. It is guided by material and conceptual resources at individuals'
disposal and conditioned by social and physical constraints (Gubrium
and Holstein 1997, chap. 8).

Again, this one simple yet profound theme—meaning is not inherent—
is arguably the core principle of interpretive social constructionism.
There are many other ideas associated with ISC, but all of them tend to
cohere around the creation of meaning as the central guiding concern.

Interpretive constructionists believe that researchers ought to study the meanings people live by and how those meanings are created. They are wary of methodologies and approaches that lead researchers to impose meanings onto those they study, rather than investigating meanings (Blumer 1969). They are not principally concerned with discovering what things "really" mean in order to dispel myths or correct misunderstandings (Berger and Luckmann 1966, p. 12). They try to suspend belief *and* disbelief in reality (Schutz 1970) in order to examine how meaning and reality are produced by and for members of various social settings (Garfinkel 1967).

Objective Social Constructionism

Objective social constructionism is different from what I have just described. Although important and useful, OSC arguments do not focus on the creation of meaning, or at least not to the extent that ISC arguments do.[3] For OSC analyses, what are made, built, or assembled are not interpretations but (for lack of a better phrase) real states of affairs. As a result, OSC arguments can be made without necessarily attending so much to what things mean to actors and the intricate processes through which those diverse meanings are created; OSC arguments can be made without suspending belief in the existence of the world as the analyst sees it.

OSC has roots in a broad range of sociological perspectives, too diverse and numerous to specify beyond the examples I provide later. Moreover, many scholars who take an interpretive constructionist approach to some issues take an objective constructionist approach to other issues, even in the same report. ISC and OSC analyses are often interwoven in complex and even contradictory ways. But to put it simply: OSC deals with the creation of "real things" as opposed to "meanings." Consequently, OSC is reflected in any arguments that suggest that real social phenomena (e.g., actual family relationships vs. interpretations of putative relationships) are produced by the actions of individual actors and groups, by constraining social forces, by the operations of class, race, gender, politics, or religion, and so on. Culture and interpretation may play a role in an OSC analysis, but only insofar as these issues can be put to use in a more standard sociological account of what is really going on and why it is happening. For example, authors who identify "self-fulfilling prophecies" often incorporate an element of interpretation into their analyses, but they may do so within a framework that takes for granted the meaning of virtually everything in order to enter debates over the real causes of social behavior (e.g., Watzlawick 2006). In the hands of somewhat more interpretive scholars, arguments about self-fulfilling prophecies may occupy an ambiguous middle ground between objective and interpretive constructionism (e.g., Loseke 1999, pp. 167–168). But again, simply put, objective constructionists argue that something is "socially constructed" when a real phenomenon (as opposed to an interpretation or meaning) derives its existence or its dimensions from other social factors.

When Maines (2003) argues that all sociology is constructionist, it is largely OSC that he has in mind:

> Sociology's fundamental domain proposition is that some combination of social things cause or are related to some other combination of social things. Insert whatever variables, factors, elements, or "constructed social realities" one wants, and the proposition holds. Parents influence their children through communication; inner-city schools disadvantage inner-city students; unemployment goes up when the economy shrinks; mobility opportunities are lower at the top and bottom of class systems; personal identities are expressed through narratives; divorce tends to have an array of negative effects on the children of divorced parents; and electronic and visual media technologies tend to give the capitalist class an advantage. We all know that [all of these factors] have been historically created and that they undergo change in different ways and at different rates, and that even some of them (e.g., television, cities, capitalism, schools) at one time did not exist at all. (p. 16)

This statement leans heavily toward the OSC side of the OSC/ISC continuum. The phrase "personal identities are expressed through narratives" seems potentially interpretive-constructionist, as long as the verb "expressed" is read in a meaningmaking way. Most of the other examples in Maines's list refer to the objective construction of social life—that is, to the creation of real states of affairs through the operation of various social forces. If this is social constructionism, then sociology truly is thoroughly constructionist and has been since its inception. Sociologists always have and probably always will try to explain *why things occur as they do.* However, this form of analysis overlaps with, but is far from identical to, the ISC focus on *how things are defined as they are.*

Take Maines's examples that "inner-city schools disadvantage inner-city students" and that "divorce tends to have an array of negative effects on the children of divorced parents." These kinds of arguments may employ verbs that imply a constructionist analysis—as in *manufacturing* students' careers, the social *creation* of children's experiences, or perhaps the *making* of delinquents. But this is fairly standard social-scientific thinking and is certainly *not* what rigorously interpretive scholars would call "constructionist." An ISC scholar would more likely focus on how these issues are interpretively constituted—that is, given meaning. For example, a social problems constructionist in the tradition of Malcolm Spector and John Kitsuse (1977) would study the different claims that are made about the issue of inner-city schools. The researcher would examine the diverse meanings that various claims-makers create as they proffer competing interpretations of the putative problem at hand, the supposed causes and effects of the problem, the suggested solutions to the problem, and so on. An ISC scholar would study how narratives—those told by everyday folk as well as by OSC scholars—create meaning by making assertions about actors, motives, conditions, causes, effects, and remedies.

Certainly, an ISC scholar may be tempted to argue that meaningmaking can lead to real, observable changes in a society. This type of argument has been a feature of ISC and OSC thought for decades. It takes us back to the middle ground I mentioned with respect to self-fulfilling prophecies. Blumer's first premise of interactionism ("People act based on what things mean to them") and William I. Thomas's oft-cited theorem ("If people define things as real, they are real in their consequences") both imply a simultaneous concern with meaning and with objective reality. Berger and Luckmann (1966, p. 91) also encouraged analyses that considered the dialectical relationship between what people do and what they think. Controversies over constructionists' selective relativism (Best 2003; Ibarra and Kitsuse 2003; Woolgar and Pawluch 1985) and solutions such as "analytical bracketing" (Holstein and Gubrium 2003) in large part also point to the ambiguous overlaps and "interactions" (Hacking 1999, p. 31; see also Loseke 1999, chaps. 6–7) between what I am calling objective and interpretive constructionism.

My first priority in this chapter is not to clarify the ambiguous middle ground between ISC and OSC. Instead, my main goal is to describe these two forms of sociological constructionism in a somewhat stark but clear manner, so that the differences between them can be appreciated. I want to reach a broad audience with a simple point: More sociologists need to recognize that the exact same constructionist language can be used in (at least) two very different kinds of analyses. Only then, once a clear image of each approach is apprehended, might readers better trace the complex moves that researchers sometimes make as they combine or alternate between one form of analysis and the other.

Objective and Interpretive Constructionism: Common Vocabularies, Different Arguments

In this section, I further explain the difference between OSC and ISC by focusing on the vocabulary that analysts use in parallel but conflicting fashion. My discussion centers on four key terms—contingency, essentialism, reification, and work—but will touch on other central constructionist concepts as well. Though OSC and ISC rely on the same terms and make similar-sounding arguments, there are often vast differences that go unrecognized. I wish to make these differences unambiguously apparent. Moreover, as an interpretive constructionist, I want to advocate more consistent and self-conscious usage of the ISC perspective. In order to pursue these goals, I draw examples from widely read textbooks and anthologies, as well as journal articles and monographs. Given my own research interests, I pay most attention to constructionist writings on family, inequality, and social problems.

Contingency

Both ISC and OSC are in superficial agreement about the contingent nature of social life. The foil for constructionist analyses tends to be arguments, whether advanced by laypersons or scholars, that treat social phenomena as natural, inherent, or automatic. As Hacking (1999, p. 12) has noted, constructionists of all sorts typically argue that what some people may take for granted and treat as inevitable actually should not be seen that way. But what is contingent? Interpretations or objective realities?

For an OSC analysis, what is contingent is some real trait, behavior, or state of affairs. Consider the following example from a widely read text on sociological social psychology. The passage uses constructionist verbs but leans much more toward OSC than ISC:

> Social institutions are *created* and *maintained* through the active participation of individuals. To the extent that we are aware of our reasons for participating in various cultural productions, we can be said to be mindfully engaged in the *construction* of reality. . . . Imagine [an attorney] explaining to her spouse and children that she does not have time to celebrate birthdays and anniversaries because she is busy fighting for an important social cause. She is often absent from family meals and other everyday rituals as well. One day she awakens to the discovery that she is no longer meaningfully engaged with her family—they seem to be living their lives without her. This example illustrates the simple but profound point that if we do not actively participate in the *production* of

those realities that we wish to maintain . . . they will be eroded by the forces of entropy. (O'Brien 2006, p. 517; emphasis added)

This passage suggests that close relationships are "constructed"—created, maintained, produced—by the careful effort people put into them. The argument is that even familial relationships are not automatic or inevitable and cannot be taken for granted. This is a useful way of thinking about things, but in my opinion is not as *interpretive* as it could be. It lies closer to the other end of the OSC-ISC continuum.[4]

ISC analyses employ a different and (in my view) deeper sense of contingency.[5] In their book *What Is Family?* Jaber Gubrium and James Holstein (1990) adopt a more thoroughly and consistently interpretive form of constructionism. They are interested in how people *define* family affairs, an issue that arguably precedes discussions of whether a family exists, what qualities it may have, and what causal factors shape it. Here contingency centers on meaning: The meaning of any (putative) familial relationship is not inherent. According to Gubrium and Holstein's version of constructionism, people define the family into and out of being through their interpretive practices. People assign various qualities to families (e.g., closeness, distance, normality, deviance) as they think and talk about ambiguous states of affairs. It is in this different sense that the authors use the exact same verbs "construct" and "produce": "We offer a view of family as a socially constructed object, a product of decidedly public actions and interactions" (1990, p. 12).

Consider an example derived from Gubrium and Holstein's (1990) observations of a family/patient support group. A father and his twenty-two-year-old son with schizophrenia offer competing interpretations of the closeness of their relationship, as well as the behavior and motivations of the son. The father accuses the son of (among other things) not being around very often and then of being quiet and surly when he is present. The father assembles these three potential "facts"—absence, silence, surliness—into a narrative that his son was more a stranger than a loving family member. In response, the son recasts the same biographical elements into a different pattern. In the son's account, absence and silence and surliness are portrayed as signs of love as well as struggles with mental illness, not as signs of alienation or disloyalty. The son says:

Come on. You know I care. It's just hard for me. I come by, but I don't want to start you worrying, so I don't say too much. I don't want to complain because I don't want you to think that I'm not doing okay. I thought I was doing something good for you by trying to stay out of your hair. . . . I get pretty screwed up sometimes, so I try to stay away when I might have a bad day. (Gubrium and Holstein 1990, p. 59)

Thus, what Gubrium and Holstein are focusing on here is not the same kind of contingency as in the previous case. In O'Brien's example, what is contingent are real families, whose existence and qualities are not inevitable. This sort of objective contingency is common in the literature on families, whether the contingent factors are wide-scale cultural and economic conditions or the daily choices of spouses (e.g., Carrington 2004; Hochschild 1989). In Gubrium and Holstein's example, family again is contingent, but this time it is the meaning of family that is not inevitable and that must be constructed. This sort of interpretive contingency is somewhat less common in the literature, but it also has been pursued (e.g., Harris 2006b; Knapp 1999; Loseke 1987; Miller 1991).

Essentialism

All constructionists tend to emphasize contingency and argue against the foil of inevitability, but there are different degrees of inevitability. A potentially weak sense of inevitability may exist when someone takes a phenomenon for granted and does not question why something appears to be the way it is. A stronger form of inevitability is reflected in "essentialism," the belief that some phenomenon has an essence or inherent nature that makes it what it is. But this term too can be put to different uses depending on the version of constructionism at hand. An OSC definition of essentialism would be one that launches analysts into debates over the real causes of real behavior. In *The Social Construction of Difference and Inequality,* Tracy Ore (2003, p. 5) offers this explanation:

[Essentialism is] the tenet that human behavior is "natural," predetermined by genetic, biological, or physiological mechanisms and thus not subject to change. Human behaviors that show some similarity are assumed [by nonconstructionists] to be expressions of an underlying human drive or tendency. In the United States, gender and sexuality are among the last realms to have their natural or biological status called into question.

This version of essentialism can lead to OSC because it encourages scholars to enter debates over *why* mundane behavior occurs. The "nature versus nurture" debate is often treated as "essentialism versus constructionism," but in my view that contrast elides the OSC/ISC distinction. ISC is not preoccupied with nature versus nurture. Interpretive constructionists sidestep such debates in order to study more carefully what people *claim* to be the reasons for behavior, as well as how those claims are advanced, confirmed, and contested. In contrast, more objective constructionists try to separate myth from reality regarding human behavior, usually by arguing against innate tendencies.

For OSC, essentialism centers on the idea that people do what they do because it is in their nature: They are inherently nurturing, they possess natural genius or talent, or they are "born bad." The objective constructionist counterargument is that these real behaviors and traits are not simply inherent but are created by social factors: Women may be expected and pressured to act nurturing (Bellas 2001; Crompton and Lyonette 2005); genius and talent may be produced by access to high-quality instruction and other social factors quite apart from the inborn capacities a person may have (Chambliss 1989; Scheff 2006); deviance and conformity can be seen as socially elicited actions rather than innate propensities (Agnew 2001; Becker 1973, pp. 26, 34). Although these sorts of OSC arguments are important, they are not the same as ISC arguments.

An interpretive constructionist take on essentialism focuses more squarely on the meaning of things—on how things are viewed or described—rather than on the causes of behavior. Representation, not causality, is the more central issue for ISC analyses.[6] Consequently, interpretive constructionism rebuts meaning-centered essentialism rather than causality-centered essentialism; its target are assertions that some actions (e.g., not wearing clothes, smoking pot, or even committing murder) are essentially or inherently wrong or that certain categories (e.g., the "alcoholic") simply reflect real features of the world. Consider Goode's (1994) definition of essentialism, from his text on deviance:

> Essentialism is the view that all phenomena in the world have an indwelling "essence" that automatically and unambiguously places them in specific, more or less unchanging categories. . . . Essentialists are comfortable with using the terms "true" and "real" when referring to categories or their representatives. Certain inherent, unchanging characteristics define, for example, "true" alcoholism or "true" homosexuality. (Goode 1994, p. 32)

I don't mean to imply that Goode's large book is uniformly interpretive. But in this passage, in this definition, essentialism is portrayed in ISC terms. Classifications, not causes of behavior, are what are at stake. The question is not "What causes alcoholism?" or "What causes good parenting?" but rather "How do different people define what 'alcoholism' or 'homosexuality' mean and decide whether particular individuals should be described in those terms?"

For a classic ISC treatment of essentialism, consider Howard Becker's (1973) influential formulation of the labeling perspective on deviance. Although Becker wavers between a realist and a radically interpretive point of view (see Berard 2003; Pollner 1987), his famous dictum on deviance can be read as ISC. It is also interesting that he so long ago articulated in embryonic form the objective-interpretive distinction that is the subject of this chapter. Notice the dual meanings of the verb "create," as well as his argument against essentialism:

> Deviance is *created* by society. I do not mean this in the way it is ordinarily understood, in which the causes of deviance are located in the social situation of the deviant or in "social factors" which prompt his action. I mean, rather, that social groups *create* deviance by making the rules whose infraction constitutes deviance, and by applying those rules to particular people and labeling them as outsiders. From this point of view, deviance is *not* a quality of the act the person commits, but rather a consequence of the application by others of rules and sanctions to an "offender." The deviant is one to whom that label has successfully been applied; deviant behavior is behavior that people so label. (Becker 1973, p. 9; emphasis altered)

In this passage, the kind of essentialism that Becker is contrasting with constructionism is different than in Ore's (2003) case, mentioned earlier. Becker is arguing against absolutist notions of deviance and respectability, such as "public nudity *is* immoral" or "abortion *is* murder." An essentialist might consider public nudity or abortion to be morally wrong now and forever, irrespective of what human beings think about those actions. An interpretive constructionist would argue that meanings are never essential, because they are socially created. People define things as deviant, normal, and so on. The ISC agenda would then be to study in detail how those meanings are created (Holstein 1993), rather than to move quickly back to examining the real causes of deviant actions, as Becker (1973, pp. 26, 34) does.

Reification

Along with essentialism, reification is a common antagonist for constructionist analyses. Berger and Luckmann (1966) provide a profound and oft-cited inspirational definition of reification, but one that can be read and used from either an OSC or an ISC perspective.

> Reification is the apprehension of human phenomena as if they were things, that is, in non-human or possibly super-human terms. Another way of saying this is that reification is the apprehension of the *products*

of human activity as if they were something else than human *products*—such as facts of nature, results of cosmic laws, or manifestations of divine will. Reification implies that man is capable of forgetting his own authorship of the human world. (Berger and Luckmann 1966, p. 89; emphasis altered)

Notice the ambiguity surrounding the constructionist idea of "production." What is being produced—actual social phenomena or interpretations of social phenomena?

For an objectivist, reification is treating an organization, a family, or inequality as if they were "things"—as if they existed outside of the interactions through which people created, enacted, and transformed them. Consider J. Kenneth Benson's (1977) programmatic article on organizations. He argues that many conventional scholars treat organizations as if they had an "autonomous, determinate structure." His constructionist approach, in contrast, treats organizations as always produced in an ongoing manner by human behavior: "Relationships are *formed,* roles are *constructed,* institutions are *built* from the encounters and confrontations of people in their daily round of life" (Benson 1977, p. 3; emphases added). These constructionist verbs seem to be used in a primarily objectivist manner as Benson argues against the reification of organizations (see also Hall 1987, p. 16).

Similarly, Michael Schwalbe and colleagues (2000, p. 420) critique sociologists who do not understand that "social entities"—and forms of inequality in particular—"must be understood as recurrent patterns of joint action." For example, they argue that "class" is too often treated as a thing—an explanatory variable. Instead, class should be studied as "a situated construction, accomplished through people's daily efforts to make a living; through struggles between workers and employers . . . ; and through cooperation among elites to control business, finance, and government" (2000, p. 441). Though the authors acknowledge the importance of meaning, their argument against reification seems in many ways more objectivist than interpretive.[7]

Melvin Pollner (1987) provides, in my view, an ISC understanding of reification. He cites the same passage from Berger and Luckmann that I quoted above, but gives it a much different spin. For Pollner (p. 100), reification occurs whenever people act or talk as if there are "determinate and objective or absolute entities"—that is, when someone posits an object whose meaning is independent of any human subject. As an example, Pollner describes how officers and judges act as if they are responding to an "independent field" of deviance, rather than (interpretively) creating the meaning of behavior through their responses to it.

During the course of their everyday routines, these actors regularly reify deviance as a thing waiting to be found rather than an ongoing human product—"product" being an interpretation of indeterminate events. In contrast to Benson (1977) and Schwalbe and colleagues (2000), Pollner (1987) is not interested in how social interaction creates the real properties of organizations or class inequality; he is interested in how people convince themselves that there are "organizations" and "inequalities" as real, independent entities in the world.

When I have cited Berger and Luckmann (1966) in my own work on equality in marriage, I have also given their work a decidedly interpretive spin (Harris 2000a, p. 131). Objectivist researchers, I have argued, are prone to reification when they assume that marital equality and inequality exist in the world and that their job is to accurately define, measure, and explain those phenomena. Reification is evident whenever scholars specify the contingent factors, choices, and practices by which some couples succeed or fail at accomplishing marital equality (Blaisure and Allen 1995; Schwartz 1994). In contrast, a constructionist would de-reify equality in order to focus on the contingent *definitional* processes that bring equality and inequality into being (Harris 2006b, p. 8).[8] Here, marital equality and inequality are both *interpretive* accomplishments—that is, meanings. Although this approach strikes some as cynical and detached, it can more favorably be seen as a way to respect and study the truths people live by. What are the different ways that people define "marital equality"? How do they interpret ambiguous instances as examples of "power," "labor," "respect," or whatever else they regard important to equality? How does the issue of equality/inequality actually enter people's lived experiences? These are the questions I asked, which are more reflective of ISC than OSC (see Chapter 5).

Work

As constructionists highlight contingency and argue against essentialism and reification, they often do so by documenting the important kinds of "work" that human beings do. Reality is not automatic, natural, or self-generating; it is created by people's actions. This broad premise has led to the development of many interesting concepts that build directly on the metaphor of humans as construction workers. Here is an incomplete list:

- authenticity work (Gubrium and Holstein 2009b)
- beauty work (Kuan and Trautner 2009)

- biographical work (Holstein and Gubrium 2000)
- body work (Gimlin 2002)
- border work (Thorne 1993)
- boundary work (Lamont and Molnár 2002)
- care work (Herd and Meyer 2002)
- category work (Ryen and Silverman 2000)
- character work (Holyfield and Fine 1997)
- control work (Ortiz 2006)
- conversational work and interactional work (Fishman 1978)
- dream work (Nelson 2001)
- edge work (Lyng 1990)
- emotion work (Hochschild 1979)
- ethnicity work (Berbrier 2000)
- identity work (Snow and Anderson 1987)
- ideological work (Berger 1981)
- image work and influence work (Prus 1999)
- kin work (Stack and Burton 1993)
- membership work (Baker 1984)
- mind work (Owens 2007)
- money work (Schweingruber and Berns 2003)
- narrative work (Gubrium and Holstein 2009a)
- nature work (Fine 1997)
- rape work (Martin 2005)
- reality work and time work (Flaherty 1984, 2003)
- recognition work and response work (Ferris 2004)
- rights work (Plummer 2006)
- risk work (Horlick-Jones 2005)
- self work (Spencer 1992)
- semiotic work (Bakker and Bakker 2006)
- sex work (Seidman 2003)
- social problems work (Holstein and Miller 2003)
- somatic work (Waskul and Vannini 2008)
- surgical work (Pope 2002)
- symbolic work (Wanderer 1987)
- teamwork, face work, and remedial work (Goffman 1959, 1967, 1971)
- thought work, family work, food work, sociability work, and support work (Devault 1991)
- trajectory work, awareness context work, composure work, rectification work, sentimental work, and trust work (Strauss et al. 1982)

The kinds of work that these concepts imply are somewhat diverse, but they can be placed along the objective-interpretive continuum I highlighted earlier. Consider the concepts of *conversational work* and *thought work*. Both emerged out of feminist analyses that sought to bring recognition to women's important contributions to social life. In Pamela Fishman's (1978) and Marjorie Devault's (1991) analyses, the authors document the often invisible work (Daniels 1987) that women perform in their close relationships. Fishman (1978) carefully describes how women actively maintain conversations via subtle comments such as "Mmm," "Oh?" and "Yeah?" Women do more of this interactional work, Fishman argues, and it is largely unnoticed and taken for granted. Devault (1991), in turn, highlights the planning and organizing that women (more than men) put into feeding their families. Such work goes well beyond selecting recipes and making shopping lists and includes frequently taken-for-granted actions such as attending to the contradictory food preferences of family members, maintaining variety, budgeting, fostering a desired mood at the table, and so on. The construction metaphor implicit in these two examples seems to be: just as it takes time, effort, and planning to build a real chair, it takes time, effort, and planning to feed one's family or to conduct an intimate conversation. Family meals and ordinary conversations, like chairs, do not exist automatically or inevitably. They all are dependent on the efforts of human beings.

Although useful and insightful, these conceptions of work seem potentially more objective than interpretive. Fishman's (1978) *interactional work* includes efforts that keep a real conversation going. Devault's (1991) *thought work* includes efforts that help put real food on the table. Much in these analyses does not entail a thoroughgoing bracketing of social reality and a consistent focus on the creation of meaning.[9] A more interpretive constructionist would probably not employ the concept of work in order to argue that our society should recognize as laborious some activities that have previously been classified as nonwork, such as volunteering, caring, and emoting (Daniels 1987, p. 413). An interpretive constructionist would probably not, at least not under the guise of analysis, enter debates over what the public should count as important or real labor. Such debates about the objective status of work rely on the various kinds of interpretive work in which ISC is interested (see also Besen 2006; Gusfield 1984; Spector and Kitsuse 1977, pp. 70–71).

Whereas OSC analyses tend to focus on the work it takes to create reality, ISC analyses tend to focus on the work it takes to create a sense of reality. This latter version of work is reflected more prominently in some of the concepts I listed previously. Discursive constructionists, such as those associated with the concepts of *social problems work* (Holstein and Miller 2003; Loseke 1999, pp. 19, 198–199) and *biographical work* (Holstein and Gubrium 2000), usually try to bracket as much of a social issue as possible—the actors, actions, conditions, and causes—in order to examine how they are categorized and given meaning. For example, analyses of social problems work might consider how people types (e.g., the "inexpressive male" or the "battered woman") are invented and popularized, as well as how these categories are employed to make sense out of ambiguous situations in everyday life (e.g., Loseke 1987, 2003). Analyses of biographical work might examine how past conversational actions (such as silence, interrupting, yelling, active listening) are given meaning by a spouse's, friend's, or therapist's narrative. An interpretive constructionist would emphasize the work it takes to link behavioral incidents into a meaningful pattern. Any social situation—a conversation, a family meal, or any other—contains "a number of evanescent, ambiguous difficulties" that may or may not be noticed and defined as some sort of "trouble" (Emerson and Messinger 1977, p. 121). The process of selecting, classifying, and narrating elements of experience is the interpretive work that ISC analyses focus on (Gubrium and Holstein 1997, p. 147; Riessman 2002). OSC scholars tend to assume or act as if they hold primary responsibility for this kind of work, rather than highlighting how members get the job done.

Concluding Thoughts

I want to make three final points about the OSC-ISC distinction. First, the difference between objective and interpretive constructionism is a matter of degree. It is unlikely that any author or report could be placed utterly at one end or the other of this continuum. I have never met or read a truly naïve realist who would deny that multiple interpretations are sometimes plausible or that some descriptors are merely arbitrary conventional symbols. Given the rise and influence of interpretive constructionism, it seems unlikely that even the most structural, quantitative, positivistic scholar would not express some recognition of the importance of meaning, culture, perspectives, and related constructionist notions. Indeed, Maines (2001) and Paul Atkinson and William Housley (2003) argue that many interactionist and constructionist ideas have pervasively infiltrated mainstream sociology, even if not all sociologists explicitly acknowledge the intellectual heritage of those ideas.

At the same time, an utterly interpretive constructionism also seems unlikely. As debates within the social problems literature have clarified, it is impossible for a scholar to bracket everything at once (Best 2003; Woolgar and Pawluch 1985). At least some assumptions about objective reality must enter even the strictest constructionist analyses.[10] James Holstein and Jaber Gubrium's (2003) solution to this dilemma is for interpretive constructionists to be deliberate, minimalist, and explicit as they import realist assumptions into their analyses, in order to highlight the local contextual factors that shape (and are shaped by) interpretations. Rather than attempting a wholesale bracketing of social reality, Holstein and Gubrium recommend a strategic "analytic bracketing" that alternates between the concrete "whats" and constitutive "hows" of social reality (Holstein and Gubrium 2008). Other interpretive constructionists recommend moving somewhat further toward objectivism. Joel Best (2003) expresses confidence in analysts' abilities to focus on meaningmaking while simultaneously comparing lay interpretations with the "facts" of the matter and locating those interpretations within larger structural contexts.

My second point flows from the first: The fact that the difference between OSC and ISC is only a matter of degree does not mean that the distinction is eradicated. Degrees can be large and consequential. Degrees matter. For example, in my own work I have tried to argue that sociologists remain largely captivated with their own conceptions of inequality, despite the proliferation of qualitative and constructionist studies of this topic (see Chapters 5 and 6). Even scholars who acknowledge the idea that "meaning is not inherent" subsequently proceed to treat inequality as an objective fact whose features can be readily observed and explained by analysts (e.g., Collins 2000; Heiner 2002; Lamont and Molnár 2002; Ore 2003). The risk of this objectivism is that we may not fully understand the diverse meanings that "unequal situations" may have for people in everyday life, as well as how those meanings are created (Harris 2006a, 2006b). In response to my critique, however, a more objectivist scholar might reasonably argue that a rigorously interpretive sociology entail risks of its own, such as missing the opportunity to correct the public's misunderstandings about the real extent and causes of inequality and other problems.

Adopting any orientation involves risks and benefits. All theoretical perspectives have strengths and weaknesses. So let many flowers bloom—but let's not treat them as if they were all from the same plant. I suggest that the distinction between objective and interpretive constructionism provides one way to summarize and clarify the different kinds of constructionist work that have proliferated in sociology (and related social sciences) in the past few decades. Clearly, this distinction is only a starting point. OSC and ISC are themselves very broad labels; more could be done to specify all of the subtypes of, as well as all the ambiguous overlaps between, these two approaches.

My third and final point is, thus, an endorsement of vigilance. Readers who are interested in understanding and using constructionist ideas may benefit from increased alertness regarding the particular form of constructionism that is in play in any given publication or passage therein. Vigilance is required because even when two scholars invoke the same theoretical source, excerpt, and concept—such as Berger and Luckmann (1966, p. 89) on reification—there is still ample room for ambiguity and divergent agendas. These agendas shape what we know and what we try to learn.

Perhaps it is fitting that the basic premises of constructionism—that meaning is not inherent, that it depends on people's purposes and perspectives—apply reflexively to the concept of social constructionism itself. If you think about it, how could it be any other way?

Outline of the Book

A theorist's selection of substantive examples is often a somewhat arbitrary act. In this book, I have attempted to demonstrate the utility of the OSC/ISC distinction by, admittedly, choosing five topics that fit my own research interests and background. However, by focusing on mind, emotions, family diversity, marital equality, and social inequality in Chapters 2–5, I have also attempted to address a range of diverse and attention-grabbing topics. These chapters begin with (seemingly) "micro" or small-scale concerns and move toward "macro" or larger-scale concerns, and they progress from (apparently) apolitical issues toward topics that are glaringly political and contentious. I say "seemingly" and "apparently" because, as most sociologists should know, adjectives such as micro/macro and political/apolitical are not straightforward. (Indeed, they are as slippery to grasp and apply as the objective/interpretive distinction). Upon closer inspection, readers will be able to see that the chapters on mind and emotions do have implications for contentious debates over large-scale social problems and that studies of "small-scale" social interactions have import for an in-depth understanding of family diversity and social inequalities.

Although these chapters delve into theoretical, methodological, and substantive details that are somewhat particular to their respective topics, there are many recurring arguments that link them. Each chapter attempts to demonstrate the utility of viewing constructionist literature through the objective/interpretive prism. Each chapter argues that objective and interpretive constructionist scholars use seemingly identical concepts to produce highly divergent research findings—and that these perspectives and findings lead to differing implications for social policy and social reform. Each chapter attempts to show that interpretive constructionism is still—despite the growth and widespread adoption of the generic "constructionism" label—a somewhat neglected and underutilized perspective in comparison to objective constructionism. Last, each chapter attempts to demonstrate that the distinction between objective and interpretive constructionism is more a continuum than a dichotomy, and that authors and readers could benefit from a greater awareness of the big difference that can result even from a number of small differences that are merely matters of degree. I hope readers find these arguments convincing. An expanded description of each chapter follows.

Chapter 2: Constructing Minds

A fundamental starting point for many sociological constructionists is the idea that the human "mind" is a social creation rather than a biological inevitability. Classic studies of children raised in relative isolation illustrate the contingent nature of our minds: unless thoroughly socialized by others, human beings have very limited ability to think and communicate. Mind is further shaped in that others teach us *how* to think. We derive our perspectives and values from the groups we associate with, both in childhood and adulthood. Many interactionist and phenomenological concepts (such as cultural beliefs and values, interpretive frames, mind-sets, role taking, social lenses and prisms, stocks of knowledge, and worldviews) all cohere around the argument that the contents and functioning of our minds—as objective (real) aspects of our being—are socially constructed.

But there is another sense in which mind is created in social interaction. Interpretive constructionists highlight how the *idea* of mind is used in everyday life. People attribute "mind" to their pets, computers, cars, and other nonhuman entities. They also debate the kinds of mind that they and others possess: bright, dim, honest, deviant, criminal, generous, selfish, insane, deliberative, confused, blank, and so on. Individuals frequently attribute specific thoughts to themselves and others as they tell stories about past and future events. All of these actions involve giving meaning to minds. Research in this tradition of constructionism demonstrates how the existence and nature of our minds are interpretively created as well as objectively created.

Chapter 3: Managing Emotions

This chapter builds on the previous one by examining a related microsociological issue: human feelings. In contrast to assumptions about the natural or biological basis of emotions, sociologists have argued that emotions are socially constructed. A major strand of research in this tradition focuses on the active effort individuals put into managing their feelings and the feelings of others. Emotion management can be given an objective or interpretive spin, however. Most authors follow Arlie Russell Hochschild (1983) and write about "emotion work" in relatively objectivist terms: the subject of analysis is how people manipulate appearances and experiences of actual bodily states.

A smaller group of scholars approaches emotion management more interpretively. For them, the goal is to understand how ideas or assertions about emotions are created. Emotional categories (from love to road rage) are developed and innovatively applied to ambiguous circumstances in everyday life. When two friends debate whether someone is "pissed off" or "only a little irritated" or "not bothered at all," they are creating emotions by defining them into (or out of) being. Research in this vein demonstrates how "real or disguised feeling states" are not just worked up or managed in the traditional sense of objective constructionism; they are interpretively constructed as well.

Chapter 4: Family Diversity

Chapter 4 begins to move the book's subject matter toward what would conventionally be seen as more "macro" and controversial topics, by focusing less on the "inner" workings of individuals' thoughts and feelings and more on "external" relationships and inequalities. Most social scientists who study the family today are fully aware that there are a plethora of family forms in the United States and other countries. Rather, the foil for many scholars is the commonsense belief in and reverence for what has been called "The Standard North American Family" or SNAF (Smith 1993): a heterosexual husband, wife, and their biological children living under one roof, preferably with the husband being the sole or primary breadwinner. Many books and articles are devoted to describing, explaining, and often extolling family diversity that has developed over time and across different cultures, such as single parent families, adoptive families, foster families, stepfamilies, polygamous families, and many others. To counter SNAF assumptions, these works seek to familiarize readers with these diverse ways of practicing family, to engender sympathy and respect for different kinds of families, and to foster recognition of the social factors that construct family life.

Not all constructionist scholars study family diversity in the same fashion. There is a second major alternative way of approaching family diversity that is somewhat less recognized in the literature. I call this approach "interpretive family diversity." Here the focus is on how the same set of interpersonal relationships can be variously interpreted. People acquire different conceptual frameworks that they creatively use to define whether a family relationship exists, what kind of family it is, and what causes and consequences are associated with that family. The existence and nature of family is something that is discussed and debated, and thereby "talked into being," in everyday life. These divergent assumptions can lead interpretive scholars to produce analyses that diverge dramatically from traditional objectivist research, even though they use seemingly identical concepts to address similar explanatory concerns.

Chapter 5: Creating Equal Marriages

Family diversity has been a serious concern of researchers and social justice advocates for some time, but so too has the issue of fairness in marriage. In the past fifty years, much has been written on marital equality, but almost exclusively from objective viewpoints. Even qualitative researchers have given constructionist verbiage an objectivist spin: marital equality is something that is "built" or "created" as a real condition. The vast majority of scholars have sought to understand the contexts and actions that lead to the "production" of factually equal or unequal relationships.

Recent interpretive research, in contrast, examines how marital equality is created *as a meaning* rather than an actual condition. In this view, "the social construction of marital equality" consists of the interpretive practices by which people define relationships as equal or unequal. Whereas objectivist researchers (1) define marital equality, (2) measure the extent to which couples have achieved equality, and (3) explain the causes and consequences of equality and inequality, interpretive researchers study how married people (and their companions, coun-selors, lawyers, etc.) accomplish those three tasks. On the one hand, interpretive constructionism can help researchers more carefully investi-gate (rather than assume) the diverse meanings that spouses may live by. On the other hand, an interpretive approach leads to a more relativistic and hesitant moral stance; it complicates advocacy and the pursuit of social reforms that might promote "real" gender equality at home.

Chapter 6: Producing Social Inequality

The topic of marital equality can prove to be a helpful launching point for an even more controversial discussion of inequality in general. The sociological literature is filled with descriptions and analyses of social inequality. Sociologists are concerned with economic stratification, health disparities, racial and sexual discrimination, educational disad-vantages, and a plethora of related issues. However, this chapter shows that social inequalities can be approached as objective situations or as interpretations. Most sociologists study the social creation of inequality by attempting to find facts: What is the nature and extent of the inequal-ity? What "produces" or causes it? What are its negative consequences? What policies or practices might ameliorate inequality?

I argue that more scholars should study the interpretive construction of inequality by focusing on the diverse claims people make about the nature, extent, causes, and effects of putative inequalities. I summarize and explain the similarities and differences between four seemingly con-structionist publications that fall in different places along the objective-interpretive continuum. In so doing, I hope to show that there is still much room for an interpretive agenda to be pursued. Rigorously inter-pretive scholars do not need to shy away from this macro, politically charged topic.

Chapter 7: Conclusion

The final chapter summarizes my argument and addresses nine ques-tions I expect readers may have, based on reactions I have received from those who have read (or listened to me present) earlier versions.

I maintain that social constructionism is of crucial importance in sociology and related social sciences, despite the ambiguities of this per-spective. Readers would benefit by being more aware of the internal con-tradictions of constructionism, and researchers could identify untapped avenues of inquiry by noticing whether current constructionist research on a topic is of the objective or interpretive variety.

Notes

1. Among other sources, see Schutz (1970) and Berger and Luckmann (1966) on phenomenological sociology; Garfinkel (1967) and Heritage (1984) on ethnomethodology; and Blumer (1969) and Mead (1934) on symbolic interactionism and pragmatism. Textbooks and readers that discuss these perspectives include those by Cahill (2004); Coulon (1995); Hewitt (1997); Lindesmith, Strauss, and Denzin (1999); Musolf (2003); O'Brien (2006); Prus (1996); Reynolds (1993); Sandstrom, Martin, and Fine (2003); and others.

2. For examples, see Fontana (2002), Manning (2001), Riessman (2002), and Zerubavel (1997).

3. I use OSC and ISC as nouns (as in construction*ism*) and as adjectives (as in construction*ist*), depending on the context.

4. For other examples, see Ulmer and Spencer's (1999) review of interactionist research on *criminal career contingencies* and compare it with Holstein and Gubrium's (2000, pp. 162–163) discussion of *interpretive contingencies.* Whereas the research on criminal career contingencies involves carefully studying the various factors that shape real phases and stages of life, research on interpretive contingencies involves carefully studying the various factors that shape how the life course (including any putative phases, stages, or causes) is given meaning.

5. O'Brien alludes to this deeper form of contingency in other places in her book. For example, her own definition of constructionism (O'Brien 2006, p. 55) is more interpretive than objective, despite her later uses of the perspective.

6. In ISC, causality or "why" questions enter in limited fashion and tend to revolve around the issue of *why interpretations happen the way they do,* with the goal of discerning the factors that shape the meaning-making process (see Gubrium and Holstein 1997, chap. 9).

7. In Chapter 6 I explain this assertion in greater detail. Schwalbe and colleagues (2000) assume that inequality exists objectively and that it is the scholar's job to define inequality, decide what the most important kinds are, find examples, and explain the causal factors that "produce" it. A more rigorously interpretive approach would bracket the existence of inequality and study how people interpretively produce inequality meanings through their own definitions, examples, and explanations.

8. Similarly, Berard (2006, p. 12) treats reification as assuming that inequality (or any entity) exists "prior to and independent of social understandings and judgments."

9. Some of this analysis does move further down the continuum toward ISC, however. Fishman (1978) and Devault (1991), respectively, assert that "doing" conversations and "doing" family are ways of "doing gender." By coordinating an in-depth conversation or orchestrating a family meal, women can be seen as assembling signs of gender propriety and thereby performing what is

taken to be "natural." Though this interesting analysis seems (to me) fairly inferential and overlaid onto the objective analysis, it does highlight the creation of meaning. It arguably occupies an ambiguous middle ground along the OSC-ISC continuum.

10. It is always possible to find realist assumptions in a constructionist's research—not the least of which is the assumption that it is possible to study and accurately describe the interpretive work that people do. Moreover, interpretive scholars are always finding something else in need of bracketing that has been overlooked by their fellow constructionists. For example, constructionist staples such as "mind" and "perspectives" have been examined as interpretive accomplishment—as I show in the next chapter.

2

Constructing Minds

A basic tenet of social constructionism is that reality does not appear "in the raw." Since meaning is not inherent, any aspect of human experience can be classified and acted toward in various ways. Human beings must therefore interpret the things they encounter. This process of interpretation is often considered to occur in or through people's *minds* as they think about things or converse with others. My application of the OSC/ISC distinction to the constructionist literature begins with this key issue. By focusing on mind, this chapter starts from the "inside"; subsequent chapters examine constructionist theory and research on more "exterior" relationships and structures.

Numerous sociological concepts—such as collective conscience, cultural beliefs and values, interpretive frames, generalized others and reference groups, mental modalities and mind-sets, role taking, social lenses and prisms, stocks of knowledge, worldviews—all tend to refer to the contents or actions of minds. Constructionists admit that mental functioning may depend partly on biological foundations internal to the individual. However, they suggest that mind's sources and applications are profoundly social. It is culture, language, and human interaction that enable human beings to think as competently and variably as they do (Berger and Luckmann 1966).

Once created, the argument goes, mind is a productive social force. Through minded behavior, human beings generate reality in both an interpretive and objective sense: People give things meaning, act on those meanings, and make concrete changes in the world. Since mind is such an important dimension of human existence, many scholars afford it a prominent place in their theory and research (Blumer

1969; Zerubavel 1997). Thinking is largely treated as a topic for researchers to conceptualize, study, describe, and explain (Brekhus 2007; Callero 1991; Meltzer 2003; Smith 1982).

Not all constructionists follow suit. An alternative stand of research asks: What if we treat "mind" itself as an *interpretive* construction rather than an actual entity, ability, or process? What might we gain by focusing on the assumptions and assertions that various people (in various contexts) make about their own and others' minds? By reframing the topic in this manner, some researchers attempt to contribute different insights about the social dimensions of mind. Mind is still considered a social "achievement," but its origins, functioning, and consequences tend to be studied more as meanings or claims and less as objective or factual realities.

In this chapter, I compare scholarship on the objective and interpretive construction of mind and attempt to demonstrate how various constructionist authors can use similar terms to make parallel but divergent arguments. Relatively objective and interpretive analyses of "the social construction of mind" can overlap in subtle ways, but their contributions are distinguishable if not contradictory.

Studying Mind as a Socially
Created Ability or Behavior

The more "objective" approach to studying mind tends to treat thinking as a skill or practice that develops within all human beings—or at least those who are physically capable (e.g., not severely brain damaged) and who are normally socialized (e.g., not feral children). Although virtually all individuals possess minds, the ability to think is considered a contingent construction not an automatic outcome or process. Objective constructionists tend to reject strong proclamations about the biological "naturalness" of mind's existence and traits. Claims about mind being a God-given ability would likely be rejected as well. Some interactional constructionists also protest analyses that treat human beings as utterly programmed by their cultures or subcultures, since minded actions are deemed partially contingent on local circumstances and human discretion. Studies of the objective construction of mind thus highlight the social factors that shape (but not necessarily determine) the development and expression of human thought.

Defining and Defending Mind:
Blumer on Symbolic Interactionism

Among Europeans and Americans at least (Lillard 1998), it is routine to speak and write assuredly about human thought. Individuals regularly describe themselves and others as involved in minded actions: assuming, believing, considering, disregarding, evaluating, forming opinions, imagining, judging, mulling things over, remembering, wondering, and so on. But of what exactly does "mind" consist? How, why, and when does "it" work? A large number of social scientists have sought to understand the nature of thinking and its relationship to emotions, actions, and the larger society (Strydom 2007). In so doing, they have put forward a wide array of competing models and metaphors of mind (Sternberg 1990; Valsiner and van der Veer 2000).

In sociology, one prominent conception of mind comes from symbolic interactionism (Blumer 1969). Following George Herbert Mead (1934) and other pragmatist philosophers (Wiley 2006), Blumer (1969, pp. 63, 95) treated mind as an inner dialogue. Sometimes this internal conversation occurs as external conversations do, as when individuals tell themselves "Remember—you're on a diet and no carbs are allowed!" before they act to satisfy a pang of hunger. On other occasions such self-interaction can occur in the form of fleeting images or abbreviated references, in a sort of subvocal shorthand (Athens 1994, p. 524). Perhaps an individual might briefly imagine the disapproval he or she might see on a companion's face before deciding whether or what to eat.

For Blumer and Mead, the human capacity to think only arises in social settings. Rare instances of severely neglected children show the importance of social interaction: individuals who grow up in relative isolation lack language and normal reasoning abilities (Blumer 1981, p. 141; Davis 2006). To be mentally competent, individuals must be taught that they are someone—that they have a self with which to interact—and they must be given the means with which to do so. Children pass through various stages of development as they practice the ability to imagine the perspectives of others (Blumer 1969, p. 13). Such role taking leads eventually to acquiring an overarching frame of reference that can be used to make sense of one's self and one's environment and to fit into the norms of one's society (Mead 1934, pp. 46–47). Socialization continues throughout one's life, with the potential for subcultural variations depending on one's interpersonal networks and associations (Shibutani 1955). Consequently, even two neighbors may live side by side yet occupy different cognitive worlds (Blumer 1969, p. 11).

Mead and Blumer both held that the ability to think separates human beings from animals and insects. Although animals appear to communicate with each other, such interactions are what Blumer (1981, p. 145) would call "nonsymbolic" and Mead (1934, p. 43) would call "a conversation of gestures." When two dogs fight each other, Mead suggested, they are merely reacting mindlessly (instinctively) to each other. Similarly, a newborn animal may prepare for the future merely out of blind impulse: "A squirrel hides nuts, but we do not hold that the squirrel has a picture of what is going to happen" (Mead 1934, p. 119). Unlike "lower" life-forms, human beings do not simply respond to stimuli. People can interpret what is going on before they act. Only human beings, via the acquisition of language and a sense of self, are able to exchange "significant gestures" (Mead 1934) or engage in "symbolic interaction" (Blumer 1981, p. 145) with others and with themselves. Only human beings can recall a past circumstance and debate its relevance for a current or future situation (e.g., a potential fight or a cold winter).

Human beings do at times engage in unthinking conduct, however. Mead (1934, pp. 42, 72, 102) invokes the examples of an absentminded professor who begins to dress for dinner, forgets what he or she is doing, and puts on pajamas; a well-trained soldier whose body responds automatically to certain orders; and an experienced boxer who may block a punch automatically. But the characteristic and predominant form of human interaction is said to be symbolic (Blumer 1969, p. 10). Whether getting dressed, performing a drill, or fighting a boxing match, people notice and classify things and prepare to act based on the meanings they've created. Before dressing, for instance, an outfit may be assessed for its cleanliness, warmth, appropriateness, and attractiveness. Mind may be especially active when people are confronted with obstacles to their actions, but Blumer (somewhat more than Mead[1]) suggests that thought is in play more or less continuously:

> For the human being to be conscious or aware of anything is equivalent to his indicating the thing to himself—he is identifying it as a kind of object and considering its relevance or importance to his line of action. One's waking life consists of a series of such indications that the person is making to himself, indications that he uses to direct his action. (Blumer 1969, p. 13)

The symbolic interactionist (SI) conception of mind conflicts with some other scholarly approaches. As Blumer (1969, p. 14; 1981, pp.

153–159) notes, SI differs from biological accounts that locate thought in the physical composition of the brain; it differs from Freudian perspectives that emphasize unconscious motives or the interplay of psychological forces (such as personality structures or the id, ego, and superego); and it differs from some sociological accounts that treat thought as the mere expression of internalized values or of an individual's gender/race/class location in society. Blumer asserted that most explanations of human behavior erroneously downplayed the importance of self-interaction; in his view, no social scientific perspective other than symbolic interactionism gave due respect to the importance of self-interaction (see Athens 1993, pp. 187, 190). He believed that any social scientist must come to terms with the fact that, by thinking, people creatively and actively guide their own responses to the situations they encounter. This self-interaction should not be dismissed, nor should it be compressed into a single form. Blumer (1972, 1981) criticized those who assumed that people always think in a particular fashion, such as exchange theorists' (Homans 1958) presumption that people continuously engage in cost/benefit calculations or dramaturgical analysts' (Goffman 1959) tendency to focus almost exclusively on actors' concerns over the impressions they make on others.

For interactionists, behavior is contingent on interpretations, which may be as variable as people's diverse purposes and perspectives. Blumer (1971, p. 305) did not rule out the search for objective information about society; at times he encouraged social-problems analyses that raise public awareness or correct factual misunderstandings. Nor did he deny that internal and external forces can influence individuals' conduct (Blumer 1969, pp. 87–88). However, he derived from Mead the firm conviction that human behavior is best understood as essentially self-directed and meaning guided: "The unraveling, analysis and comprehension of what takes place in the interpretive process as human beings form their social acts becomes in Mead's scheme the central task of social science" (Blumer 1969, p. 64; 1981, p. 151).

If mind is central to human conduct, then one's research practices must reflect that. Thus, Blumer (1969, p. 51) argued that good research depends centrally on scholars' ability to imagine the perspective of others. This ability is enhanced by achieving a first-hand familiarity with respondents' lives and by assiduously avoiding the all-too-common practice of imposing foreign (e.g., scholarly) orientations onto their conduct (Blumer 1969, pp. 51, 86). Many qualitative sociologists have attempted to follow Blumer's advice (Lofland 1976; Prus 1997; Reynolds and Herman-Kinney 2003). Participant observation, in-depth interviews, analysis of personal documents, and other strategies have been developed and deployed to investigate how various individuals and groups "see" or think about the objects in their worlds (see Gubrium and Holstein 1997, chap. 2). Many of the research articles that have adopted an interactionist orientation can be found in periodicals such as *Symbolic Interaction, Studies in Symbolic Interaction,* and the *Journal of Contemporary Ethnography,* among others.

Theoretically inclined scholars, too, have adopted or expanded upon Mead and Blumer's approach toward mind as an inner dialogue. For example, Randall Collins (2004) has incorporated Mead's ideas into his work on interaction ritual chains; Thomas Scheff (1993) has forged connections with his perspective on emotions and social bonds; and Norbert Wiley (2006) has sifted out the subtle differences and similarities between the portraits of mind that were offered by Mead, Blumer, and other pragmatist philosophers (see also Athens 1994).

Mind's Actions and Traits: Zerubavel on Cognitive Sociology

A second important example of and inspiration for constructionist research on mind can be found in Eviatar Zerubavel's (1991, 1997) cognitive sociology. Like Mead and Blumer, Zerubavel's influential program also rests on the assumption that our minds create a sense of reality. However, he disavows any enduring interest in the thinking of specific actors, instead preferring to focus exclusively on cultural and subcultural patterns of thought.

Zerubavel contrasts his approach with respect to two other orientations. The first—labeled cognitive universalism—focuses on the way "everyone thinks the same" due to our common physiology. This perspective is reflected in lay and scholarly discourses that locate thinking in the generic operations of the human brain. The second orientation—cognitive individualism—treats people as solitary thinkers each with a distinctive mind-set that is a product of a particular personal background. "Everybody is different" is the catchphrase of this perspective. In between lies cognitive sociology, an approach that "reminds us that we think not only as individuals and as human beings, but also as members of particular communities with certain distinctive cognitive traditions that affect the way we process the world in our minds" (1997, p. 112). Thus, like others who work in this vein (Brekhus 2007; Cerulo 2002), Zerubavel emphasizes the normative dimension of mind by gathering evidence of cultural differences in how people think.[2]

Like Blumer, Zerubavel (1997, p. 28) asserts that "there is always more than only one way to perceive something. No single 'view' of any object . . . is inevitable." People learn from others how to experience things. Such instruction can take place explicitly—as when a child is told outright not to eat bugs but to relish lobster—or tacitly—as when a child observes others brushing away flies or reacting with joy to the underwater delicacy. Zerubavel (1997, p. 19) also distinguishes between *primary cognitive socialization* ("where we are inducted into society at large and acquire the knowledge and cognitive skills expected from every single one of its members") and *secondary cognitive socialization* ("where we acquire the more specialized knowledge and skills that are required in specific sectors"). For example, an adult wine connoisseur or recreational marijuana user may become so only after entering certain social circles and learning from others which physical sensations to notice and how to define them as pleasurable (see Becker 1953). The notion of "pure" perception is doubtful, Zerubavel (1997, pp. 23–24) argues, because "what we experience through our senses is normally 'filtered' through various interpretive frameworks." For instance, he finds it quite telling that people can sometimes enjoy food that they would normally consider repulsive, as long as they are not told exactly what is on their plates (Zerubavel 1997, p. 77).

Via scores of brief but intriguing examples, Zerubavel suggests that thinking occurs on a "supra-personal" yet "sub-universal" level. To continue with the example of food: Zerubavel suggests that what people find edible or delectable is often not so random to be a matter of personal taste or so universal as to be a biological imperative; instead, it is socially patterned. The cognitive line between edible/inedible foods varies among different societies, or by different subcultures within a society, or by the same society over time (Zerubavel 1997, p. 77). Some groups do enjoy worms, snails, frog legs, deer penis, and bull testicles, while others abhor bacon and steak. The animal rights and environmental movements have over time encouraged a portion of Americans to reject all consumption of meat and even dairy products, which has generated controversy.[3]

Although Zerubavel frequently invokes the constructionist idea that meaning is not inherent, he combines this premise with the assertion that reality consists, in fact, of continuums rather than discrete chunks. He suggests that "the world presents itself not in pure black and white but, rather, in ambiguous shades of gray, with mental twilight zones and intermediate essences" (Zerubavel 1991, p. 71). Day and night, mountains and valleys, male and female, childhood and adulthood, self and environment—everything bleeds into everything else. Any act of classifying reality into insular components thus involves a degree of consequential arbitrariness—arbitrary because the fine lines people draw could always be drawn differently, and consequential because classifications reflect and shape subsequent thoughts, actions, and institutionalized practices (Zerubavel 1991, p. 29). However, human beings cannot escape this dilemma. In order to mentally grasp any entities at all, people must draw boundaries by somewhat crudely "lumping" and "splitting" elements of experience (Zerubavel 1991, p. 21; 1997, p. 27). The question for Zerubavel is how different people view the relationship between the boundaries they draw and the nature of reality.

Some groups tend to exhibit a rigid mind-set. They deny the fluid nature of reality and perceive their own classification schemes as merely reflecting the truth. They forget that all distinctions are conventional and insist, ethnocentrically, on the superiority of their own arbitrary perspectives. For example, to speak as if beef tacos were "naturally" food but worm tacos were "of course" disgusting would be to engage in arbitrary reification. Rigidity, though, is itself a matter of degree; some individuals and groups exhibit more or less of it than others. Zerubavel traces the development of rigid thinking to a number of possible psychological and sociological sources. For instance, an individual may feel a "a craving for rigid structures" as a result of "not having had limits set on one's actions early on"; or, collectivities may exhibit an "obsession with boundaries" as a consequence of "perceiv[ing] themselves as minorities in constant danger of extinction" (Zerubavel 1991, p. 49). Particular domains within a society—such as law, science, and religion—can also be more rigid than others. The rigid mind-set, with its "purist effort to force reality into exclusive mental compartments," underlies and guides many efforts designed to separate legal from illegal, fact from fiction, or sacred from profane (Zerubavel 1991, pp. 57–60).

The opposite of the rigid mind is fuzzy thinking, which is "a virtually structureless mind-set distinctively characterized by an aversion to any boundary that might prevent mental interpenetration" (Zerubavel 1997, p. 57). Fuzzy is how the world appears to infants. Without socialization and especially language, human beings are unable to differentiate one thing from another, including themselves from the world. According to Zerubavel (1991, p. 81), such boundaries are "discernible only through society's mental glasses." Infants typically gain a sense of self and the ability to categorize a continuous reality into discrete entities. However, Zerubavel asserts that even adults can exhibit fuzzy thinking, at least to a degree, depending on the psychological and sociological factors that shape their mind-sets. For example, women tend to "experience reality in a somewhat more fluid manner than do men" in part because of the manner in which young girls slowly separate themselves from their mothers and because of the overlapping nature of women's work and home lives; some religious traditions (e.g., Buddhism) and historical developments (e.g., globalization and cosmopolitanism) may also promote an undifferentiated view of the world (Zerubavel 1991, pp. 84–85). Finally, fuzziness may be encouraged within particular contexts or realms (as in playful and artistic behavior) just as rigidity can be.

The third and final mind-set Zerubavel identifies lies in between these polar extremes. The "flexible" mind is one that recognizes both the benefits and drawbacks of rigid and fuzzy classification, remembering that distinctions can be both arbitrary and useful. Flexible people rely on categories but think in terms of "both/and" instead of "either/or" (Zerubavel 1997, p. 57). For example, Eskimos sometimes eat as food the same frozen fish they earlier rode as a sled (Zerubavel 1991, p. 122). Or, a professor with a flexible academic identity would feel comfortable reading and conducting research that spanned different disciplines or fields—such as philosophy, psychology, and economics—without denying the loose differences between those intellectual perspectives (Zerubavel 1995). Human creativity in any realm is enabled by flexibility, Zerubavel asserts, since one can only innovate within some kind of recognized structure. Moreover, flexible mind-sets are associated with optimum mental health: "Rigid and porous selves are equally pathological and overindividuation and underindividuation can both lead to suicide" (Zerubavel 1991, p. 120).

Espousing no specific quantitative or qualitative methodology, Zerubavel instead advocates an eclectic but analytically focused system of data collection. Cognitive sociologists should look broadly and comparatively for evidence of cultural mind-sets, which will inevitably be expressed through people's statements, actions, and artifacts (Zerubavel 2007). Karl Mannheim (1952) once proposed the "documentary method of interpretation" as a research strategy whereby a scholar collects and compares a wide array of ambiguous instances in order to discern the underlying "styles of thought" and "worldviews" that connect them. Zerubavel (1991, p. 55) adopts this method when he looks for the diverse "mental lenses" that shape how various "thought communities" classify the world into insular components (e.g., edible/inedible). His distinction between rigid and fuzzy thinking also involves treating disparate examples as indicators or underlying cognitive patterns. For instance, Zerubavel (1991, p. 55) identifies rigidity within the collective worldview of Orthodox Jews: "It is hard not to see the mental affinity between the attribution of impurity to bodily discharges, the abomination of ruminants that have no parted hooves, the taboo against wearing clothes made of both wool and linen, and the practice of mourning and mock burying members who marry nonmembers. These are all different manifestations of a single rigid mind-set."

Zerubavel's approach to cognitive sociology has influenced the work of many sociologists. Wayne Brekhus (2007) refers to a "Zerubavelian tradition" of students and colleagues associated with Rutgers University, such as himself (Brekhus 2003), Mary Chayko (2002), Jamie Mullaney (2006), and others (Cerulo 2002). Indeed, insofar as Zerubavel's goal is to infer the contents and actions of people's minds based on what they say, do, or create, then his aspirations are common to huge swathes of classic and contemporary sociology. Countless scholars have attempted to study what different groups of people think, why they think that way, and what the consequences are. This can be seen in classic examples such as Emile Durkheim's (1984) notion of collective conscience and David Riesman's (1950) study of inner, outer, and other-directed personalities, or in modern day ethnographies and run-of-the-mill opinion polls and focus groups (cf. Maynard 2006; Prus 1997; Puchta and Potter 2002). A very high percentage of social science investigations rely on data derived from closed and open-ended interviews, which are often seen as providing access to cultural or subcultural beliefs and understandings (see Holstein and Gubrium 1995a, p. 1).

Studying Mind as an Interpretation or Claim

Many scholars have in one way or another studied mind as an actual entity or behavior, but some take a different constructionist approach. There is another way to study the social origins, contents, traits, and actions of people's minds. Instead of viewing mind as a socially created ability that people use to define reality and guide behavior, mind itself can be studied as something that actors define into being. The presence or absence of mind, as well as its putative traits and actions, is a topic that laypersons themselves discuss and debate. By orienting toward mind itself as an interpretively constructed phenomenon, a second form of scholarship thus problematizes a fundamental concept in much constructionist theory and research.

Studying "Questionable" Attributions of Mind

As Harold Garfinkel (1967, pp. 40, 78) once suggested, the "documentary method of interpretation" is not only a methodological strategy that scholars (such as Mannheim and Zerubavel) can use to infer the presence of mind-sets or worldviews; it is also a procedure that everyday folk also use to infer the existence and functioning of mind.[4] Such "mind work" (Owens 2007) or "minding" (Gubrium 2003) occurs when people treat indeterminate experiences as signs of mental processes—thinking, desiring, intending, imagining, manipulating, responding, and so on. To demonstrate this point, a number of researchers have examined what might be called conventionally questionable or extreme cases, by focusing on how people attribute mind to animals (Alger and Alger 1997; Sanders 2003b), to individuals who are severely handicapped or ill (Bogdan and Taylor 1989; Gubrium 2003; Pollner and McDonald-Wikler 2003), or to violent offenders undergoing rehabilitation (Fox 2001).

Clinton Sanders (2003a) has forcefully challenged the symbolic interactionist precept that nonhuman animals do not possess minds because they are incapable of spoken language. Mead (1934) enjoyed invoking dogfights as examples of thoughtless or nonsymbolic interaction. In contrast, Sanders focuses on people who regularly interact with their pet dogs as if they were capable of all sorts of cognitions: forming intentions, possessing memories, planning revenge, engaging in trickery and manipulation, expressing loyalty, and so on. Sanders (2003a, p. 419) cites an example of a pet owner whose dog Toby would stare and sigh longingly at the butter when it was placed on the dinner table. On one occasion, when this seemingly strategic behavior did not yield a taste of butter, Toby retrieved a pig's ear from another room in the house and laid it at his owner's feet. The owner viewed her dog's behavior as evidence of thoughtful conduct. She concluded that Toby had "reasoned and came up with the idea of a trade," and she responded by giving him some slabs of butter on bread (Lerman 1996, as cited in Sanders 2003a, p. 419).

Conventional symbolic interactionists would dismiss the dog owner's claims as fallacious anthropomorphism—the misattribution of human thoughts to merely reactive animals (Mead 1934, pp. 182–183). Sanders disagrees. He suggests that Mead's unfortunate attitude has kept interactionists and other sociologists from incorporating human-animal relationships into their analytic purview. Many people interact with pets on a regular basis, as more than half of US households contain companion animals of one sort or another (Sanders 2003a, p. 421). It is very common for people to assume their pets possess distinctive personalities and the ability to think for themselves. Surely Mead and Blumer would not protest this extension of interactionist premises: If people act based on what things mean to them, then it is important for interactionists to study how people attribute mind, selves, and other identities to animals. Such studies could not only illuminate human-animal relationships but could, through extrapolation, explicate the generic processes through which minded identities are constructed in human-human interactions as well (Sanders 2003b).[5]

More controversially, Sanders argues that animals do in fact think and that the actual difference between human and animal intelligence is only a matter of degree. He suggests that qualitative sociologists should carefully observe and interact with animals and attempt to understand their perspectives and cultures, much as conventional ethnographers do with human beings (Sanders and Arluke 1993, p. 384).

Like Sanders, Gubrium (2003) has also studied the attribution of mind in "questionable" circumstances, but he did so without arguing or investigating whether such attributions might be correct. Gubrium's work focuses on attributions of mind to human beings whose cognitive status is in doubt due to the effects of Alzheimer's. This disease seems to degrade the mind to the point where the afflicted can no longer recognize the faces of family members or accomplish routine activities (such as bathing and eating). Consequently, caregivers wonder how much of the person is still "there" or "gone." Spouses, children, and other companions look for signs of a mind that may have not yet been completely eradicated or that remains hidden behind their loved one's apparent incapacitation. Subcultural rules of thumb guide their search. Caregivers learn what to look for by interacting with medical personnel and support group members, reading related newsletters, and other sources of information on the disease. For example, one publication advised that pacing and restlessness could be signs that a patient is anxiously wondering "What's wrong with me? Can't you see that I am getting worse? How much worse will I get?" (Gubrium 2003, p. 186). Caregivers were told to pay active yet selective attention to the victim's words and gestures in order to discern what patients are truly communicating, because some of what they say or do would inevitably be meaningless, random, or unintended[6] (Gubrium 2003, p. 186).

Whereas Sanders took a stance on the existence of thought in animals, Gubrium brackets the issue of mind's objective status in order to study how its supposed existence is interactionally achieved. Using another action verb—"preserves"—as a synonym for "constructs," Gubrium (2003, p. 185) takes the position that "mind experientially persists to the extent that some agent preserves it, be the agent the one whose mind is at stake or some other." The truth of the matter enters the picture for Gubrium primarily as a matter of debate among caretakers and their companions. For example, support groups sometimes attempt to guide individual members toward the interpretation that their severely afflicted loved one is gone and that their continuous searching for signs of lucidity has become unrealistic and unhealthy. In such discussions, the foundations as well as the content of such truth claims can be contested, as the value of first-hand familiarity (e.g., "I know my own spouse!") is juxtaposed with the benefits of an outside perspective or professional training (Gubrium 2003, p. 188). Those with intimate familiarity can be said to be in denial just as those with credentialed expertise can often be described as having inaccurate or irrelevant knowledge with respect to specific cases (see also Bogdan and Taylor 1989, p. 140).

Alzheimer's victims sometimes cannot be asked about their own cognitive status. However, as Kathryn Fox's (2001) research on violent inmates shows, claims to self-knowledge can be disputed even among those who can speak intelligibly on their own behalf.[7] Fox studied a prison rehabilitation program for violent offenders entitled Cognitive Self Change (CSC). The guiding philosophy of CSC was that criminal actions spring from criminal mind-sets. Prisoners who chose to participate in the program could obtain an earlier release date, but they would have to accept CSC premises—that criminal behavior is generated by criminal thought patterns, and that the inmates needed to learn to identify and change those thought patterns within themselves in order to prevent future bad behavior. CSC staff encountered some resistance. One inmate named "Todd" denied that he had a criminal mind-set because the few acts of violence he committed in his life were all situational. According to him, there were contextual reasons and, at most, some momentary lapses in good judgment that led to his behavior. Because he refused to describe his past thoughts and actions as indicative of criminal thinking, Todd was given a negative performance evaluation in the program.

Generally, prisoners who resisted staff portrayals of their biographies were regarded as engaging in "distorted concrete thinking" rather than possessing authoritative understandings of their own thoughts and actions (Fox 2001, p. 180). If an inmate complained about the conditions in the prison or the treatment he received from guards, the CSC staff suggested this, too, was evidence of a criminal mind-set. When multiple prisoners voiced the same complaints, their claims were portrayed by CSC staff as indicators that they all shared the same faulty cognitive patterns—such as perceiving themselves as victims and being quick to anger (Fox 2001, p. 179).

Studies by Sanders, Gubrium, and Fox provide just a few examples of research on minding in controversial or unusual contexts. Other scholars have examined conventionally questionable attributions of mental competence or agency to animals, human beings, and even non-biological objects (Holstein 1993; Owens 2007; Pollner and McDonald-Wikler 2003; Weinberg 1997). Also worth mentioning in this context are those interpretive constructionists who have conducted more historical studies of how contentious mental categories were originally invented and subsequently applied. Addiction, attention deficit disorder, IQ, pre-menstrual syndrome, and other concepts can be shown to be temporally contingent ways of making sense of "problematic" behavior rather than simply accurate reflections of inner realities (Conrad and Schneider 1992; Figert 2003; Reinarman 2005).

Invoking Mind to Accomplish Everyday Goals

It is useful to study inferences and attributions of mental states in con-troversial or unusual circumstances, as (arguably) scholars such as Sanders, Gubrium, and Fox have done. However, once one begins look-ing for the interpretive construction of mental phenomena, its ubiquity becomes readily apparent. Some researchers have advocated a broader and more systematic examination of mental attributions. As preliminary examples, consider the following four lists:

1. People regularly avow intentions or impute them to others:
   - I went to the store today in order to buy some milk.
   - I thought I should call you because . . .
   - I've always believed that honesty is the best policy.
   - You're just trying to get some attention.
   - You don't think about anyone but yourself.
2. Individuals also routinely ascribe intelligence and other traits to their own minds and those of others:
   - She is as sharp as a tack. He is as dumb as a post.
   - I must be dense. I'm an idiot.
   - You've lost your mind. You're crazy.
   - My mind is a blank.
   - You're a fuzzy-minded liberal.
   - You're so closed minded.
   - I'm concerned about you.

3. Many statements seem to suggest mind's actions and accomplishments:
   - I don't pay attention to their opinions.
   - I wonder what would happen if . . .
   - I understand your position.
   - I couldn't agree more.
   - I know just what you mean.
   - You've got the experience needed to make good judgments.
   - Don't be so judgmental.
   - You're like an elephant—you never forget.
4. Some commonly used expressions seem to involve denying mental capacities:
   - I don't know why I did that.
   - I can't believe you did that.
   - I can't read your mind.
   - You can't predict what their reaction will be.
   - You just don't get it.
   - You don't know how it feels.

As these short lists indicate, people frequently reference mental phenomena of one kind or another. So routine is mental claimsmaking that it may be easy for analysts to treat such assertions as unremarkable or to assume they are mere "reality reports" provided by respondents. Some researchers, however, make such mental claimsmaking the central subject of their inquiries (Coulter 1979; Edwards 1997; Potter 2006). By problematizing[8] the reality of minds, researchers can investigate the meanings that may be created and the interactional goals that may be served by invoking or implying the existence of a mental action or trait.

Consider the expression commonly invoked among friends—"I can't believe you did that!"—where "that" can be kissing someone at a party, achieving a remarkable grade, saying something controversial, wearing a questionable outfit, or some other action. The expression "I can't believe" could be treated as a more or less accurate report on the inner workings of the person's mind: The individual lacks the capacity to believe that a particular action occurred. Alternatively, another route would be to examine how the phrase gives meaning to the act in question (which is perhaps deemed "outrageous" in a relatively serious or humorous sense), to the actor who performed the act (who perhaps is being portrayed as a major deviant or a minor prankster), and to the speaker (who may imply something about his or her own character via this description). These meanings may serve one or more interactional goals, such as teasing, complaining, praising, and so on. The specific sense and purpose the phrase "I can't believe" acquires depends on the circumstances of its use.

Similarly, consider politician Mitt Romney's claim that "the idea of Bill Clinton back in the White House with nothing to do is something I just can't imagine." This statement, which was made in 2008 during a nationally televised debate,[9] can be seen as an attempt by Romney to define his own political identity and garner the support of Republican voters across the United States. It is not necessarily an objective or first-hand account of his mental incapacity to envision possible futures.

In this way, mental assertions can be studied for their *reflexive, indexical,* and *consequential* properties (Edwards 1997, p. 65). That is, mental claims can be seen as simultaneously *giving* meaning to the contexts in which they are invoked, *deriving* meaning from the contexts in which they are invoked, and *performing actions* within the contexts they are invoked (see also Heritage 1984).

Positive claims to knowledge can be similarly analyzed for the meanings they create and the functions they serve. In his helpful article, Charles Antaki (2004) quotes from a videotaped interaction where a woman named "Zoe" offers her mother "Lyn" a cigarette. Lyn pauses before answering reticently, and then Zoe subsequently invokes a knowledge claim:

> Zoe: Do you want one?
> Lyn: Well, I've already had a cigarette of yours.
> Zoe: That's alright 'cause I know you're going to buy me some.
> (Antaki 2004, p. 675)[10]

The phrase "I know" could be treated as accurately or honestly conveying information about the future that is contained in Zoe's mind. Alternatively, Antaki suggests, Zoe's statement can be seen as performing "social action" of some sort: "Zoe is up to something, not clinically reporting some inner reality. . . . It could be a hint (that it is Lyn's turn to buy cigarettes) or perhaps a complaint (that Lyn is always on the scrounge)" (2004, p. 675).

This approach to studying mind's meanings and consequences differs noticeably from more objectivist approaches to mind espoused by Blumer, Zerubavel, and other social scientists. However, it does resonate fairly well with two extant and more widely known strands of literature.

Research on "motive talk"—the intentions or reasons that people ascribe to their own or others' conduct (Mills 1940; Hunter 1984)—can be used to justify and support the development of more interpretive approaches to mind.[11] Authors working in this vein have been largely skeptical or at least agnostic toward claims about motivations and causality (Hopper 1993; Scott and Lyman 1968). Excuses, justifications, and other forms of accounts are seen as cultural "vocabularies" that actors employ to manage impressions and protect their identities. Accusations of bad conduct can be parried by claiming a lack of understanding ("I did not know my action would lead to negative results") or a lack of desire ("I did not want to perform this action—I was forced to"). Even explanations of positive accomplishments regularly involve attributions of some underlying intentions or mental states, such as determination or adherence to high ideals (Benoit 1997).

To pursue a broader interpretive sociology of cognition, however, motive-talk analysts would need to expand their interests in "intentions" and "reasons" to include claimsmaking about all kinds of mental phenomena (see Coulter 1989, p. 6). As ethnomethodologists and discourse analysts have shown, new insights can be gained by carefully examining the interpretive and interpersonal production of "forgetting" (Lynch and Bogen 2005), "being honest with someone" (Edwards and Fasulo 2006), "holding an opinion" (Puchta and Potter 2002), "becoming surprised" (Heritage 2005), and other mental states. An exclusive focus on motivations is unnecessarily narrow.

Recent developments in qualitative methodology also have an affinity with an interest in the interpretive construction of mind. In some circles, research interviews are no longer treated as procedures for mining respondents' minds for nuggets of information or opinion (Holstein and Gubrium 1995a). Instead, researcher-subject encounters are coming to be seen as claimsmaking or meaningmaking occasions that "construct" more than simply "reveal" the perspectives of informants (Atkinson and Silverman 1997; Baker 2002; Koro-Ljungberg 2008; Potter and Mulkay 1985; Rapley 2001). If descriptions of mental contents are responsive to specific interactional settings and goals, then this complicates naturalists' efforts to obtain accurate understandings of respondents' beliefs and other inner experiences (see also Gubrium and Holstein 1997). Mind becomes less an internal feature of individuals and more a rhetorical or interactional move, a contingent outcome of the particular encounter that produced it. Studying that production process is different than documenting shared cultural mind-sets (Zerubavel 1997) or investigating the idiosyncratic details of an individual's inner dialogue (Blumer 1969, pp. 94–96).

Conclusion

Constructionists have a long tradition of advancing thoroughly social conceptions of human cognition. Mind has repeatedly been described as a socially constituted ability and as a reservoir of cultural knowledge (Berger and Luckmann 1966; Mead 1934). Again and again, constructionists assert that human beings learn how to think by internalizing the mind-sets of the groups with which they associate (Shibutani 1955; Zerubavel 1997). These socially acquired perspectives are said to profoundly influence—but not necessarily determine (Blumer 1969)—how individuals define reality and pursue their courses of action.

I have argued here that there is a smaller tradition of constructionism that revolves around a different set of questions: What if mind is studied as an indeterminate "object" that is variably interpreted in the course of everyday life? What would result if mind itself were treated as an idea or claim rather than as a container and conveyor of ideas and claims? This second camp shows that new insights can be gained about the meanings that may be created and the purposes that may be served when people invoke, affirm, and contest the existence of mental phenomena. In so doing, these researchers attempt to bring a wide range of mental phenomena into consideration as *interpretive* rather than *objective* constructions: thinking, intending, imagining, possessing opinions, forgetting, predicting, and so on.

Though I have written this chapter as if there are two distinct constructionist approaches to the study of mind, I also acknowledge that the division is not clear-cut. Complicated variations and overlaps can be found both within and between each camp. For example, both Blumer (1969) and Zerubavel (1997) confidently treat mind as a real human ability, but the former scholar emphasizes individual discretion much more than the latter. Sanders (2003b) and Jeff Coulter (1979), in turn, share some interests in studying attributions of mind, but they combine those predilections with divergent agendas: Sanders suggests that *animals* are *more* cognitively endowed than they are conventionally assumed, whereas Coulter argues that *human beings* are *less* cognitively active than conventionally assumed.[12] Meanwhile, Jaber Gubrium (2003), Derek Edwards (1997), and Jonathan Potter (2006) attempt to remain more noncommittal about the objective status of mind as they conduct their studies.

Despite such complexities, I suggest that my rough distinction does have merit. At least as a starting point, it seems useful to recognize that mind can be analyzed as a social "achievement" in a relatively objective or interpretive sense. The difference tends to hinge on whether the constructionist premise that "meaning is not inherent" is applied to objects that minds perceive or to the idea of mind itself. Those who read or conduct constructionist research could benefit from recognizing this difference and tracing out its implications for their areas of interest.

In the next chapter, I examine theory and research on a related microsociological issue, emotions. Human beings are often described as doing one of three things: thinking, feeling, and acting. In the past few decades, research on the second aspect of human experience has grown dramatically in the social sciences, challenging previous understandings of our feelings as exclusively or primarily biological phenomena. Scholars have achieved some profound and fascinating insights about the cultural and interactional dimensions of emotions. As with the extensive literature on mind, though, there is still much room for more rigorously interpretive studies of emotions. Despite the proliferation of avowedly constructionist research, most scholars take a relatively OSC rather than ISC approach when they argue that emotions are socially created, produced, and worked on.

Notes

1. On this issue, Charon (2007, p. 102) and Low (2008, pp. 332–333) notice a difference in emphasis between Mead and Blumer.

2. Blumer (1969, p. 2) might say that Zerubavel emphasizes the second premise of interactionism ("The meaning of . . . things is derived from, or arises out of, the social interaction that one has with one's fellows") but neglects the third premise ("These meanings are handled in, and modified through, an interpretive process used by the person in dealing with the things he encounters").

3. Here and elsewhere, I have mixed in some of my own examples with those Zerubavel provides in my attempt to provide a clear and concise explanation of his approach.

4. For Garfinkel (1967), the documentary method of interpretation actually occurs in *all* acts of classification, not just those involving mind. See also Heritage (1984).

5. For example, when people observe a human companion "quickly" eating a food item at the dinner table, they may wonder or inquire what that behavior signifies. Does the person think the food is delicious? Is she especially hungry or perhaps in a hurry to get somewhere else? Has he learned unhealthy eating habits or forgotten his manners? Any particular answer might involve the imputation or avowal of mind.

6. As with Sanders's research, ideas from Gubrium's study can be applied to interaction more broadly: Even among normally functional individuals, it is not uncommon for people to look for cognitive patterns that lie behind behavior

while simultaneously recognizing that there will be accidents, exceptions, and flukes that need to be disregarded or weighted less significantly.

7. Actually, in many quite ordinary social settings, individuals are not necessarily assumed to have authoritative knowledge about their own mental states (see Coulter 1979).

8. This problematizing can occur by either *doubting* the accuracy of claims about human cognition (e.g., its assumed pervasiveness) or by *bracketing* human cognition (i.e., setting aside the issue of veracity). Coulter (1979) tends to adopt the first strategy whereas Edwards and Potter (2005) tend to adopt the latter.

9. According to the website of the *New York Times,* Romney made this statement during the Republican national debate that was held on January 24, 2008, in Boca Raton, Florida. He likely repeated similar statements on other occasions as well.

10. Readers are encouraged to consult Antaki's original article for a more precise transcription.

11. In US society at least (Lillard 1998), people are regularly assumed to have an understanding of and control over what they are doing. Consequently, lay (and scholarly) debates about the morality and causality of conduct frequently implicate the mental components of "knowledge" and "will" (Scott and Lyman 1968, p. 48).

12. Similarly, some analysts prefer to treat vocabularies of motive as mere rhetorical devices (Hopper 1993) whereas other scholars grant that such vocabularies can sometimes serve as actual (or objectively accurate) reasons for conduct (Mills 1940).

3

Managing Emotions

Since Arlie Hochschild's (1983) groundbreaking research, the sociology of emotions has grown exponentially. Sociologists now frequently document the social dimensions of emotional experiences and displays, as evidenced by hundreds of journal articles and a recent handbook (Stets and Turner 2006). Following Hochschild's early example, probably the most popular and prolific strand of research centers on the active role that individuals and groups play in shaping their own and others' emotional experiences and expressions (Kemper 1989, p. 16). The influence of her concept of "emotion management" can be seen in a plethora of research projects on a variety of roles, occupations, and settings, such as those involving baseball players (Snyder and Ammons 1993), casino card dealers (Enarson 1993), detectives (Stenross and Kleinman 1989), gymnasts (Snyder 1990), litigators and paralegals (Pierce 1995), married couples (Duncombe and Marsden 1998), medical students (Smith and Kleinman 1989), nurses (Bolton 2001), prison inmates (Greer 2002), professors (Bellas 1999), rape workers (Martin 2005), salespeople (Schweingruber and Berns 2005), search and rescue volunteers (Lois 2001), support groups (Wolkomir 2001), undergraduates (Albas and Albas 1988), wheelchair users (Cahill and Eggleston 1994), and staff at an abortion clinic and animal shelter (Arluke 1998; Wolkomir and Powers 2007), just to name some. Consistent with general constructionist principles, and contrary to assumptions about emotions being primarily natural or physical phenomena, these scholars study how people "work" on emotions, and in so doing help create feelings and displays (Lively 2006; Peterson 2006; Thoits 1996).

47

The management of emotion can be given an objective or interpretive spin, however. Some authors also study the creation and manipulation of emotions and make parallel arguments, but on a different level (e.g., Edwards 1999; Gubrium 1992; Staske 1996; Whalen and Zimmerman 1998). In keeping with the theme of this book, this chapter attempts to clarify the similarities and differences between research on what I call objective emotion management (OEM) and interpretive emotion management (IEM), two distinct yet partially overlapping ways of arguing that emotions are "socially constructed."

Objective Emotion Management

In the objective approach, emotions are treated as real properties of human beings. People think and act, but they also feel. OEM scholars argue that this aspect of human relations has been underappreciated in past research, and they want to remedy that neglect. OEM scholars do so by formulating definitions of emotion that go beyond the biological, by studying the strategies through which emotional states are generated or suppressed, and by highlighting the potentially problematic consequences for those who are paid to perform OEM as an implicit or explicit part of their jobs.

Beyond Biology: OEM Conceptions of Emotions

The foil for OEM analyses are scholarly and lay beliefs that emotions are primarily biological or automatic responses to environmental cues. Some psychologists, for example, follow Darwin in arguing that at least some emotions may be innate features of our anatomy—that is, "hardwired" reactions that have been inculcated within us via the process of natural selection (Cosmides and Tooby 2000; Ekman 1994). Emotions such as anger or fear have aided in the survival of the species: they prepare human beings for action (e.g., fight or flight) and signal information to others (e.g., "back off!"). Lay conceptions of emotions sometimes also downplay the social and contingent dimensions of emotion. In everyday life, people speak of themselves and others as having "natural" reactions to events, including grief at loss, happiness with success, and love for their children. Sociologists of emotion often challenge these scholarly and lay viewpoints by arguing that our feelings are not necessarily automatic. They suggest that emotions are contingent upon and shaped by social forces and human action—from cultural norms to demography to ad hoc interpretive processes—and cannot be reduced to biological or psychological determinants (Hochschild 1983; Lofland 1985).

Defining emotions. It is often difficult if not impossible to define scientific concepts clearly (Agger 2000); however, even a rough definition can guide research and inform readers of an author's theoretical stance. Thus, it makes sense that some scholars would attempt to specify what they mean by "emotions" in the first place. OEM researchers attempt to go beyond biology, but they still assume that emotions are things— actual sensations that people can create and manage—and their conceptions of emotions reflect this assumption. Most famously, Hochschild (1983, pp. 17, 219) defined emotion as a biological *sense,* like sight and smell, that tells us information about the world and prepares us for action. Our feelings are another way we learn about and navigate within the world around us. At the same time, Hochschild (1983, p. 28) asserted, emotions give us clues to our own perspectives. We can work back from what we feel to discover what we thought about or expected from a situation. For example, a feeling of frustration at a traffic jam might be traced to expectations about how a particular freeway usually works (or how it ought to work) as well as to assumptions about the value of time spent inside one's car versus outside of it. Even fear of danger, which may seem an almost instinctive response, has a social dimension. Fear is prompted and shaped by socialization: danger matters to us because we are taught to have a strong sense of self, a self that we don't want to lose. "Without this prior expectation of a continuous self, information about danger would be signaled in fundamentally different ways" (Hochschild 1983, p. 221).

Many researchers find Hochschild's (1983, pp. 201–222) conception of emotion as a perspective-guided sense to be well-argued and plausible. However, it is important to note that a single definition has not been universally adopted by sociologists and other scholars. Steven Gordon (1990), for example, once proposed to treat emotion as "relatively undifferentiated bodily arousal," leaving "sentiments" as the more proper subject matter of sociological research. Sentiments he defined as "socially constructed pattern[s] of sensations, expressive gestures, and cultural meanings organized around a relationship to a social object, usually another person" (Gordon 1990, pp. 563, 566). Gordon Clanton (1989, p. 179) offers a more minimalist definition at the outset of his research on jealousy: "Emotions are responses to situations interpreted on the basis of previous social learning." In general, researchers' particular conceptions of emotions are, rightfully, intertwined with their theoretical perspectives and explanatory goals (Smith-Lovin 1995, p. 119).

In an important article, Jaap van Brakel (1994, pp. 203–204) lists over twenty different definitions of emotions appearing in scholarly publications during the 1980s and early 1990s.[1] His list reveals complicated overlaps and discontinuities among various social scientists and philosophers regarding the proper definition of emotions.[2] Further complications arise from the incompatible distinctions that scholars make between key terms, such as "affect," "feelings," and "moods." Some scholars distinguish "basic" from "secondary" emotions—with the former argued to be more biologically grounded or universal than the latter—but their lists of what counts as basic emotions do not completely converge (van Brakel 1994, pp. 184–186). Some scholars reject that there are any basic emotions (Gordon 1990, p. 567) or question the utility of the basic/nonbasic distinction (Averill 1994), whereas other scholars claim that all emotions are basic (Ekman 1994). Some biologically oriented scholars attempt to objectively define certain emotions by looking for recurring patterns of physiological changes (e.g., in the face, brain, body) that constitute or correspond to those specific emotions, but these efforts have produced questionable results (Barrett 2006).[3] Still other scholars do not explicitly define emotions at all; in particular, many researchers who write about objective emotion management must simply trust that readers will have a rough idea of what they mean by "emotion" (or by "anger," "sadness," etc.). This too is understandable, given the Sisyphean challenges involved in clearly defining concepts (Agger 2000, pp. 143, 239).

In short, OEM scholars challenge biological conceptions of emotions but still approach emotions (and feelings, sentiments, moods, etc.) as actual sensations that people experience bodily. Some follow Hochschild in attempting to specify precisely what emotions consist of—such as a mixture of biological, cultural, and interactional elements—while others rely on implicit definitions. However, defining emotion remains a controversial and unresolved issue among OEM scholars and across the social sciences.

Creating and Manipulating Emotions

A useful purpose is served by conceiving of emotions as more than biological and as malleable to human effort: it opens up space for OEM research on how people "construct" their emotional states alone and in concert with others. Hochschild proposed two key concepts to guide such studies: surface acting and deep acting.

Hochschild (1983, p. 216) traces the theoretical roots of surface acting to Erving Goffman's (1959) dramaturgical orientation, which highlights the intricate strategies people employ to conform to social norms and manage the impressions they make on others. According to Goffman (1963, p. 11), people learn what the proper emotional tone should be for a given occasion and then attempt to "fit in." They can smile at a party even though they are unhappy; they can express gratitude for a birthday present that they do not actually want; they can feign disappointment when they are actually pleased by a deal they have made. All of these behaviors are examples of surface acting, the management of feeling displays (Hochschild 1983, p. 33).

Whereas Goffman's version of dramaturgy tends to stop at the surface of the skin, Hochschild attempts to go further with the concept of deep acting. Human beings not only manage how they appear to feel, Hochschild argues; they also try to control what they are actually feeling. People do not just smile when they are unhappy—they remind themselves of why they should be happy (perhaps by focusing on a positive aspect of a situation or redefining a negative event as positive in some way). People don't just feign gratitude—they sometimes focus on the effort someone put into an unwanted gift in an attempt to create a real feeling of appreciation. People don't just cover up nervousness— they breathe deeply, meditate, or take other steps to reduce their anxiety. People *work* not only on their displays but on their actual feelings, either for their own benefit or so that others can observe the more true or felt emotion being expressed. This latter form of work Hochschild (1979, p. 551, n. 2) originally termed "emotion work" or "emotion management" and contrasted it with the mere surface acting that Goffman focused on. However, for the purposes of this chapter, I consider (objective) "emotion management" and "emotion work" as broader categories that encompass both surface acting and deep acting, as others have done (Kemper 2000, p. 51).

The focus on objective emotion management draws attention to efforts of individuals—and the discretion they may exert—in "constructing" their emotions; however, this work does not take place in a vacuum (Copp 1998). In several respects, it is guided by and embedded within social contexts. First, deep and surface acting are prompted and constrained by cultural rules that govern how we ought to feel or at least appear to feel on various occasions. Generally, people are expected to express gratitude for gifts and mourn the loss of loved ones. However, emotion rules are cultural not biological. They vary by time and place. Different cultures or subcultures may develop their own expectations for how to mourn the death of a child (Lofland 1985), how much sympathy should be shown to victims of catastrophes (Clark 1997), or how much affection spouses should show one another (Derné 1994). Other people teach us the emotion norms of our (sub)culture as well as strategies for conforming, as evidenced by the simple but frequent reminders parents give to their children to express gratitude (i.e., "Say 'thank you'!").

A second social dimension of OEM is that it can be performed *between* individuals and not simply *within* individuals. Human beings frequently attempt to shape the emotions of their companions (Thoits 1996). After a breakup, one friend may console another by suggesting that "There are plenty of fish in the sea" or "At least now you won't have to deal with his or her annoying friends." Either statement could be considered an example of cognitive emotion work—attempting to modify feeling by redefining a situation—that is accomplished interpersonally rather than merely intrapersonally. Even bodily emotion work—trying to shape feelings by affecting physical arousal—can be prompted interpersonally. Football players may try to generate excitement and confidence in themselves *and* their teammates by pounding on each others shoulder pads and screaming loudly (Zurcher 1982).

A third social feature of OEM is that it can occur within one's place of employment as well as in one's personal life. Emotion rules and emotion management can be endorsed (if not strictly enforced) by employers. In her study, Hochschild (1983) argued that airlines trained flight attendants to suppress hostile emotions toward unruly customers. Trainees were instructed to perform surface acting (e.g., by always maintaining a smile) as well as deep acting (e.g., by thinking of the passengers as houseguests or as children). Attendants were also told to perform interpersonal emotion management on their coworkers (e.g., by allowing a frustrated attendant to "vent" complaints out of earshot of passengers) as well as on passengers (via attendants' polite and calm demeanors). This emotional labor—being paid to perform surface and deep acting at an individual or an interpersonal level—has become a very popular subfield (Lively 2006; Steinberg and Figart 1999). Much has been written about paid emotion management performed by various kinds of employees (Bolton 2005). Special attention has been given to the issue of gender differences in the expectations that employers, employees, and customers have about emotional labor (Bellas 2001), stemming in part from Hochschild's (1983, p. 171) assertion that female flight attendants have more demands placed upon them than male attendants. Related but distinguishable from gender is occupational stratification: OEM researchers argue that individuals who hold higher status occupations (doctor vs. nurse, executive vs. secretary, manager vs. waitress) tend to be shielded from much of the burden of emotional labor in addition to receiving higher pay.

In sum, OEM scholars study the active effort people put into shaping the display and experience of emotional states. OEM researchers document the various strategies people use to perform "work" on their own and others' feelings. The creative work of generating or suppressing emotions—whether through surface or deep acting—is guided by cultural norms, the requirements of paid employment, gender expectations, and other constraining factors.

The Consequences of OEM: Inauthenticity and Potential Social Ills

Part of the appeal of Hochschild's *The Managed Heart* (1983)—in addition to the useful concepts she coined for describing emotion management—is the book's moral stance. Hochschild does not simply describe how emotions operate; she simultaneously raises concerns over social justice, particularly for those who perform emotion management as part of their jobs. Hochschild argued that emotional labor is frequently underrecognized and poorly compensated, despite the effort, skill, and sacrifices it can require. Many scholars have followed up on Hochschild's concerns, by expanding, refining, and sometimes challenging aspects of her argument.

Hochschild contends that the management of emotions in one's personal life is usually a healthy practice. In interactions with their relatives and friends, people can exchange "gifts" of sympathy, gratitude, love, and other emotional experiences and displays. They can "work up" (or "work down") their feelings as they see fit, while navigating within the context of cultural norms and interpersonal expectations. If a person experiences anger, they might use that feeling as a "clue" to their perspective: perhaps they will discover that they think a companion's action was a sign of disrespect and subsequently decide whether or how they want to respond.

According to Hochschild (1983, p. 19), a "transmutation" occurs when this "private emotional system" moves into the public realm of paid employment. Emotional gifts become commodities to be bought and sold, informal emotion rules become set and enforced by employers, and a wage is substituted for reciprocity (Hochschild 1983, p. 86). For example, customers may repay polite service with rudeness or indifference, but workers may be required to always maintain a friendly demeanor. Many service industry employers emphasize the need for a "positive attitude" and suggest that "the customer is never wrong," leading their workers to perform a myriad of surface and deep acting strategies. Alternatively, some workers may be paid to display and foster negative emotions. Bill collectors may be instructed to assume that delinquent borrowers are either loafers or cheats rather than individuals suffering from unfortunate financial setbacks or expressing legitimate complaint about a product or service. In this way, collectors are encouraged to use their voices to display anger and create alarm, instead of showing sympathy. However, whether performed in an aggressive or (more often) pleasant style, Hochschild contends that negative consequences can accompany emotional labor.

When emotions are managed for company purposes, workers risk becoming burned out or alienated from their feelings. As a result of continuous deep acting, they may feel "numb" or they may start to question what their own thoughts and feelings mean. In other words, emotional laborers may begin to lose some of the "signal function" Hochschild (1983, p. 29) identified in her definition of emotions. Workers may either begin to feel less—as with burnout—or they may begin to question whether their feelings reflected their own perspectives or the perspectives of their employers. Hochschild (p. 192) sees in modern society increased concerns over "authenticity," or being honest with one's self. With the increasing commercialization of human feeling, Hochschild (p. 197) believes that more and more people now wonder if their emotions are their own or their company's. One solution she proposes—in addition to increasing the recognition, respect, and compensation given to emotional labor—is to provide emotion workers a greater degree of control over their own jobs (p. 189).

In subsequent studies, scholars have tended to soften or complicate Hochschild's argument. Some scholars note that emotional laborers may not suffer ill effects from emotion management at all. Certain people may actually enjoy managing their emotions on the job—or at least *some* workers may, *some* of the time. For example, Allen Smith and Sherryl Kleinman (1989) found that detectives dreaded interacting with crime victims (who vented anger and made frequent bids for sympathy), but relished interacting with criminals (whose belligerence was defined as merely a strategic move in an engaging game). Other scholars highlighted the complex array of variables that might contribute to emotional burnout or alienation: a person's responsibilities at home as well as at work, the status of their occupation, the culture of their workplace, their individual personalities, and other factors. These researchers have found that the complexity of social life makes it difficult to generalize about the positive and negative effects of emotional labor (Erickson and Grove 2008; Lively 2006; Steinberg and Figart 1999; Wharton 1999).

Interpretive Emotion Management

Many researchers now study how people "work" on emotions, but not all do so in the same way. When some authors write about "managing" emotions, they use a similar vocabulary to mean something different than those who follow in the tradition of Hochschild. In this section, I explain research that demonstrates how "real or disguised feeling states" are not only managed in the traditional sense of surface and deep acting, but also through the interactive process of labeling feelings. These more interpretive scholars tend to sidestep or reframe the issues with which objectivist scholars are concerned, including defining and distinguishing emotion states, describing the processes through which emotions are "worked up" or "worked down," and explaining the problems associated with emotional labor.

Studying Conceptions of Emotions

Recall that OEM scholars wrestle with a difficult question in the course of their research: What exactly *are* emotions? Attempting to answer this question brings sociologists in competition with philosophers, psychologists, and others who have proposed their own definitions of emotions. Are emotions primarily social or biological? Is it primarily nature or nurture, or some intricate combination, that leads human beings to feel the way they do? Do social contexts tend to draw forth innate responses or do cultural regulations shape the feelings that arise out of cognitive appraisals of situations? What precisely is "it" that people "work on" when they perform OEM?

For the most part, IEM scholars do not need to rely on explicit or implicit definitions of emotions. That is because IEM scholars are primarily interested in how other people think and talk about emotions—how people assert, confirm, negate, and act on their own ideas about the existence and functioning of various "emotions," "feelings," "moods," and so on. Rather than answering questions about how emotions *as things* operate within individuals and groups, IEM researchers tend to bracket those questions in order to focus squarely on how understandings and claims about emotions are developed by various individuals and groups. By approaching emotions *as interpretations,* IEM scholars bring an overlapping but discernibly different perspective to studying the role of emotion in social life.

Folk theories and vocabularies of emotion. Social scientists are not the only ones to theorize and analyze emotions; laypersons do too. Just as there is controversy in the scientific community regarding the nature of emotions and the definitions of terms used to refer to them, there is cross-cultural diversity in lay conceptions of the nature, varieties, and functioning of emotions.[4] In terms of physiology, various cultures connect emotions alternatively to the brain, heart, liver, or intestines (Russell 1991, p. 429). Different societies develop their respective understandings of the kinds of events that trigger emotions, what those emotions will be, and who will experience them (Lutz 1988; White 2000). More local or subcultural conceptions of emotions can also be developed, as Gubrium (1992) found in his comparative study of two family therapy facilities. In addition, individuals have some discretion to selectively and creatively apply popular understandings about emotions as they communicate with others and pursue their interactional goals (Edwards 1999; White 2000).

It is true that OEM scholars attend to cultural diversity—particularly the emotion rules that different groups develop to control their members' emotional displays and experiences. But there is a key difference: IEM scholars are more likely to adopt a *constitutive* rather than *regulative* view of norms (see Heritage 1984; Ibarra 2008). When an emotion rule is invoked—perhaps about the proper expression of gratitude—it becomes a tool for characterizing a situation. Situations are indeterminate, and many norms can be said to apply at any given time; consequently, the selection and application of a "rule reminder" can be seen as a constitutive, meaning-making tactic as much as a regulative one. The statement "You should try to show a little more gratitude" would likely create different meanings and serve different purposes than statements suggesting that someone is "focusing quite naturally on their self-interests" or "acting like a total ingrate." Speakers create meaning and guide conduct when they choose to invoke a particular norm and express it in a particular way. An interest in emotions as interpretations thus causes IEM scholars to more closely examine the specific words people use to depict feelings and rules (see Edwards 1999; Staske 1999).

When IEM scholars draw from cross-cultural research, they are more likely to do so in an attempt to problematize assumptions about the one-to-one correspondence between emotion categories and the bodily states to which they purportedly refer. Is there some "thing" that people call "fear"? Is there a bodily sensation that goes by the name "love"? One way to open up space for research on the creation of emotional states as inter- pretations is to highlight the contingent nature of emotional vocabularies.

Ethnographers who study the vocabularies of emotion that exist in different languages have found much overlap but some diversity too.[5] There are at least two interesting points of contrast. First, sometimes other cultures make finer distinctions than English speakers do. The word "disgust" can be used by English speakers to refer to moral indignation as well as a physical reaction to an unpleasant smell; "surprise" can be used to refer to unforeseen circumstances that are pleasant or unpleasant; "fear" can be used when a person is faced with physical injury or with a social injury. In contrast, the Ifaluk use two separate words for the two forms of disgust and the two forms of surprise; the Utku similarly distin- guish between the two types of fear (Russell 1991). Second, sometimes other cultures make looser distinctions than found in English. Many cul- tures appear to use a single word to describe emotions that English speakers would characterize as either sadness or anger; where English speakers distinguish shame, guilt, shyness, and embarrassment, the Javanese use one word—*isin* (Russell 1991). The conclusion interpretive scholars tend to draw from these sorts of comparisons is that the identifi- cation of emotional states is not a natural or automatic process. Different languages provide different sets of resources for making sense of feel- ings. What people think or claim they feel is influenced by the terms they have inherited from their ancestors and contemporaries.

The ambiguity of physiological states. In contrast to the role Hochschild's (1983) book has played in OEM scholarship, there is no one text that serves as the foundation for IEM research. Some interpre- tive researchers, though, draw inspiration from Stanley Schachter and Jerome Singer's (1962) early experimental studies. Schachter and Singer attempted to show that social factors influence perceptions of bodily experiences. The researchers injected study participants with the drug epinephrine (an adrenaline that produces a state of physical arousal) while varying certain contextual factors. They found that participants' self-reports of their emotional states were influenced by the actions of those around them—specifically, research assistants who pretended to be similarly dosed research participants. By speaking and behaving as if they were amused, angry, or euphoric, research assistants could shape participants' self-perceptions of their own bodily states. Schachter and Singer's study has been followed by much psychological research. Collectively, this work demonstrates that the physiological differences between emotions are small, that different emotions are accompanied by overlapping sensations, and that cognition plays a significant role in the interpretation and labeling of these elements (Barrett 2006; Loseke and Kusenbach 2008).

A more sociological perspective on emotional identification can be found in Morris Rosenberg's (1990) symbolic interactionist discussion of "reflexivity," which he defines as human beings' capacity to reflect and act upon themselves. In his theoretical article, Rosenberg devotes two sections to the reflexive control individuals can exert over their emotional experiences and displays; these ideas overlap with Hochschild's discussion of deep acting and surface acting. One section of Rosenberg's paper, however, focuses on the agency individuals exert when they consider and interpret their own emotional states.

Rosenberg starts by "admitting" (to more objectivist readers) that emotional states may occasionally manifest themselves in a clear and easily labeled fashion, but he then argues that emotions are very often ambiguous and require reflexive cognitive work for their identification. He identifies four factors that generate this ambiguity and the need for reflexive self-interpretation. First, Rosenberg (1990, p. 5) suggests that "different emotions may have similar physical manifestations." Anger, anxiety, excitement, and fear may all involve overlapping sensations. Second, ambiguity can result from "the fact that emotions may be mixed" (1990, p. 5). On a roller coaster, for example, a person may experience both fear and pleasurable excitement, or a person may feel both sad and elated at a graduation ceremony. Third, emotional ambiguity can arise "because there is no touchstone by which an internal experience can be measured confidently" (p. 5). Unlike checking the fluid levels in an automobile, there is no dipstick to determine whether a person is "full of rage" or "all out of love." Consequently, individuals lack clear-cut means for discussing their feelings and comparing them to the feelings of others. Fourth, Rosenberg notes that people may find it "difficult to label an emotion accurately [because their] language may not provide an appropriate term for it" (p. 5). For example, since Americans don't often use the German term "schadenfreude," they may be less equipped to identify their own experiences of pleasure at the misfortune of others. Rosenberg argues that all of these factors can create uncertainty and complicate individuals' recognition of their emotional states. As a result, it takes reflexive cognitive work to label emotions: "We do not simply 'feel' an emotion; we also 'think' an emotion" (p. 5).

Work by Schachter and Singer and by Rosenberg can certainly aid and inform research on the labeling of emotions. However, there are at least two potential drawbacks to relying on these authors for theoretical inspiration on IEM. One problematic tendency is the need to "prove" that some emotions are actually ambiguous, as a matter of fact. This concern can lead scholars into a complicated—and objectivist—debate. Instead, IEM scholars could simply rely on the constructionist premise that "meaning is not inherent." All conditions—whether bodily, interactional, or societal—can be understood or described in multiple ways. By operating under this assumption, IEM scholars can attempt to conduct coherent and cumulative research on labeling feelings, while bracketing objective questions about the actual degree of ambiguity that labelers face.

This leads directly to a second and more important limitation of using Schachter and Singer and Rosenberg as sources of inspiration for research on IEM: it may be unnecessarily restrictive to frame emotional identification as primarily a matter of resolving bodily ambiguity. When people ascribe emotions to themselves and others, there are a host of considerations that could come into play, and researchers need not assume by default that the body is central among them. For example, during job interviews and in letters of application, people may claim that they are "thrilled" by an opportunity, or they may tell a friend or a romantic partner "I'm afraid our relationship isn't going to work out." In either case, the emotional claims makers may be oriented more—if not entirely—toward external circumstances than toward their own internal bodily states.

Thus, the labeling of feelings could be conceptualized in broader terms: Emotional identification is not necessarily about resolving bodily ambiguity. It is a meaning-making project that may be oriented to interactional goals, past and future situations, and other social (rather than physiological) concerns.

Identifying and Modifying Instances of Emotions

As I mentioned earlier, there is a very large literature on the strategies people use to manage their emotions in the more objective sense. Much has been written about the techniques that individuals use in order to evoke or suppress emotion at work or in their private lives. A much smaller body of research focuses on an arguably equally important topic: how people "work up" and "work down" interpretations of emotional states. By conceiving of emotions as labels that are applied to indeterminate states of affairs, IEM researchers open up space to study how descriptions of feelings are invoked, debated, and modified in intensity. Gubrium (1989, p. 249) refers to this as another form of emotion work that largely escapes Hochschild's analytic purview (see also Frith and Kitzinger 1998).

For an IEM scholar, an emotion exists when it is defined into being. Someone must perceive or claim that an instance of an emotion has taken place. Shirley Staske (1996) calls this process the "instantiation" of emotion. Instantiation can be studied by simply examining the ordinary and daily claims that people so often make about the feelings they purportedly undergo, as well as the reactions that those claims elicit. Once a feeling has been instantiated, it can be "upgraded" or "downgraded" by either the speaker or by listeners in their subsequent discussions.

Downgrading and upgrading emotions. Consider the following two examples of the interpretive modification of emotion, which I have adapted from Staske's (1996, pp. 121–122) research on relational talk between college-aged friends and romantic partners.[6] After administering a brief questionnaire, Staske asked her respondents to discuss emotionally influential topics while a video camera taped their interaction. In the first example, two female friends discuss a past interaction they had on campus:

J: Well, let's see. The only thing I thought about was like one day last week, when we were walking down the quad, and you were like complaining, complaining, complaining.

D: (laughs)

J: I mean MORE, a lot more than usual (laughs). And I was just like ready to hit you. . . . And the whole way back from the cafeteria, you didn't have anything good to say. It was all dada da da da.

D: (laughs)

J: I was like mad about that. Not mad, just kinda frustrated.

D: Irritated.

J: Irritated. I mean, two minutes after we got in the elevator I didn't care anymore. You know it was like—

D: Mmm hmm.

What Staske (1996, p. 121) notices in this excerpt is how an oblique reference to a strong emotional state—"I was just like ready to hit you"—is subsequently downgraded by the speaker to "frustrated" and then again by her companion to "irritated." All of these candidate descriptions constitute a kind of discursive emotion work. The reality and the strength of this college student's feelings are being worked on, but in a definitional sense. Whereas an OEM researcher might study how an individual tries to suppress a real feeling of being "mad," "frustrated," or "irritated," IEM researchers are more interested in how people conjure up these emotions as purported or perceived instances of feeling.

In another example that I have adapted from Staske (1996, p. 121), a romantic couple discusses the man's emotional state.

> M: I'm not always—I'm hardly ever depressed.
>
> F: Because everything is going right right now.
>
> M: Was I ever depressed this summer or whenever you met me when—
>
> F: YES.
>
> M: Why?
>
> F: For weeks you agonized, "Should I leave Florida, should I move to Connecticut, should I move to Illinois with you, should I go to school, should I quit, what should I do?"

In this excerpt, the female respondent attempts to convince her partner that her characterization of his emotional state as "depressed" was not unwarranted or exaggerated. In response to her partner's protestations, the woman claims that the man "agonized" over various issues in his life. This second description constitutes an upgrade in severity from depression (Staske 1996, p. 122) and provides rhetorical support for the woman's initial assessment.

The social aspects of identifying emotions. Earlier I described OEM as social in at least three respects: Objective emotion management is shaped by cultural norms (and other constraining factors); it is something individuals perform upon themselves and upon others; and it takes place in private relationships and in public interactions at work. Like OEM, IEM is social in similar but subtly different ways.

First, people have a great deal of authority to characterize their own feelings, and they even assume license to describe the feelings of others. But these claims cannot be made merely at will. Not just any description will do, as there are some social constraints. Emotional claims makers must use (or at least improvise upon) the vocabularies they inherit from the groups with which they associate. Moreover, they must speak or write in ways that are sensitive to their audiences, to whom they are accountable (Locke 2003). A contemporary American who says "I love that movie" is not likely to elicit a negative response or sanction from companions. The statement "That comedy scared me to death," on the other hand, might raise some concerns. Or consider a political example: Barack Obama, when campaigning for the Democratic nomination in 2008, discovered that a large segment of the voting population did not appreciate his description of them as "bitter" over their economic situations. In other statements, though, Obama successfully characterized portions of the US population as "proud" with no negative response, as that emotion is now considered a highly positive one (despite its history as a "deadly sin"). My point is that historical, cultural, and interactional contexts provide guidelines for positing instances of emotions. Emotional expressions such as "tough love" and "road rage" might seem quite strange but for the validation they have received among many in US society (Best and Furedi 2001; Gubrium 1992).

IEM also parallels the social dimensions of OEM in that it takes place at an interpersonal as well as individual level (Staske 1998). Just as people (objectively) try to shape their own feelings and the feelings of others, they also (interpretively) try to define or characterize their own feelings and the feelings of others. In friendly or contentious discussions, interactants propose, consider, modify, and accept or reject candidate labels. Two siblings may lightheartedly argue over whether a prior event was "totally embarrassing" or "no big deal." The descriptions they put forward and ultimately agree upon (assuming they do agree) can be seen as the products of concerted *social* interaction rather than the musings of isolated individuals. Readers should also recall the earlier example that I adapted from Staske (1996), where the feeling "I was ready to hit you" was collaboratively downgraded to "frustrated" and then "irritated" during a conversation between two friends. As such IEM research shows, people may pursue a variety of context-sensitive goals (e.g., creating humor, avoiding conflict, criticizing, etc.) as they postulate and debate instances of emotion (see also Edwards 1999).

The third social dimension of OEM—that it occurs as a part of paid employment as well as in private life—is also generally applicable to IEM. Many companies announce via advertising and through their representatives that they are "proud" of the services they provide their customers. (A national company called MerryMaids televised commercials claiming that their employees "love to clean.") Teachers, counselors, doctors, office managers, and other workers often try to decipher and assess the emotional states of students, patients, clients, or coworkers (e.g., see Gubrium 1992; Forsberg and Vagli 2006).

One helpful study of workplace IEM was conducted by Jack Whalen and Don Zimmerman (1998), who examined emotional claimsmaking made by call takers at a 911 dispatch center. In the course of answering emergency telephone calls, the center's employees would fill out a form devised to succinctly convey information (via a dispatcher) to the police, fire department, and other responders. On this form the call takers would sometimes describe callers as "hysterical." Whalen and Zimmerman argued that the reason for this characterization was not primarily due to caller's states of agitation, since not all agitated (e.g., shouting or sobbing) callers were labeled hysterical and some callers spoke in a monotone, as if in a daze, and did receive the hysterical label. The label "hysterical" was applied, the authors argued, to callers who were deemed to be poor sources of information. Call takers' training and workplace concerns lead them to focus on a specific goal: conveying precise and complete description of the problem at hand so that appropriate responders could arrive promptly and well-informed. Call takers were held accountable for any failures in this regard; hence, the label "hysterical" can be seen as part description (of callers and their situations), part explanation (for why some essential information may be missing from the form), and part excuse (missing details are attributed to the caller rather than the call taker). In short, Whalen and Zimmerman argued that call takers' descriptions of emotions were oriented to professional concerns as much (or more) than to callers' bodily conditions.

Studying Claims About Authenticity and Problems Involving Emotions

Recall that as Hochschild (1983) described the various surface and deep acting strategies that individuals use to manage their emotions, she simultaneously engaged in social problems claimsmaking. Hochschild raised questions about the consequences of commercialized emotion management on workers, including whether they risked becoming alienated from their own "true" feelings. It is certainly reasonable for Hochschild and for the scores of researchers following her (Lively 2006; Steinberg and Figart 1999) to ask and attempt to answer these questions. However, a more interpretive approach would be more cautious about designating the ontological status of both feelings and social problems. The focus of interpretive analyses would be on competing claims about "what someone really feels" and "what has gone wrong here."

Reframing authenticity. Hochschild's OEM framework relies on comparisons between "actual" emotions with feelings that may be less genuine or authentic. Via the concept of surface acting, Hochschild provoked much interest in how people can sometimes fool others by feigning a feeling that they may not really have. The concept of deep acting, on the other hand, has drawn attention to how an individual can fool him- or herself by cognitively embracing an alternative interpretation of the events that are provoking (or failing to provoke) a particular emotion. Finally, Hochschild's concern over the consequences of commercialized OEM—the estrangement of workers from their own feelings—suggests that individuals can lose touch with what their emotions really are. Workers doing continuous emotional labor may wonder, at the end of the day, whether the feelings they experienced (and the perspectives that generated them) are their own or their employers' (Hochschild 1983, p. 198).

An interpretive approach to studying emotion management would be less inclined to distinguish either appearances from reality or authentic from inauthentic emotions. What concerns IEM scholars is how these contrasts themselves are invoked and applied as people describe and debate their own and others' feelings (Edwards 1999; Pollner and Stein 2001). For example, Gubrium (1992) focused extensively on the issue of "who knows what" about emotions in his study of two therapy clinics. His approach, however, did not presume that emotion workers could ever possess privileged access to the true nature of their emotions. Rather, his goal was to study how people make claims about why they are in a position to know about emotions at the same time as they make claims about the nature, causes, and consequences of those emotions (see also Gubrium 1989).

Sometimes, individuals do claim that no one else can tell them what they feel. People do depict themselves as authorities on their own emotional states—as in "I know my love is real" or "You can't imagine how I feel." However, these sorts of claims may be rejected by others. Listeners may contradict a self-avowed emotional state by asserting that the person's actions "say" more about his or her feelings than a verbal proclamation does (Edwards 1999). Or listeners can suggest that the person is "in denial," that the person lacks an "objective" or "outside" perspective to make sense of their feelings, or that professional training and credentials are needed to help provide a more "realistic" assessment of the person's emotional experiences (see Gubrium and Holstein 1990, chap. 6; Gubrium 1992). Individuals may even undermine their own previously confident descriptions of their own emotional states (Staske 1998). It is not uncommon for people to assert that they have acquired new or better perspectives on what they previously thought they were feeling—as in "Now I know I was only infatuated and was not in love."

Hochschild's OEM framework seems to imply that sometimes actors know what they really feel while on other occasions they can be in error. A more strictly interpretive approach would refrain from entering this debate in order to closely study how people attempt to legitimize or criticize the foundations of claims about emotions (see also Gubrium and Holstein 2009b).

Emotions and social problems. Hochschild is within her rights to raise an alarm over the treatment and well-being of emotional laborers. In doing so, she followed in the venerable sociological tradition of locating individual "troubles" in their larger social contexts (Mills 1959). There is another sociological tradition, however, that deviates from the practice of documenting and explaining social problems as objective realities. More interpretive scholars tend to treat social problems as claims-making activities that apply meaning to indeterminate conditions or behaviors (Holstein and Miller 2003). This line of research tries to carefully distinguish between (on the one hand) making or adjudicating claims about social problems and (on the other hand) studying the processes through which such claims are made, debated, and acted upon (Spector and Kitsuse 1977). This more meaning-centered perspective leads to a different approach to studying the relationship between emotions and social problems.

Earlier in this chapter, I discussed the interactional construction of emotional troubles by focusing on Edwards (1999), Gubrium (1992), Staske (1996), Whalen and Zimmerman (1998), and others. In contrast to these more microapproaches, Joel Best and Frank Furedi (2001) demonstrate a more macroapproach to studying the interpretive creation of social problems related to emotions. These two scholars traced the creation and evolution of the concept of road rage, which has been used to make sense out of the behavior of drivers in the United States and in the UK. British newspapers first publicized this putative problem in 1994, and two years later it attracted widespread attention from Americans (Best and Furedi 2001, p. 107). Many automobile insurance companies, journalists, lawmakers, psychologists, and laypersons treated the problem as a genuine and serious one. Despite this attention, road rage never achieved a clear-cut definition. Consequently, many behaviors were portrayed as indicators of road rage, from momentary feelings of anger to obscene gestures, honking, and tailgating, to car accidents, fist fights, and shootings—even driving an automobile into a building (Best and Furedi 2001).

Once invented and popularized, a diverse array of claims makers linked road rage to their social agendas and perspectives. In Britain, for example, conservatives lamented the rise of road rage as another sign of the breakdown of civil society; environmentalists depicted it as a further reason to reduce driving and undermine people's detrimental reliance on automobiles; feminists described it as a problem involving aggressive men and vulnerable women (Best and Furedi 2001, pp. 110–111). At a 1997 congressional hearing in the United States, one representative discussed road rage as being related to an impending bill designed to improve an aging and unsafe highway system; a clinical psychologist characterized road rage as a psychological disorder afflicting over half of all US drivers (p. 113). In both countries, commentators freely extrapolated from "road rage" to posit (either seriously or humorously) the existence of other formulaic "x-rage" problems, including "air rage," "hotel rage," "parking lot rage," "shopping cart rage," and "golf rage."

In their analysis, Best and Furedi do not necessarily deny the reality of the feelings, behaviors, and situations described as road rage. But they do put a slightly different spin on C. Wright Mills's (1959) injunction to locate individual troubles in their social context. Best and Furedi study the diffusion of the problem of road rage across various nations and groups as a category available to interpret indeterminate feelings, actions, and events. Perceived instances of "rage" become more common, perhaps "upgrading" (in Staske's [1996] terminology) what might otherwise have been described as mere aggravation, annoyance, exasperation, frustration, impatience, irritation, or vexation. This form of analysis is much different than that of Hochschild (1983), who speaks of the diffusion of an objectively real phenomenon—workers becoming alienated from their feelings—as emotion management becomes increasingly commercialized.

Conclusion

In this chapter, I have suggested that there are two discernibly different approaches to studying emotion management: objective and interpretive. I have drawn contrasts in three major areas. First, OEM scholars attempt to implicitly or explicitly define emotions as entities whereas IEM scholars attempt to focus their attention on other people's conceptions of emotions. Second, OEM scholars study how experiences and displays of emotions are "worked up" or "worked down," whereas IEM scholars study how descriptions of emotional states are invoked, modified (upgraded and downgraded), and acted upon. Third, OEM scholars try to document and explain the real problems that result from paid emotion management, whereas IEM scholars study how our understandings of emotions and social problems are the result of interpretive claimsmaking.

Though the differences between OEM and IEM sometimes appear stark, there are many overlaps. OEM scholars are clearly not naïve realists. Hochschild (1983) and those who follow in her tradition do speak repeatedly of the importance and variability of meaning. There are explicit recognitions in the OEM literature that situations can be interpreted in many different ways. However, in OEM research, the idea that "meaning is not inherent" tends to be applied primarily to explain how emotions *as entities* are worked on. Cognitive deep acting, for example, is defined as the process through which individuals modify their actual feelings by changing their interpretations of surrounding events. In contrast, IEM scholars apply the idea that meaning is not inherent to emotions themselves. It is the perceived or proclaimed nature of emotions—not simply the thoughts or situations that provoke or modify feelings—that is the subject of IEM analyses. Thus, OEM research does attend to issues of meaning and interpretation, but not in the same way or to the extent that IEM research does.

As I have attempted to show, both OEM and IEM research also share an interest in cultural diversity and rules. OEM scholars study the various norms that cultures and subcultures create about the "proper" way to feel in specific social situations. Emotion management is framed as a process of individuals "working" on feeling and/or its display in order to conform to societal expectations. IEM scholars, in turn, rely on an overlapping but more complicated view of norms as both regulative and constitutive. When speaking of the regulative function of norms, IEM scholars tend to focus on the rules that guide discourse about feelings—that is, on the norms and vocabularies governing how people depict feeling states. When speaking of the constitutive function of norms, IEM scholars turn Hochschild's concept of "emotion rules" on its head. From the interpretive perspective, norms about emotions are selectively and creatively applied as people "talk into being" the various feelings, actions, and situations that concern them (Edwards 1999). People are not so much given simple "rule reminders" (Hochschild 1983) as they are subjected to interpretive claimsmaking about what feelings, actions, and situations are purportedly in play given the particular rule that someone has invoked.

The differences between OEM and IEM research can be difficult to see not only because authors in both traditions tend to rely on similar terminology—such as meaning, work, management, and norms—but because they employ similar methodologies. Both Hochschild (1983) and Gubrium (1992) conducted in-depth qualitative observations, and their reports present direct quotations from their research participants, as well as some interactional details about when and where those quotations were spoken. Nonetheless, Hochschild's and Gubrium's analyses are dramatically different. As Hannah Frith and Celia Kitzinger (1998) show in detail, the same kinds of qualitative data yield much different results depending on whether the emotion work in question is approached in a more objective or interpretive manner.

The complicated differences and overlaps between OEM and IEM research are often ignored when both sorts of analyses are lumped together under the broad umbrella of "constructionism" or "interactionism" (Loseke and Kusenbach 2008; Marvasti 2008, p. 319; Thoits 1989). This lumping, I argue, also contributes to the continuing underappreciation of interpretive emotion management as an already existing and viable strand of research. Hochschild (1983, pp. 223–229), for the most part, relegated the issue to an appendix.[7] Perhaps due to Hochschild's early example and influence, Jan Stets and Jonathan Turner's (2006) massive edited collection *Handbook of the Sociology of Emotions* does not contain a chapter devoted to IEM research, nor does their text *The Sociology of Emotions* (Turner and Stets 2005). Article-length overviews (e.g., Smith-Lovin 1995) also give IEM short shrift.[8] Such neglect is unfortunate, given the centrality of IEM to people's everyday encounters with emotions.

I have written this chapter to help readers recognize the differences and similarities between objective and interpretive emotion management and to encourage more scholars to consider conducting more consistently interpretive research on the topic. In the next three chapters, I move away from (seemingly) microissues of mind and emotion and begin to consider literature that focuses explicitly on social relationships and inequalities. My contention is that the objective/interpretive distinction is useful for making sense of divergent uses of constructionism even within these more macro and politically charged areas.

Notes

1. Interestingly, the term "emotion" can be traced to the Latin verb "to move" (as in e-motion). This seems a rather quaint origin in comparison to the

complicated and nuanced meanings it has been granted in scholarly and popular discourse.

2. The same dilemma occurs with respect to definitions of specific emotions, such as anger (van Brakel 1994, p. 181; Schieman 2006).

3. After reviewing biological approaches to studying emotions, Barrett (2006, p. 24) concludes that "there is no clear objective way to measure the experience of emotion. Scientists are not able to use any single measurement, or profile of measurements, to indicate when a person is in a state of anger or fear or sadness, and so on."

4. In some societies, there are apparently no equivalent words for "emotion" at all (Russell 1991, p. 429; Wierzbicka 1999, p. 3).

5. Many ethnographers appear to have little trouble translating terms from other languages into English. However, some researchers report significant cross-cultural differences that earlier ethnographers may have neglected to look for or appreciate (Russell 1991). Cross-cultural comparisons are further complicated by the irremediable ambiguity of language (Agger 2000; Heritage 1984). Even speakers from the same culture may give many different meanings to emotion categories (e.g., "love" or "fear") depending on the specific contexts within which, and purposes for which, those terms are invoked.

6. Readers are encouraged to consult the original article as well. I have removed and altered much of the author's transcription to increase the clarity and reduce confusion. I have made these changes in order to make Staske's data more accessible to readers, but what I have done would not satisfy the conventions of conversation analysis.

7. Hochschild (1983, p. 206) does mention that the label people give to an emotion may help evoke or shape the actual feeling at hand; but here interpretive emotion management is invoked merely as a subsidiary or support to objective emotion management (cf. Gubrium 1989, p. 249).

8. Although this paragraph may sound overly critical, I do not intend it as such. The ignoring of IEM and its lumping into the same theoretical perspective as OEM are both reasonable and understandable practices. All reviews of the scholarly literature reflect the purposes and perspectives of reviewers, who must set somewhat arbitrary boundaries around the scholarship that is considered (see Agger 2000, chap. 3; Fine and Kleinman 1986; Zerubavel 1995). Admittedly, I inevitably have done my own share of ignoring and lumping in this chapter and book.

.

4

Family Diversity

Virtually all social scientists who write about "the family" today are aware that there are a plethora of family forms in the United States and other countries. While some express concern about the potentially negative consequences of diversity (Glenn, Nock, and Waite 2002), many if not most family scholars could be described as "diversity defenders" (cf. Cherlin 2003). They are, at minimum, uncomfortable with the idea that one kind of family could be deemed the most natural, effective, or divinely dictated form of kinship. In fact, arguing *against* those ideas seems to be a primary goal of hundreds of articles and books on marriages and families—in the plural, as such works are more likely to be titled now (Coleman and Ganong 2004; Coltrane 1998; Coontz, Parson, and Raley 1999; Lamanna and Riedmann 2006; Schwartz and Scott 2007).

The foil for many scholars' publications is the commonsense belief in and reverence for what Dorothy Smith (1993) called "The Standard North American Family," or SNAF. SNAF consists of a heterosexual husband, wife, and their biological children living under one roof, with the husband being the primary breadwinner when feasible. Many Americans still consider SNAF the most real or ideal family form—perhaps even the "essence" of family—even though they frequently don't practice it. Single-parent families, gay and lesbian families, foster families, childless couples—these and other family forms are often perceived as deviant, broken, or less genuine forms of family in comparison to SNAF (Erera 2002).

Perhaps to encourage awareness and acceptance of "nontraditional" families, social scientists have devoted many publications to describing, explaining, and extolling family diversity. Historians, anthropologists, sociologists, and other scholars document the contrasting forms of kinship that have been practiced by different groups and in various eras. "Diversity" appears explicitly in the titles of numerous books on family (Baca Zinn and Eitzen 2005; Erera 2002; Stockard 2002), including an important handbook (Demo, Allen, and Fine 2000).

All of this attention to family diversity seems necessary and important. In recent years, laws and policies have been enacted based on the assumption that the nuclear family should be defended and promoted at the expense of other families (Erera 2002). The recurring calls to prohibit same-sex marriage indicate, arguably, that there is still much intolerance and ignorance about the family. Politicians and pundits often confidently claim that the "5,000-year-old" institution of marriage—as a heterosexual and monogamous union—is the cornerstone of the United States and other societies (Dobson 2006). Family scholars are right to challenge such arguments. It is erroneous to assume that heterosexual monogamous marriage is universal, and it can be misleading to gloss over the diverse ways that such marriages are practiced. When loosely applied, the labels "nuclear family" and "traditional marriage" can obscure the large variations in how families have been organized over time and across cultures. Documenting these objective variations is an important task.

However, not all "diversity advocates" study family diversity with the same goals or assumptions. There is an alternative way of approaching family diversity that also challenges commonsense beliefs about family, but from a more interpretive rather than objective perspective. This interpretive perspective is less recognized in the literature, even though a growing number of family researchers accentuate the importance of meaning, contingency, interactional work, and other constructionist themes. While scholars who study objective family diversity (OFD) are interested in documenting factual variations in kin relations, scholars who study interpretive family diversity (IFD) are interested in documenting the diverse ways that any familial relationship can be given meaning. For IFD researchers, any set of social bonds can be described or understood in many different ways. For them, the goal is to study how various familial *interpretations* are constructed, rather than examining how real family diversity is made.

In this chapter, I explain the distinction between objective and interpretive family diversity by focusing on three central questions: What is the definition of "family"? How does family diversity manifest itself? What causes or creates family diversity? I hope to show that scholarship on OFD and IFD is distinct, even though authors frequently employ similar terms and address parallel concerns. OFD and IFD scholars can both claim to adopt a constructionist orientation, even though their analyses differ in important ways. Acknowledging these differences can help us, as authors or readers of family research, recognize that focusing on one form of diversity may obscure diversity of another kind.

Objective Family Diversity

Defining Family

In order to study family diversity, it seems sensible to assume that one must have a working definition of "family." A scholar needs at least a rough understanding of what a family is if he or she is going to research and write about it. Additionally, defining family is significant for more than research. Census counts, healthcare policies, legal and administrative decisions regarding child custody and adoption, and other important matters are influenced by conceptions of family (Dolgin 1997; Seccombe and Warner 2004).

Defining one's terms inevitably involves drawing boundaries of inclusion and exclusion. However, social scientists interested in OFD are wary of leaving anybody out of their conceptions of family. Indeed, OFD scholars tend to argue explicitly against conservatives who put restrictive limits around what qualifies as a "real" family (i.e., mom, dad, and their children) and what does not (e.g., homosexual partners and their children). Consequently, OFD authors frequently provide tentative definitions that are highly inclusive, for example, "We define family as any relatively stable group of people bound by ties of blood, marriage, adoption; or by any sexually expressive relationship; or who simply live together, and who are committed to and provide each other with economic and emotional support" (Schwartz and Scott 2007, p. 3).

These sorts of conceptions allow a wide range of relationships to be classified as family. For example, a group of college students sharing an apartment could potentially fit these definitions. But they are precise enough for OFD scholars to proceed to discuss a number of issues in relation to families, such as courtship, childcare, employment, divorce, aging, and other topics. OFD authors devote chapters to describing and explaining the functioning of single-parent, adoptive, Asian American, Muslim, and other diverse forms of families, after offering a broad definition of "family" or refraining from settling on a single definition (Coleman and Ganong 2004; Demo, Allen, and Fine 2000).

While OFD scholars approach family as an objective entity that exists in the world, they are not naïve realists. They acknowledge to some degree that "family" is in the eye of the beholder. This is evident in at least two ways. First, OFD scholars mention the importance of "subjective" factors in their definitions of family. Authors suggest that family members "consider their identity to be significantly attached to the group" (Lamanna and Riedmann 2006, p. 9) or are at least "committed to each other" (Schwartz and Scott 2007, p. 3). These phrases imply that it is important to investigate whether potential family members deem themselves as such. But that implication is rarely pursued with vigor—at least in comparison to research on interpretive family diversity.

Second, OFD scholars do allude to the indeterminacy of the meaning of "family" by highlighting the debate over its proper definition. Conventional textbooks tend to review a number of potential definitions before settling on one that is more comprehensive or at least useful for their purposes (Seccombe and Warner 2004). In so doing, these authors sometimes explicitly admit a degree of arbitrariness is involved in defining family (Lamanna and Riedmann 2006, p. 9) or even acknowledge that "a single, all-encompassing definition of 'family' may be impossible to achieve" (Erera 2002, p. 3). Nonetheless, objectivist family scholars seem to operate under the principle that they know a family when they see it. Despite their wariness about the adequacy of their own and others' definitions, these authors persist in the reasonable assumption that "family" refers to real relationships that researchers can identify, count, describe, and explain.

Discerning Diverse Family Forms

If family should be defined inclusively rather than narrowly, as OFD scholars contend, then many different kin relationships may come into view. Researchers can choose to specify family diversity in various, often overlapping ways. One might speak of diversity in terms of disciplinary concerns, as in anthropological family diversity (Stockard 2002) and historical family diversity (Coontz 2000), which might respectively examine diverse kinship practices cross-culturally or within certain cultures over time. Or one could identify diverse families via categories of race or ethnicity (Coles 2006), region or nationality (Roopnarine and Gielen 2005), class (Rank 2000), sexual orientation (Kurdek 2004), or religion (Dollahite, Marks, and Goodman 2004). One could also locate diversity in the structural arrangements of households—such as single-parent (Amato 2000) or multigenerational (Cohen and Casper 2002) families—or by the nature of marriage, as in monogamous, polygynous, and polyandrous (Stone 2000, chap. 6). One can also examine diversity *within* families, by highlighting the contrasting experiences that individual family members may have—perhaps due to their sex, their age, or their biological status (e.g., child by birth, stepmarriage, or adoption) (Erera 2002). In addition, one could distinguish between diverse interactional processes and dynamics, such as parenting styles, which may vary by group or over time (Fine, Demo, and Allen 2000, p. 441; Greder and Allen 2007).

Some of the most compelling examples of objective family diversity come from anthropologists (Jankowiak 2008; Pasternak, Ember, and Ember 1997; Stone 2000), including Janice Stockard's (2002) exceedingly readable book. Consider these five points of contrast that Stockard highlights:

• Societies differ in how they trace descent. Not all groups trace kinship bilaterally—through both the men and women of one's family—as many Americans do. The historical Iroquois treated as kin those individuals who are biologically related through the women, the traditional Chinese and the Nyinba of Nepal trace kinship via the men.

• Societies differ in how they structure marriage in many respects, including the number of spouses that can be involved. Some cultures tolerate or encourage polygamy instead of monogamy. Men in the !Kung San and traditional Chinese societies sometimes had more than one wife; among the Nyinba, the moral and statistical norm is for one wife to marry a group of biological brothers (i.e., fraternal polyandry).

• Sometimes cultures provide a great deal of individual discretion in the selection of a spouse, other times an individual has little or no vote in whom they marry. An infant Nyinba male grows up married to whomever his eldest brother chose for him, whereas an Iroquois marriage would be arranged by the mothers of the bride and groom.

• Societies also differ in their conceptions of the proper age for marriage. A young (8–12 years) !Kung San bride could expect to marry a groom who was around ten years older; interestingly, a deceased Chinese daughter would be married posthumously, to ensure her security in the afterlife.

• Societies differ in their postmarital residence practices. While most Americans are expected to establish a new home, a traditional Chinese or Nyinba bride would move into her husband's home and live with his family, whereas a !Kung San or Iroquois groom would join his wife's camp.

These points of contrast merely scratch the surface of the kinship diversity that Stockard (2002) and other anthropologists emphasize. But through these and similar examples, OFD scholars clearly and persuasively challenge the notion that there is one version of "family" (e.g., SNAF) that is natural or universal—the "essence" of family. Even throughout the United States, the monogamous heterosexual nuclear family is not always the moral or (especially) statistical norm (Erera 2002). OFD research successfully demonstrates the diverse ways that family can be practiced.

Explaining the Construction of Objective Family Diversity

Perhaps to counter conservative claims that "the family" forms the foundation or cornerstone of society, OFD scholars treat families as merely one variable among a wide array of social forces that mutually affect each other. Social scientists by training tend to adopt a somewhat deterministic frame of reference, by viewing human relations as embedded within a complex matrix of causal variables (Babbie 1986; Berger 1963). This is true of family studies as well. OFD scholars often highlight the social factors that shape families, such as economic inequalities, religious beliefs, the enactment and reversal of laws, and so on (Dollahite, Marks, and Goodman 2004; Erera 2002; Rank 2000). Increasingly, scholars also acknowledge the active efforts that family members put into creating their relationships and by extension their societies, while emphasizing that those efforts are either enabled or limited by larger social conditions (Baca Zinn and Wells 2000, p. 255; Stockard 2002, p. 9).

As one example of OFD analysis, consider Stockard's (2002) portrait of the Nyinba once more. Drawing on a number of ethnographic and historical sources, Stockard (2002) explains fraternal polyandry among the Nyinba as a result of cultural and environmental factors. The Nyinba live on a plateau high in the Himalayan Mountains of Tibet. The arable land is limited and cannot support much population growth. Brothers must work together to maintain the prosperity of their households by specializing in different economic pursuits, including agricultural work, raising cattle, and long-distance trading (p. 87). The fruits of their labor are passed down to the subsequent generation of sons, who will continue to share the same residence and property, rather than dividing it up. In this geographical location, with the modes of subsistence available, striking out on one's own would likely lead to a life of relative destitution. In light of these conditions, fraternal polyandry can be seen as a strategy that the Nyinba developed to limit offspring and maintain wealth. However, Stockard (pp. 83, 93) also distinguishes between "first causes" and later causes, suggesting that whatever the reasons that spurred the development of polyandry, it became firmly engrained in their culture and "integral to Nyinba identity." The practice separates them from outsiders in the surrounding area; it even distinguished them from their own slaves, who they forbade (until being freed in 1926) from engaging in fraternal polyandry (p. 98).

With this case study and others throughout her book, Stockard supports her argument that family is not uniform or natural. Kinship is always "a product of a specific culture, within a particular history and environment"; it is "culturally constructed" (Stockard 2002, p. 2).

Maxine Baca Zinn and Barbara Wells (2000) provide a second example of an OFD analysis in their chapter on diverse Latino families. Drawing on research by Patricia Fernandez-Kelly (1990) and other scholars, Baca Zinn and Wells argue that social class and employment opportunities play a large role in shaping family structure and functioning. The authors compare Cuban Americans with Mexican Americans, suggesting that while both groups highly value marriage and family, the latter Latino immigrants have faced more difficult economic circumstances. For example, Mexican Americans have more often been recruited for low-status occupations and purposefully excluded from opportunities for advancement, which has resulted in a higher rate of poor female-headed households in some communities (Baca Zinn and Wells 2000, pp. 259–260).

With this comparison and others, Baca Zinn and Wells (2000, p. 254) support their OFD argument that "structural arrangements . . . produce and often require a range of family configurations." Latino families should not be approached as if they had some "essential characteristics" that distinguish them from other kinds of families; rather, family diversity is created by the "social context and social forces that construct families" (pp. 255, 267).

Interpretive Family Diversity

Research on objective family diversity is important. It is sensible and justifiable for scholars to assume families are real, to identify different forms of family, and to explain the processes that create families. However, there is a discernibly different way of studying family diversity that is arguably just as reasonable and valid. Studies of interpretive family diversity tend to derive from different assumptions and lead to different results, even though they examine similar issues and employ identical terms as those found in OFD publications. When IFD scholars write about the "construction" or "production" of families, they are primarily interested in the creation of meaning rather than the creation of real family relationships (Gubrium and Holstein 1990; Harris 2006b; Loseke 2001; Miller 1991; Rosenblatt 1994). IFD arguments thus draw theoretical insights from narrative analysis (Bruner 1987; Foley and Faircloth 2000; Riessman 1990, 2002; Walzer 2006), studies of motive talk and claimsmaking (Hopper 1993; Knapp 2002), and other meaning-centered perspectives inspired by interactionism, phenomenology, and ethnomethodology (Blumer 1969; Garfinkel 1967; Gubrium and Holstein 1993; Schutz 1970). However, vigilant reading is required to detect the differences between OFD and IFD scholarship, because both kinds of analyses can incorporate ideas from any of these scholarly traditions.

If the search for objective diversity is reflected in the argument that there are many different kinds of families "out there," the search for interpretive diversity is reflected in the argument that any set of relationships can be viewed or described in different, often contradictory ways. For IFD scholars, diversity lies in the purposes and perspectives that guide people's interpretations rather than in the objective properties of actual familial bonds.

Studying the Process of Defining Family

It is true that many OFD scholars admit (or at least imply) awareness of the subjective and arbitrary nature of any definition of family. But this awareness is not part of an overarching perspective that puts interpretation and indeterminacy at the center of analysis. If "meaning is not inherent" is the guiding premise of one's research, then controversy over the proper definition of family provides useful though expected fodder for research instead of an obstacle to objective description and explanation. Whereas an OFD researcher may attempt (implicitly or explicitly) to define family in a more comprehensive or inclusive fashion, IFD scholars refrain from judging the adequacy of lay or scholarly definitions (Holstein and Gubrium 1999, p. 15). IFD scholars do this by bracketing the concept of family—that is, they attempt to set aside any preconceptions about or interest in what "really" does or does not constitute a family.

As a methodological strategy, bracketing facilitates the careful investigation of all the diverse ways that putative families, and their putative characteristics, are defined into and out of existence. To be sure, kinship may often be invoked in a culturally conventional fashion (Schneider 1980), but IFD scholars also highlight the flexible and idiosyncratic application of familial descriptors. A group of college roommates may claim they are a family of sorts. In some households a pet dog or cat may be described as part of the family and may receive lavish attention, framed photos, and even Christmas presents. In some communities, individuals may portray their coworkers, support-group members, coaches, neighbors, and other companions as "just like" a brother, sister, mother, father, son, or daughter; they may also portray coresident biological relatives as strangers and not kin at all (see Gubrium and Holstein 1990; Stack 1974). Then, at a later time, these individuals may contradict their own assessments, reversing their earlier claims about kinship in light of new considerations. The point for an interpretive constructionist is not whether or which of these familial understandings is correct. The point is to investigate the meanings these descriptions create and the factors shaping their production (Broad, Crawley, and Foley 2004). IFD scholars bracket "family" in order to study all the creative ways that people use the familial concepts they've inherited to pursue their goals—such as persuading, praising, criticizing, or amusing others—as they interact in casual settings or in formal engagements with social institutions (Gubrium and Holstein 1990).

While IFD scholars bracket family, it would be somewhat misleading to say that they abstain entirely from defining family. IFD scholars do articulate a way of understanding family. For them, "Family is a usage, not a thing" (Miller 1991, p. 610). Terms of kinship are treated as "a set of conceptual resources for accomplishing the meaning of social relations" (Holstein and Gubrium 1999, p. 5). Thus, while it is somewhat accurate to argue that IFD scholars join OFD scholars in defining the concept of family, the IFD definition is of an entirely different sort. Both OFD and IFD scholars seek to highlight "family diversity" by opening up consideration of what constitutes a family. Arguably, however, the IFD challenge to common sense or conservative conceptions of family is deeper and more radical than the OFD challenge. While OFD scholars seek to broaden the label of family to encompass additional social forms, IFD scholars suspend belief in virtually *any* conception of family as a concrete entity in order to better investigate its full range of meanings and applications (Holstein and Gubrium 1995b, p. 895).

Discovering Forms of Interpretive Family Diversity

OFD scholars are interested in gathering factual information about family diversity: How many adoptive, foster, and stepfamilies are in the United

States? How are spouses selected in different cultures around the world? What factors shape the prevalence of certain family forms over others?

In contrast, IFD scholars tend to be more interested in understanding the distribution and production of diverse family meanings: How might the same families tend to be depicted differently, depending on the social setting they find themselves within? How do local cultures, metaphors, narratives, clinical training, interests and agendas, audiences, and other factors influence understandings of familial bonds (Broad, Crawley, and Foley 2004; Gubrium 1992; Loseke 2001; Haney and March 2003)?

Given their orientation, IFD scholars exhibit more caution when specifying the possible range of diverse family forms. The categories, classifications, and terms of distinction should be studied and discovered, not assumed or imposed. Gubrium and Holstein (1990) examined family discourse that occurred in courtrooms, support groups, nursing homes, and other locations, in order to investigate people's diverse descriptions of (potentially) familial relations. In discussions and debates, family members and others inferred meaning from indeterminate signs (1990, p. 77). Is a household too crowded or does it provide an opportunity for intergenerational learning experiences (pp. 90–92)? Does a messy or dilapidated home indicate a family is falling apart, or is it a sign that a parent is setting appropriate priorities by putting relationships above trivial physical concerns (p. 82)? Is a frequent change of address necessarily an indicator of family instability (p. 87)? Family members, social workers, prosecutors, judges, and other individuals interpret these ambiguous indicators in various ways—and thereby create family diversity—depending on how their goals, orientations, and companions influence their understandings and descriptions.

Rather than including chapters on single-parent families, African American families, and so on, interpretive scholars are likely to organize a book around competing perspectives on or claims about families. Paul Rosenblatt (1994), for example, has described a number of different metaphors that can be used to think about any given family. In order to challenge and stimulate the development of family systems theory, Rosenblatt demonstrates how viewing families through various metaphorical prisms can shape therapeutic understandings and actions. According to him, merely thinking of family as an actual "entity" (like a rock or an automobile) is metaphorical (1994, p. 35). This metaphor is operative when families are portrayed as existing independently ("the Smith family") and as being more than the sum of their individual parts. Families are likened to entities when they are treated as if they were alive, as if they had their own personalities ("an angry family") and interests ("for the good of the family") beyond those of individual members. Families can be thought of as nonsentient entities, too. The metaphor "families are like rivers" emphasizes the manner in which kinship stretches forward and backward in time, is ever changing, and is not necessarily dependent on any single individual for its nature and existence (p. 42). Families can also be conceived as "houses," as structures that (with varying levels of success) protect members from outside forces or confine and subjugate members to certain locations and expectations (p. 45).

In principle, there is no limit to the number of metaphors that might be applied to families. Rosenblatt demonstrates how families can be compared to aquariums, tapestries, governments, and other social and nonsocial phenomena. There is always a degree of arbitrariness when a family member, theorist, or therapist employs one metaphor rather than another, since many different metaphors could be applied to any given family (see also Knapp 1999). However, the choice of metaphor shapes what aspects of family relations are noticed, the meanings those behaviors and conditions are given, and the subsequent actions that are pursued (Rosenblatt 1994, p. 31).

Recall that objectivist scholars highlight family diversity by focusing on underappreciated kinship experiences. OFD researchers highlight (for example) "Latino" families, or perhaps kinship variations within Latino communities, or perhaps even interactional variations within families depending on the age or sex of individual members. Interpretive scholars, as I have tried to show in this section, tend to spend more time highlighting diverse meanings rather than diverse objective realities. IFD researchers study how the same element of familial experience—a putative action, condition, relationship, or whatever—can be defined in different ways. As I discuss next, what a particular family is "objectively" (whether Latino, adoptive, poor, and so on) becomes relevant to IFD analysis only if the researcher can show the impact of such factors on interpretive processes and outcomes (Holstein and Gubrium 1995b, p. 899).

Explaining the Construction
of Interpretive Family Diversity

For OFD scholars, families are enmeshed in a field of social forces. The economy, law, politics, religion, gender ideology, and other factors—along with the daily actions and choices of individuals—shape the diverse range of family forms that exist in any given society. Somewhat similarly, IFD analyses also place families in a broader social context. Here too, families are shaped or constructed by forces larger than themselves. But instead of focusing on the production of real families, IFD researchers study the social factors and processes that encourage competing depictions of family forms.

Interpretive constructionists highlight the active work that people engage in as they define reality. Although this interpretive work is creative, it is not random or indiscriminate (Holstein and Gubrium 1999, p. 7). People can use "family" to refer to just about anything, but there are limits and patterns in how they do so. Family meanings tend to be socially distributed, and thus partially predictable, depending on where, by whom, and for what purposes family relations are being considered.

For example, in their studies of a variety of different settings, Gubrium and Holstein (1990) demonstrated the impact that professional perspectives and agendas can have on interpretations of family. In an example derived from an involuntary commitment hearing, Gubrium and Holstein recount the case of "Mr. Biggs," whose psychiatrist believed should be released to his family rather than hospitalized against his will. The judge, upon learning that the family with whom Biggs would reside consisted of a girlfriend, her two children, and her sister, was less convinced.

> [Judge:] Now who is it that takes care of him? You say these two ladies are going to be able to keep him out of trouble. How long has he lived with them? What happens when he gets delusional again? . . . Who's going to make him take his medication? . . . I just don't see any family there to look out for him. (Gubrium and Holstein 1990, p. 127)

The psychiatrist, in response, insisted that Biggs needed to be "close to his family" if he was going to get the sense of security and support he needed to succeed in his treatment program: "His family wants him there and they make him feel like he belongs. He needs that kind of security—the family environment—if he's ever going to learn to cope" (Gubrium and Holstein 1990, p. 127).

In this example, the existence and nature of Biggs's putative family is discursively worked up (and down), in accordance with the purposes and perspectives of the judge and psychiatrist. The judge, whose training and occupation leads him to focus on containing trouble, views things differently than the psychiatrist, whose orientation leads to an interest in treatment and recovery. The same "family" situation,

Gubrium and Holstein (1990, p. 12) argue, is constructed in different ways. Though the judge and psychiatrist have some discretion in their portrayal of the facts, their interpretations can be seen as somewhat predictable and patterned rather than haphazard. The artfulness elicited by the indeterminacy of meaning is tempered and guided by the agendas and concerns of particular groups and settings. In this example and others, Gubrium and Holstein (1990, chap. 7) show how interpretive family diversity is shaped by social forces just as objective family diversity is.

IFD analyses thus parallel OFD analyses in their attention to the factors that produce family life, although "production" is reconceived as more a matter of meaningmaking rather than concrete relationship building. IFD scholars can be differentiated further by noticing the special attention they give to *attributions* of causality beyond causality itself. More often than in OFD research, IFD scholars frequently eschew studying the actual causes of behavior in order to focus on competing claims about motivations (Dunn 2005; Gubrium and Holstein 1990, chap. 8; Higginson 1999; Knapp 1999; Loseke and Cahill 1984).

Recall how OFD scholars invoke the importance of economic factors in family functioning and form. Earlier I described Stockard's argument that the Nyinba developed polyandry out of their difficult struggle for subsistence in the Himalayan Mountains, as well as Baca Zinn and Wells's argument that some nonconventional Latino families may be a result of limited employment opportunities. Perhaps to counter conservatives' claims that "financial success" is a consequence of "proper" or "normal" families, more liberal OFD scholars frequently reverse the causal arrow. Families may be shaped by economic conditions just as much if not more than the other way around, they assert.

Rather than entering these sorts of debates, more interpretive scholars tend to sidestep them. IFD scholars enjoy turning arguments over causality into the subject of *rhetorical* analysis. By drawing on constructionist literature on "accounts" and "motive talk," IFD researchers treat causal claimsmaking as another discursive, meaning-making process (see Sarat and Felstiner 1988; Sterponi 2003). Gale Miller (1991) did this in his research on a Work Incentive Program (WIN) designed to reduce dependency on welfare. Miller examined the assumptions and assertions that WIN staff made about family life and its relation to economic success. In Miller's analysis, WIN staff interpretively *constituted* rather than simply assisted their clientele when they referred to their clients' good and bad attitudes, legitimate and illegitimate excuses, normal and abnormal families, and work successes and failures. For example, if a WIN client suggested that she was impeded from seeking a job because she had to help a mother-in-law take her insulin, a staff member would classify that explanation as either a "legitimate" or an "illegitimate" reason (Miller 1991, p. 615). Invoking and applying the legitimate/illegitimate distinction involved making assumptions about proper family duties and relationships, and interpretively arbitrating between genuine and fictional causes in response to clients' arguments and counterarguments. In this way, IFD scholars tend to study how meaning is made as motives and explanations are presented, contested, negotiated, and acted upon, rather than trying to discern the objective factors that determine familial behavior.

Conclusion

In this chapter, I have attempted to clarify the differences between two forms of family diversity—objective and interpretive. While interest on family diversity has arguably never been higher, most of this scholarship is of the more objective variety. For example, the massive *Handbook of Family Diversity* (Demo, Allen, and Fine 2000) and *Handbook of Contemporary Families* (Coleman and Ganong 2004) are both primarily objectivist (except see Laird 2000). In general, there could more be attention and research devoted to interpretive family diversity. But for this to happen in a rigorous way, scholars must also recognize that the same analytical terms—such as "construct," "create," and "produce," as well as "family diversity"—can be used in somewhat contradictory fashion. Recognizing this can help better illuminate the theoretical assumptions of existing scholarship and open up potential avenues for future work. Readers and authors can ask themselves: Which form of family diversity is being highlighted in a given publication? How might the analysis differ if the topic switched from OFD to IFD, or vice versa?

Across the field of family studies, the findings that scholars publish are very much at stake when they choose to adopt OFD or IFD frameworks. But so too are the moral implications of their research. Clearly, family scholarship is not merely informational but can have consequences for the political, institutional, and personal decisions that people make about familial affairs.

Objectively inclined scholars are well positioned to enter public discussions—sometimes called "wars" or "feuds"—over families. There is a legitimate need for researchers to insert factual analyses into debates over the pros and cons of gay marriage, cohabitation, divorce, single parenting, gender roles, and other issues (Berger and Berger 1983;

Benokraitis 2000). Ideologically left- and right-leaning activists, politicians, and pundits often dispute the causes of objective family diversity and whether particular family arrangements have positive or negative impacts on individuals and society. Many OFD scholars have attempted to contribute to the discussion by providing research-based facts and opinions (Coontz 1992; Erera 2002). This is a reasonable choice, but more interpretive scholars tend to choose differently.[1]

Because they focus on what things mean to other people and on how those diverse meanings are made, interpretivists are less disposed to providing evidence or judgments regarding the true costs and benefits of various forms of kinship. The goal of IFD analyses is not to arbitrate between the myths and realities of family life or to authenticate any particular person's or group's account (Gubrium and Holstein 1990, chap. 6). The interpretivist's guiding premise—that "meaning is not inherent"—works against those kinds of contributions.

However, IFD scholarship can make positive contributions to public, scholarly, and interpersonal debates over the functioning of various families. By explicating the interpretive practices through which understandings of family are created, by showing how all assertions about families tend to convert ambiguity into appearances of "reality," IFD analyses can at minimum insert a healthy dose of humility into such discussions. IFD scholars can also compare the diverse meanings that are generated in different contexts, thereby "rescuing" or spotlighting interpretations that otherwise might have been obscured by the narratives propounded by more prominent or powerful claims makers (Gubrium 1993; Haney and March 2003; Harris 2006b; Knapp 2002). Interpretivists can raise awareness about the many different ways that any familial situation could be defined or portrayed. Some audiences may find this illuminating and helpful (Gubrium and Holstein 2005; Miller 2003).

I have drawn a fairly bright line between OFD and IFD approaches. Yet, I have also acknowledged that there can be some complicated overlaps between scholarship on OFD and IFD. Authors who are primarily objectivist do sometimes attend to the meanings that family relations have for different groups and individuals; more interpretive authors pay attention to objective realities when they examine the social conditions that influence the meanings people give to family affairs. But the distinction between OFD and IFD seems genuine and useful, even though the divergence between the two types of scholarship is a matter of degree and emphasis. The difference can usually be seen in the assumptions and answers that researchers bring to fundamental questions: What is family diversity? What are the causes and consequences of family diversity? How can scholarship contribute to debates over family diversity?

In the next chapter, I continue to focus on family relations—while sharpening the focus on social justice—by raising the issue of equality in marriage. As with research on family diversity, almost all studies of marital equality have taken relatively objectivist approaches. The vast majority of scholars treat marital equality primarily as a thing rather than as an interpretation. Despite authors' avowedly constructionist leanings, the emphasis has been on the factors and processes that produce real equalities and inequalities (Deutsch 1999; Knudson-Martin and Mahoney 2005). Sociologists, psychologists, and anthropologists have studied the various constraints (such as social class or gender identity) and individual choices (such as the use of a communication strategy) that help to create equal or unequal relationships among heterosexual or lesbigay couples (Carrington 2004; Schwartz 1994; Stockard 2002).

In contrast, in Chapter 5 I use my own research (Harris 2006b) to advance some ISC arguments: Married people—and their friends, relatives, counselors, lawyers—may define and measure marital equality using criteria that diverge sharply from those used by researchers. Though laypersons operate within cultural and interactional constraints, they have considerable discretion to formulate their own idiosyncratic accounts of the definition, causes, and consequences of equality in marriage. These everyday meanings, and the factors and processes that create them, are what interpretive researchers should try to faithfully represent. ISC research thus takes us into difficult moral territory, but it is not nihilistic. By encouraging us to attend to the meanings people live by, ISC counterbalances objectivist researchers' imperialistic tendency to impose understandings of marital equality onto others' lives.

Notes

An earlier version of this chapter appeared previously as "What Is Family Diversity? Objective and Interpretive Approaches," *Journal of Family Issues* 29, no. 11 (2008): 1407–1425.

1. Stacey (2004) offers an important cautionary tale about the complexities of engaging in public sociology regarding family diversity.

5

Creating Equal Marriages

M any people are interested in having fair, egalitarian relationships with their spouses or significant others. Research has reflected and encouraged this interest. In the past fifty years (and especially in the last two decades), hundreds of articles and books have been written on marital equality. But what is an equal marriage? How can a married or cohabitating couple create one? What factors promote or inhibit marital equality?

In this chapter, I argue that there are two general ways of answering these sorts of questions: objectively and interpretively. The objective approach has been extensively researched (e.g., Blaisure and Allen 1995; Deutsch 1999; Hochschild 1989; Knudson-Martin and Mahoney 2005; Schwartz 1994). The interpretive approach, which is newer and has been pursued less often, constitutes a viable alternative to conventional ways of understanding the creation of marital equality and inequality (Harris 2001; 2003; 2006b), even though the objective-interpretive distinction is more a continuum than a dichotomy.

Marital Equality: The Objective Approach

The objective approach views marital equality as a real entity in the world (Hochschild 1989; Schwartz 1994). Equality is simply an objective characteristic that relationships possess to varying degrees. However, in the objective view, equality is also complex. It has many dimensions. A couple can be relatively egalitarian in some areas of their relationship, but less so in others. The degree to which equality can be achieved depends on a wide array of societal, individual, and interactional variables. Objectivist scholars spend much time (a) identifying

the major dimensions of equality, (b) measuring the extent to which couples have achieved equality, and (c) studying the causes and consequences of equality and inequality.

The Dimensions of Marital Equality

The majority of books and articles devoted to the issue of equality and
inequality in marriage focus on one or two aspects of marital equality
(Harris 2000a). "Marital equality" thus becomes whatever particular
issue is relevant to the scholar at the time. In division of labor studies,
equality becomes fairness in the distribution of household tasks (Shelton
and John 1996). In studies of power, equality might be treated as evenly
sharing the privilege of making major decisions about one's family
(Straus and Yodanis 1995).

   Some scholars, though, have discussed at length what separates
equal from unequal marriage (Haas 1980; Knudson-Martin and
Mahoney 2005; Rosenbluth, Steil, and Whitcomb 1998). The works of
Jean Stapleton and Richard Bright (1976), Gayle Kimball (1983), and
Pepper Schwartz (1994) are especially pertinent because they deal
specifically with "how to have an equal marriage." Each book is as
much descriptive as instructive in that the authors explain what an equal
marriage looks like as they provide strategies for successfully achieving
equality. All three use a variety of techniques—such as introspection
and personal experience, previous literature, interviews and observations of spouses—to define an equal marriage. Their books tend to
cohere around a number of criteria. First, the labor needs to be fairly
divided. Egalitarian partners must share responsibility for financially
supporting their family and for managing the housework and childcare.
Second, power needs to be shared evenly. Each person must have an
equal voice in major decisions. Third, egalitarian partners communicate
in a nonhierarchical fashion. Each must reciprocate concern for the
other's thoughts and must avoid disproportionately interrupting the
other. Fourth, sexual relations must be conducted fairly, so that the
needs and desires of each partner are taken into account. Fifth, feelings
of love and respect must pervade the marriage. Neither partner views the
other as inferior or simply as a means to an end (such as financial stabil-
ity or sexual companionship); rather, the marriage should be perhaps the
most intimate and important relationship each spouse has (Kimball
1983; Schwartz 1994; Stapleton and Bright 1976).

   From an objective perspective, these are the kinds of issues that separate egalitarian from inegalitarian relationships. However, it is impor-

tant to note that scholars have not achieved complete consensus on this definition. Different authors give different amounts of attention and, by implication, importance to different dimensions of equality. For example, whereas Stapleton and Bright (1976, pp. 133–140) devote several pages to the importance of wives keeping their own last names, Kimball (1983, pp. 29–30) mentions the issue only briefly and Schwartz (1994) not at all. Moreover, even among the themes that overlap, the different authors emphasize them differently. Stapleton and Bright (1976) and Schwartz (1994), for example, devote entire chapters to sexual equality, whereas Kimball's (1983, pp. 80–81, 154) treatment of the subject leaves the impression that sex is a relatively minor issue. Carmen Knudson-Martin and Anne Mahoney (2005) discern four aspects of equality, but include categories (such as "mutual accommodation") not used by other scholars. Meanwhile, Francine Deutsch (1999), Arlie Hochschild (1989), and others have conducted major research projects centering on the division of labor, implying that that is the main component of marital equality.

Measuring Marital Equality

A second major goal of objectivist research is to develop and use procedures for adequately measuring how much equality or inequality exists in a marriage. Some dimensions of equality, such as respect, have not been studied much (Hendrick and Hendrick 2006). Other dimensions, such as decisionmaking power or the division of labor, have been investigated via many imaginative measurement strategies (McDonald 1980; Mizan 1994; Shelton and John 1996; Warner 1986). It is reasonable to assume that, in order to study couples who have failed or succeeded in creating marital equality, researchers must be able to carefully evaluate and categorize marriages.

The issue of household labor demonstrates the objectivist approach to measurement. It has often been treated as the core component of marital equality. Researchers began arguing in the 1980s that many employed wives were experiencing "role overload" (Pleck 1985) as they returned home after work and completed a "second shift" (Hochschild 1989). Since then, researchers have noticed that even women who earn more income than their husbands still sometimes report doing more housework (Brines 1993; Bittman et al. 2003; Tichenor 2005). Much research has examined the conflicting demands of domestic and paid employment (Hochschild 1997; Stebbins 2001), with marital equality remaining as an important element within that issue.

The simple question that drives many studies of marital equality—
"Who does what?"—is difficult to answer with precision. How can a
researcher determine the degree to which wives and husbands share the
household labor? Following Robert Blood and Donald Wolfe's (1960)
early example, the technique most frequently used has been the "relative
distribution method" (Warner 1986). This strategy measures the division
of household labor via a brief scale that limits attention to a small number of central tasks. Respondents are asked to think about issues such as
"Who washes the dishes in your household?" and "Who pays the month-
ly bills?" and then choose between the fixed responses such as "husband
always," "husband more than wife," "husband and wife about the
same," "wife more than husband," and "wife always." By assigning
numerical values to these responses and tallying the scores for each
task, a quantitative representation of the level of equality can be created
and correlated with other variables. Over the years researchers have
revised the kinds and number of tasks in their scales, but the general for-
mat has been replicated many times (e.g., Baxter 1997; Hank and Jürges
2007; Himsel and Goldberg 2003; Smith and Reid 1986; Twiggs,
McQuillan, and Ferree 1998).

Blood and Wolfe's (1960) method has been criticized for a number
of reasons. One central issue has been raised by researchers who are
interested in comparing the number of *hours* that spouses spend on
housework: the "relative distribution method" tends to give equal
weight to tasks that take different amounts of time to complete. For
example, it probably takes much less time to process the bills each
month than it does to do the dishes every day. Researchers have pursued
a variety of tactics to overcome this weakness (Shelton and John 1996;
Warner 1986). One strategy is to assign weights to various tasks, based
on their expected frequency and duration (e.g., Model 1981; Kamo
1988). These weights qualify the values assigned to categories such as
"husband always," "both equally," and "wife more than husband."
Another strategy is to ask respondents to estimate or systematically
record how much time they devote to household labor during a particular time frame (Bittman et al. 2003; Warner 1986). By using these sorts
of innovations, researchers continue their attempts to accurately gauge
the levels of inequality that exist in different marriages.

The Causes of Marital Equality

A third major goal of objectivist research is to examine the factors that
increase or decrease the likelihood of marriages becoming equal. Some

scholars adopt an optimistic tone by highlighting the new objective conditions that have set the stage for increasing marital equality. Linda Haas (1982), Kimball (1983), and Schwartz (1994) claim that egalitarian marriages, though in the minority, are on the rise due to larger changes in society. Other scholars strike a more pessimistic note, focusing on the structural factors that are impeding equality. For example, Hochschild (1989) writes of a "stalled revolution" that began with women's increasing participation in paid labor. A problematic culture lag is inhibiting equality in marriage, because (among other reasons) women have changed faster than workplaces have: "A society which did not suffer from this stall would be a society humanely adapted to the fact that most women work outside the home. The workplace would allow parents to work part time, to share jobs, to work flexible hours, to take parental leaves" (Hochschild 1989, p. 12).

Along with the external social constraints that affect the practice of marital equality, there are also internal social constraints that have been inculcated within individual husbands and wives (see Berger 1963, chaps. 4–5). Childhood background, previous marital experiences, religious beliefs, personality traits, gender identity, income, and education are a few of the many factors that could affect an individual's desire and ability to achieve marital equality (Haas 1982; Hochschild 1989; Bittman et al. 2003). Most objectivist scholars do acknowledge spouses' capacity to resist and sometimes overcome societal factors that inhibit equality, however (Knudson-Martin and Mahoney 2005). The implicit assumption is that husbands and wives are profoundly shaped and controlled, yet they have discretion. Through their daily decisions and actions, couples play an important role in "creating and maintaining" the (in)equality that exists in their marriages (Schwartz 1994, p. 191).

Deutsch (1999) provides a nice example of the tension between freedom and constraint that is highlighted by objectivist analyses. Deutsch describes a nuanced relationship between prior marital experiences, sense of entitlement, and interactional strategies. She argues that most egalitarian wives have internalized a strong sense of entitlement—they feel confident that they deserve to be treated equally by their husbands. This leads these wives to make effective choices when confronting their husbands: They "communicate their expectations clearly and directly" (Deutsch 1999, p. 64). In contrast, women in inegalitarian marriages possess an ambiguous sense of entitlement; consequently, they let feelings of resentment build and build before "venting" angrily to their husbands. Inegalitarian wives tend to have emotional "meltdowns" and then ask for more help with a particular *chore,* instead of negotiating more calmly about the *principle* of equally sharing domestic responsibilities as egalitarian wives do. However, a woman's sense of entitlement is not static; it is shaped by cultural factors and the reactions of her husband. Depending on how he responds to negotiations, a wife may revise her sense of entitlement in a less egalitarian direction, which then influences her subsequent choices.

* * *

In summary, the objective approach to studying equality in marriage assumes that equality is (1) a real, observable property of marriages; (2) has a number of dimensions that can be measured by researchers; and (3) is "created" or "constructed" out of the interplay between social constraints and individual discretion (Deutsch 1999, p. 12; Schwartz 1994, p. 196).

Marital Equality: The Interpretive Approach

The interpretive approach to studying marital equality is more recent and, to date, not as popular as the objective approach. It offers a viable alternative to conventional research on the subject (Harris 2000a, 2001, 2003, 2006b). Interpretive constructionism begins with different assumptions that lead to different research practices and understandings. A rigorously interpretive scholar would assume that equality and inequality are labels or meanings that human beings apply to the world, rather than objective features of it (Harris 2000b). Consequently, an interpretive scholar would either set aside or rethink the issues of concern to objectivist scholars. Defining, measuring, and explaining equality would be studied as topics in their own right, as processes of meaningmaking that occur between spouses and their friends, relatives, therapists, lawyers, and other companions.

From Dimensions to "Domains of Relevance"

Whereas objectivist scholars attempt to define what an equal marriage consists of, interpretive scholars bracket that issue. Interpretive scholars do not assume that they know "what equality really means," nor do they attempt to discover the one best answer to that question—even though that may be a reasonable objectivist goal (Hendrix 1994; Rosenbluth, Steil, and Whitcomb 1998). Instead, the interpretive approach studies other people's definitions of equality and how they are applied to the ambiguous circumstances of married life. From this perspective, everyday interactions do not have inherent meaning. They must be interpreted. Terms such as "power" and "labor" do not simply capture or reflect the objective properties of a marriage; instead, they give meaning to indeterminate states of affairs, even as those terms are themselves clarified by the circumstances in which they are applied (Harris 2006b, p. 18).

Following Schutz (1964), objectivists' "dimensions of equality" can be reconceived as "domains of relevance" that married people may use to make sense of social life. Domains of relevance are interpretive schemes that are mapped onto marital actions and events. The act of "deciding what to cook for dinner" may be viewed as a chore if someone is analyzing a marriage through the prism of the division of labor. However, the same behavior might also be portrayed as an example of a fair/unfair decisionmaking privilege or communication style. If one is primarily concerned with equality in sexual relations, then deciding what to cook for dinner may be treated as irrelevant. If "power" and "the division of labor" are reconceived as "domains of relevance," we can see that these dimensions of equality actually play a role in *creating* the equality one finds in a marriage. Whether a marriage is perceived as equal—and to what degree and in what specific way—depends on the domains of relevance of interest to an observer. These domains guide the selection of relevant examples and influence how the examples are interpreted.

Objectivist scholars sometimes assume or argue that some dimensions of equality are more important than others. Even an objectivist's choice of studying a particular issue—be it housework, power, sexuality, communication, or something else—implicitly suggests that an area of social life deserves special consideration. The interpretive approach, in contrast, studies what different groups and individuals treat as most relevant and important. The assumption is that if people act based on what things mean to them, then it is important to pay attention to the criteria that those individuals use to evaluate their own or others' relationships.

Not only may some married individuals rank domains of relevance differently than scholars would, but spouses may focus on domains somewhat foreign to scholarly analyses (Harris 2006b). While many social scientists are secular, individuals may invoke religious terminology as they carve out meaningful realms of experience in their marriages. Consider "Matthew," who argued that his marriage was equal because his wife "submitted" to him, he "relinquished" his life to her, and they both respected and "elevated" each other. "Submitting," "relinquishing," and "elevating" can be seen as flexible constructs useful for interpreting the

degree of equality in a marriage, and they do not correspond straightfor-
wardly to scholarly definitions. Or consider "Alicin," who claimed that
the biggest inequality in her marriage, and the source of many problems
in her life, was intelligence. Her husband was intellectually inferior to
her, and his lack of smarts caused him to be a poor conversationalist, a
financial liability, and an insecure person.

Even if an individual seems to employ the same domain of relevance as (some) scholars do, there can be important differences in how
marital equality is interpreted. A spouse may be interested in "the division of labor," for example, but tell a marital story that would differ
from many scholars' accounts. "Lucy" lamented that her husband would
not do more work around the house. However, Lucy did not treat all
tasks (or even hours of work) as equal. As a stay-at-home mother of two,
she focused on home improvement, a specific chore she wanted her husband "Sam" to do. As a carpenter, Sam was uniquely qualified (in a way
Lucy was not) to do the kinds of repairs their house desperately needed,
but he delayed or refused to take on such tasks during his evenings or
weekends. Lucy explained to me that things would be "close enough" to
equal if he would only do more in this area. While there is much in
Lucy's account that resonates with (some) objectivist analyses, her story
does focus on particular tasks (e.g., remodeling the bathroom) that may
be neglected on a division-of-labor index or else weighted the same as
other tasks in a researcher-generated list (Harris 2006b, pp. 86–93).

In short, the interpretive approach attempts to respect and study how
people define marital equality. Rather than seeing only one legitimate
definition, interpretive scholars study what issues other people deem relevant to equality, as well as how different people rank the relative
importance of these issues.

Measurement Dilemmas as Mundane Concerns

Objectivist researchers have employed imaginative strategies to carefully measure the division of household labor. As ingenious as these strategies are, even objectivist scholars recognize that they have not resolved
complexities of meaning that pervade measurement (Harris 2000a). For
example, some doubt that every kind of household task should be interpreted as an undesirable chore (Coleman 1988; Tichenor 2005, pp.
58–59). Should playing with the children, cooking the evening meal,
and cleaning the bathroom be treated as homogenous "domestic work
items"? Should an hour of "nasty" bathroom cleaning count more than
an hour of food shopping? Researchers even question whether some

tasks—such as cooking or childcare—should actually be defined as "leisure," or as neither work nor leisure (Blair and Lichter 1991, p. 96; see also Ahlander and Bahr 1995; Shaw 1988). Additionally, some scholars wonder how hours of labor can be simply counted when certain nebulous activities, such as emotional and cognitive labor, seem to defy quantification (Devault 1991; Stevens, Kiger, and Riley 2001). Last, assuming hours of labor can be counted accurately, objectivists express at least implicit concern regarding the difficulty of setting an exact cutoff point for separating equal from unequal divisions of work (Harris 2000a). Is a 45/55 division required (Hochschild 1989, p. 282), or will a range of 40/60 or even 35/65 suffice (Haas 1980, pp. 290–291; Wilcox and Nock 2006, p. 1330)? Do spouses' total hourly contributions need to fall within seven hours per week of each other (Piña and Bengtson 1993, p. 905), or should some other cutoff points be established (Benin and Agostinelli 1988, p. 353; John, Shelton, and Luschen 1995, p. 363)?

Objectivist scholars have adopted various strategies in order to address the interpretive dilemmas that complicate the accurate measurement of marital equality. Yet by taking a different approach, these sorts of problems can be seen as fascinating research topics rather than measurement problems. From an interpretive perspective, the goal is not to precisely measure the reality of equality, but to study how people manage the interpretive dilemmas that arise whenever they attempt to gather evidence of fairness or unfairness in marriage. If one's interest is in married people's behavior, then it makes sense to carefully study how spouses select and weigh examples of potential fairness or unfairness. Although married people may not be as quantitatively precise as some researchers, they also can be seen as coping with problems of "measurement" as they discuss and debate their marriages with their husbands or wives, or their friends, relatives, coworkers, ministers, and others. Spouses may ask themselves or their companions: Is a particular activity really or only a "task"? How much is it "worth"? Am I "making too much" or "not getting my due" out of a particular event or series of events? Is my marriage equal in part or overall? Is it seriously unequal or only mildly so? Does my spouse (or friend, etc.) agree with my assessment of my marriage?

As spouses select and weigh examples that are thought to constitute equality, they may adopt a different time frame than conventional scholars. Researchers who study the division of labor, for example, often compare the number of hours spouses spend on housework on a daily or weekly basis. Some individuals, however, may take a longer view when comparing who does what. For example, "Sally" described her marriage as "equal" in the sense that "each of us has gotten to take a turn doing what we wanted to do" (Harris 2003, p. 219). In her account, Sally selected and weighed (as equivalent) two multiyear sequences of action in her life. At one point in time she worked in order for her husband to concentrate on finishing school; since finishing, he works while she gets to care for their baby at home. Sally portrayed these events as fair because she and her husband were each taking turns getting to do what they wanted. By creatively applying this notion of "taking turns" to her relationship, Sally offers her own solution to the challenge of measuring marital fairness. Certainly, not everyone would agree with her interpretation; some might feel that Sally is being utterly exploited. However, from an interpretive perspective, it is important to understand the meanings people give to their own experiences rather than quickly imposing a definition onto the lives of others via an "objective" analysis or political critique (see also Gubrium and Lynott 1987, on members' measurement strategies).

From Causal Explanations to Narrative Analysis

What are the factors that affect the creation of marital equality? For objectivist scholars, we saw that external constraints, internal constraints, and individual discretion all shape the degree to which a marriage becomes equal or unequal. Workplace conditions, personality traits, and daily choices were among the many factors that objectivist scholars suggest could influence the practice of marital equality. The goal of objectivism is to study the real causes—and discern their relative contributions—to the production of (in)equality. Interpretive scholars, in contrast, bracket the reality of equality *and* its putative causes. They study causal explanations as meaning-making processes. Whenever someone tells a story about equality, including the reasons why equality does or does not exist, that narrator can be seen as giving meaning to the situation, the actors, and their behavior (see Knapp 1999; Loseke 2001). There are always more ways than one to account for a situation (Bruner 1987; Gergen 1999). This does not necessarily lead us to disregard someone's story; rather, it encourages us to investigate the stories by which people live.

Consider two respondents from an interpretive study of marital equality (Harris 2006b). "Wayne" felt that his marriage was unequal because his wife, "Tonya," exercised more power than he did. Tonya would override Wayne's wishes and make purchases, take vacations, and visit family as she saw fit. In Wayne's account, this imbalance arose slowly over time. The main cause of Tonya's behavior and the resulting inequality was a small amount of prestige that went to her head. After marrying Wayne, Tonya joined him as comanager of an important hotel in a small community. In Wayne's interpretation, her new status eventually led her to be dismissive and bossy. Meanwhile, "Deborah"—a woman from a different marriage—formulated a parallel but inverted causal sequence. In her marriage, it was her husband, Bill, who dominated the relationship. He yelled at her for no good reason, questioned her purchases, and even discouraged her attending college. In Deborah's account, Bill felt entitled to such actions, because she had brought no financial resources when she started living with him in *his* house. That initial economic difference and his continuing higher income helped bolster Bill's assumption that he could order her around.

Though they are not as carefully researched nor as wide ranging as scholarly objectivist analyses, Wayne's and Deborah's stories do incorporate multiple factors—variables involving social context and personality traits, as well as individual choices—in explaining why their respective marriages are unequal. From an interpretive perspective, what is most important is not whether these lay explanations are thorough or accurate. What is significant is how Wayne's and Deborah's narratives simultaneously give meaning to the nature of their marriages *and* to the reasons their relationships are purportedly unequal. Their causal accounts also give meaning to the actors involved, with Wayne and Deborah coming across as fairly blameless victims suffering from the improper behavior of their spouses (see also Holstein and Miller 1990 on the construction of victims). The interpretive approach attempts to reconceive "explaining the real causes of equality" as a meaning-making process. Interpretivists do at times engage in a causal analysis of sorts, but on a different level; they examine the factors that shape understandings and descriptions of "equal" and "unequal" situations. Like objectivists, they invoke a variety of external and internal constraints to account for why interpretations happen the way they do.

One of the most important constraints is whether one's culture (or subculture) has developed and encouraged the use of egalitarian concepts (such as equal, fair, just) in relation to marriage. Obviously, people cannot use a word to describe their experiences or observations unless they have socially acquired it and learned how to "properly" use it (Gergen 1999). The concept of equality has a long history (see Condit and Lucaites 1993) and has been imaginatively applied by a number of social movements. Feminist writers and activists have done much to bring the concept of equality to the forefront of people's minds when they think about marriage. Some cultures may or may not be so "fortunate."

At a more local level, different socially organized settings may promote divergent understandings and applications of egalitarian notions as they pursue their own agendas. Gubrium's (1992) ethnography of two family therapy agencies, Westside House and Fairview, provides a helpful example. At both of these agencies, family members' choice of seats were interpreted as conveying important meanings about hierarchy and domestic order, but not in the same way. If the staff at Westside observed the father occupying a "power seat," they would tend to view this as positively functional; the father is taking charge of his family. At Fairview, the same sort of behavior would be seen as a sign of trouble, as their goal is to foster democratic relations where everyone feels free to voice their thoughts and feelings. Thus, from an interpretive perspective, understandings of equal and unequal states of affairs (though not automatic or inevitable) are somewhat patterned and influenced by the cultures and agendas of the settings individuals occupy (Gubrium and Holstein 1997; see also Bartkowski and Read 2003). Still, on any given occasion, an individual might (arguably) be said to possess some discretion, even deviating from prior socialization, audience expectations, and other influencing factors (Berger 1963; Blumer 1969). In light of his or her goals at the moment, a spouse might choose to start or avoid an argument by describing some aspect of their marriage as "fair enough" or "totally unequal." An interpretivist may engage in causal analysis of this sort, but very cautiously (Gubrium and Holstein 1999) and with the goal of appreciating the full diversity of meanings any "equal" or "unequal" situation may be given, as well as the interpretive processes that create those meanings.

Overlaps Between Objective and Interpretive Approaches

Despite their contrasting tendencies, it is sometimes difficult to tell objectivist and interpretivist approaches apart. There are other overlapping practices and concerns that join objectivists and interpretivists—though sometimes only on a superficial level—including their shared interests in meaning, qualitative methodologies, and the moral significance of research.

Overlapping Concern with Meaning and Perceptions

Interpretive scholars are meaning centered in assuming that the meaning of things is not inherent; their central task is to understand the diverse meanings people live by and how those meanings are created. However, objectivists do not ignore meaning. Quantitative and qualitative objectivist researchers do inquire about their respondents' perceptions and interpretations. They even recognize the contingency of meaning. The difference between objective and interpretive analyses is a matter of degree.

For example, consider again Schwartz (1994), who conducted in-depth and open-ended interviews with her respondents and then carefully analyzed and presented their stories. In doing so, she was somewhat cognizant of the possibility of divergent perspectives on equality. She remarks, "There was an element of 'I can't define it but I know it when I see it' to my initial search [for egalitarian couples]. There is certainly more than one way of conceptualizing fairness" (p. 4). However, she proceeds to offer her own scholarly definition of marital equality, which emerges from and guides her analysis; then, she confidently distinguishes between those respondents who *she thinks* truly have achieved equality and those who are mistaken (Schwartz 1994, pp. 3, 60). Although she acknowledges the possibility of multiple conceptualizations, it is clear that it is Schwartz's conceptualization that counts.

While primarily objectivist in orientation, Schwartz is certainly not oblivious to the indeterminacy of meaning. In her chapter on sexuality, she argues against the notion that heterosexual intercourse is inherently hierarchical. Much like an interpretive scholar would, Schwartz challenges the assumption that the meaning of intercourse is automatic: "The peer theory . . . takes the position that acts are imbued with meaning from the social circumstances of people's lives. Hierarchy is not the only imagery that must be evoked by penetration" (Schwartz 1994, p. 89). But Schwartz makes this analytical move in order to bolster her argument that heterosexual marriages really can be, objectively, egalitarian. She moves quickly from acknowledging the indeterminacy of meaning back to guidelines for achieving real equality in the bedroom. As with other qualitative objectivists, meaning arises as only one of many factors that influence the creation of real equality and inequality (Blaisure and Allen 1995; Deutsch 1999; Haas 1980; Kimball 1983; Knudson-Martin and Mahoney 2005; Risman and Johnson-Sumerford 1998).

Quantitative objectivists also express interest in meaning and perceptions. Even if they only ask about "who does this chore" or "who makes that decision" via closed-ended survey questions, researchers are expressing at least *a little* interest in respondents' thoughts and beliefs. There is even a fascinating literature that focuses explicitly on spouses' "perceptions of fairness" with respect to the division of labor (Baxter and Western 1998; Blair and Johnson 1992; Hawkins, Marshall, and

Meiners 1995; Himsel and Goldberg 2003; Lennon and Rosenfield 1994). Because so many studies have found that wives do more than their "fair share" of housework (Shelton and John 1996), scholars have asked why women often seem to put up with or not be bothered by such unequal arrangements. A number of explanations have been proposed to explain this seemingly paradoxical behavior (Major 1993; Thompson 1991). For example, it has been suggested that women may compare their workloads to the workloads of other women they know, rather than making cross-gender comparisons between their own efforts and those of their husbands. Or, it has been argued, women may recognize their objectively unequal division of labor but still desire primary responsibility for domestic tasks due to gender role socialization (Major 1993).

Underlying the objectivist literature is a confidence that equality exists and that researchers know what it is. Researchers tend (at least implicitly) to assume that the division of labor is the most important dimension of equality and that their respondents agree. In order to compare spouses' perceptions with the "reality" of their situations, studies of the perceptions of fairness also tend to adopt the same sorts of measurement practices previously described. It is the researchers who make the difficult decisions about which chores to focus on, how to weigh the importance of those chores, and where to draw the line between couples who are "really" equally or unequally sharing the labor. In contrast, an interpretivist studies how spouses (and their friends, therapists, lawyers, etc.) attempt to resolve measurement dilemmas. The "perceptions of fairness" researchers are interested in meaning, but not as fully as they could be, and only insofar as it furthers their main goal—understanding the creation of objective equalities and inequalities (see also Harris 2006b, pp. 26–28, 35–36, 40–43).

Overlapping Methodologies

There is a tendency in marital equality research (and other areas of social research) to associate qualitative research with constructionism. The argument seems to be that qualitative interviews, observations, and similar techniques can provide researchers with greater access to the interactional work that people do to "build" reality. But is the assembly work being done in primarily an objective or interpretive sense? Consider Veronica Tichenor (2005), who examines whether there is a connection between spouses' income and the power they wield in their marriages. She first suggests that quantitative studies have succeeded in demonstrating that gender can trump income as a source of power, by documenting how many higher-earning wives still do more housework than their husbands. Then she argues that such quantitative research is "unable to describe . . . the ways couples come to construct relationships where wives contribute so much and husbands so little" (p. 7). Her qualitative research aims to fill that gap in knowledge. Her goal is to use in-depth interviews to study how "spouses work together to reproduce men's dominance within their relationships" (p. 7). Although her analysis is insightful, it examines the construction of marital equality as an objective phenomenon.

Objectivist assumptions lead researchers to implement qualitative methods in objectivist fashion. Like Tichenor, many researchers set out to study marital equality via loosely structured, in-depth interviews (Deutsch 1999; Kimball 1983; Schwartz 1994). The goal may be to learn from the "experts"—those spouses who have either succeeded in achieving equality or who have learned from their failed attempts. But objectivist researchers assume they know the proper way to define marital equality. A researcher who thinks equal parenting is crucial may seek respondents with children living at home (Deutsch 1999). Selection criteria may also be used to screen out respondents whose marriages do not meet the researcher's definition (Haas 1980; Risman and Johnson-Sumerford 1998). Then, once a proper sample has been assembled, researchers ask questions (such as "How do you divide up housework?") and analyze the answers they receive, with an eye toward discovering how *the scholars' versions* of equality and inequality are practiced by respondents. All of these techniques are reasonable and defensible, but they are objectivist (Harris 2003).

An interpretive scholar may adopt similar methodological strategies, but applies them somewhat differently. When assembling a sample of respondents, an interpretive constructionist seeks spouses who are experts—though in a different sense. Objectivists seek "expert informants" who can convey factually correct details about their marriages (although researchers are also on the lookout for myths and mistakes). In contrast, interpretivists seek expert practitioners—broadly defined as "anybody who can employ the concept of equality to make sense of everyday life in a locally comprehensible manner" (Harris 2006b, p. 58). In this view, a person "practices" marital equality when, in the course of their ordinary actions and conversations, they interpret their own or another's relationship as equal or unequal. One's sample would thus not be restricted to researcher-generated definitions of equality; the goal would be to study other people's definitions and measurements. Like objectivist scholars, an interpretive scholar might solicit in-depth interviews with individuals who view their own marriages as equal or unequal. But questions would be asked and answers analyzed in slightly different ways. Instead of, or perhaps before, asking questions such as "How do you handle the housework?" (or childcare, sexuality, communication), an interpretive scholar investigates the domains of relevance that respondents tend to apply to their lives. Broad questions such as "Tell me about the equality (or inequality) in your marriage" might be used in order to provoke respondents into elaborating their own understandings of equality, while recognizing that the answers respondents give are shaped by the interview context (Harris 2003). Or, just as an objective ethnographer might do (Hochschild 1989), an interpretive ethnographer collects data by directly observing spouses' interactions with others, inside or outside their homes. But the interpretive scholar focuses primarily on the local vocabularies, agendas, audiences, and other factors that shape how depictions or understandings of marital equality are created (Harris 2000a, pp. 136–138; Gubrium 1992), not on the enactment of objective equalities or inequalities. These examples show that the difference between objective and interpretive approaches does not hinge on whether a researcher is quantitative or qualitative, even though qualitative methods are sometimes considered "constructionist" by default.

Overlapping Concern with the Moral Implications of Research

Many social scientists argue that social phenomena are not inevitable; society is the product of social forces and human action (see Chapter 1). The same holds true with marital equality and inequality. Both objective and interpretive scholars argue that (in)egalitarian marriages are not inevitable. Their analyses reveal the processes through which equality and inequality are created. Because equality is a valued moral ideal, such research is not merely technical or informational; it has direct implications for social justice and social reform. Objectivist and interpretivist scholars can both claim that their research has serious moral import, but not in the exact same way.

Objectivists appear to be on clear moral ground. In their studies of successfully egalitarian couples, they express their desire to do their part to promote equality and reduce inequality—as many social scientists do (Cancian 1995). They want to give readers "guideposts" to help spouses achieve equality (Stapleton and Bright 1976) by providing descriptions of relationships that are "worthy of emulation" (Kimball 1983, p. ix) as well as informative "analyses of those couples who have made it to the other side" (Schwartz 1994, p. 3). Objectivists hope to educate therapists on how to successfully counsel troubled couples and thereby create more egalitarian relationships (Hawkins et al. 1994; Knudson-Martin and Mahoney 2005). Even in their studies of nonegalitarian couples, objectivists can make strong moral arguments. They present their work as identifying the structural conditions and interactional practices that uphold real inequalities, so that those inequalities may be better understood and undermined. Thus, close-up studies of persistently unfair relationships still offer positive implications: "By showing us how . . . [they] support the status quo, these couples open up the possibility that gendered expectations can also be reworked to dismantle conventional privilege and support new, more egalitarian relationships" (Tichenor 2005, p. 11). Succinctly put, objectivist researchers suggest that inequality is contingent, not inevitable; that it is possible to construct real egalitarian relationships; and that their analyses help illuminate inequality and encourage equality. This is an optimistic moral message.

Interpretive scholars occupy rockier moral terrain. Their analyses also have moral import, but less obviously. The starting point of interpretive analysis—the premise that "the meaning of things is not inherent"— entails the morally relativistic assumption that "nothing is inherently equal or unequal." Any marriage can be defined in a number of different ways: functional or dysfunctional, happy or unhappy, equal or unequal, and so on. Even where there is agreement that a relationship is unequal, the exact nature, extent, and causes of the putative inequality can be viewed or described differently. From these assumptions flow the main goals of interpretive analyses, which are to investigate the diverse meanings of marital equality as well as how those meanings are invoked, applied, contested, negotiated, and acted upon. These are valid goals, but they have more limited moral implications. Compared to objectivism's clear moral stance—there is something wrong with the world (i.e., inequality) and our research is aimed at remedying that wrong—interpretivism appears noncommittal or even nihilistic.

But this is not entirely the case. There are moral positions to be found within interpretive analysis, though sometimes only implicitly (see Barber 1991; Gubrium 1993, pp. 180–186). In our attempts to conduct research and to improve the social world, we should be wary of applying notions of equality in imperialistic fashion. Interpretivism assumes the moral stance that it is good to be sensitive to the meanings that people live by, and that confidently imposing our meanings upon them (even in the pursuit of equality) may be an injustice in itself.

Drawing inspiration from John Dewey (1989), interpretivism challenges us to try to study and remedy potentially "unequal situations" while recognizing that situations can always be defined in a multitude of ways and that the definitions of the people whose lives comprise our "data" deserve careful consideration and respect (Harris 2006b, pp. 19–22). Consequently, interpretivism resonates with postmodern forms of therapy (Freedman and Combs 1996; Miller 2001) and with reflexive forms of activism that seek to "do good" while not confidently reifying problems or solutions (Harris 2006b, pp. 159–163; Gergen and Gergen 2006). Interpretive scholars do not necessarily deny the existence of exploitation and mistreatment, but, when conducting their analyses, they prefer to closely examine the various ways such phenomena may be portrayed (see Edwards, Ashmore, and Potter 1995).

Arguably, interpretivist researchers can claim that their studies exhibit more of this respect for respondents' meanings than objectivists do. But the difference is one of degree and emphasis. While qualitative objectivists might reasonably assert that they give more consideration to their respondents' viewpoints than quantitative objectivists do, interpretivists might reasonably assert that their own research is conducted in an even more inquisitive, meaning-centered way.

Conclusion

This chapter has highlighted some of the choices that researchers face after they have decided to study marital equality. Different researchers may use the same methods and the same analytical terminology to study the same topic, but in practice have very divergent theoretical agendas: They may be studying the creation of marital equality in a more objective or a more interpretive manner. Each approach has value, but each leads to different kinds of results.

As producers and consumers of research, it is important for us to recognize the implications of conducting a study from one or the other perspective. Is marital equality a real entity or an interpretation? Is the analysis attempting primarily to uncover the factors that create objective inequalities or the factors that shape interpretations of putative inequalities? What might be missed if a researcher tends to adopt one or the other orientation?

This chapter attempted to distinguish between objectivism and interpretivism, while simultaneously encouraging more researchers to adopt the latter approach to studying marital equality. If this is a controversial suggestion, then the next (and final) substantive chapter of this book is certain to raise hackles. Despite all the attention that sociologists give to the study of social inequalities—those injustices stemming from class, race, gender, sexual orientation, and other factors—my argument is that a rigorously interpretive constructionist approach has not yet been, but should be, pursued.

Note

An earlier version of this chapter appeared previously as "Objective and Interpretive Approaches to Equality in Marriage," *Journal of Constructivist Psychology* 22, no. 3 (2009): 213–236.

6

Producing Social Inequality

Most sociologists regularly assume that inequality exists in society and that it is their job to document and explain it. Indeed, the central message of much sociological research is that inequality is ubiquitous and deleterious and ought to be reduced (see also Cancian 1995). Sociologists are not alone in their concern over inequality and their desire for equality; scholars from related disciplines share the same sentiments. But sociologists, it seems, give inequality more attention than any other social scientists. Questions such as "Which groups are better off than others?" are at the heart of innumerable sociological studies and can also be traced back to the field's founders (such as Weber and Marx). A typical introductory sociology textbook not only has chapters on "social stratification" and "global stratification" but also large sections on race, gender, work, education, and families—all of which are pervaded by the issue of inequality (e.g., Anderson and Taylor 2001). Or, for additional institutional evidence of the conventional wisdom, consider the themes of three recent annual meetings of the American Sociological Association: "Allocation Processes and Ascription," "Oppression, Domination, and Liberation," and "Inequality and Social Policy."

A second assumption common in sociology is that there are two major approaches to the study of inequality: functionalism and conflict theory (Marger 1999). To put it simply, the popular belief is that one can treat inequality as a potentially positive feature of an integrated organic system, or one can treat inequality as a matter of unnecessary exploitation and unfair advantage between groups. Few sociologists claim to be functionalists today. Consequently, Kingsley Davis and Wilbert Moore's (1945) article on the importance of inequality to a smoothly functioning society remains the focal statement of the functionalist perspective on

107

inequality, while conflict-related studies of inequality continue to prolif-
erate (e.g., see edited collections by Arrighi 2001 and Shapiro 1998).
Textbooks on stratification and on introductory sociology often summarize functionalist and conflict perspectives on inequality in tables that
provide point-by-point comparisons of the two approaches (Kerbo 2009,
p. 87; Anderson and Taylor 2001, p. 176).

What's missing from the conventional picture of the sociology of
inequality is an appreciation of what interactionist, social constructionist
approaches can contribute and how that contribution differs from other
approaches. Certainly, there are many different brands of interactionism
and related interpretive traditions that derive from pragmatism, phenomenology, and ethnomethodology.[1] As I have shown in earlier chapters, even
research derived from these traditions can exhibit relatively objective or
interpretive tendencies. At minimum, though, an interactionist-inspired
approach would likely emphasize such issues as meaning, interaction, and
the qualitative investigation of real-life experiences. Recently, three
attempts have been made to set agendas that would move the sociology of
inequality in this general direction: Collins's (2000) "Situational
Stratification: A Micro-Macro Theory of Inequality," Johannes Han-Yin
Chang's (2000) "Symbolic Interaction and Transformation of Class
Structure: The Case of China," and Schwalbe et al.'s (2000) "Generic
Processes in the Reproduction of Inequality: An Interactionist Analysis."
In what follows, I compare these three statements about the future direction of research on inequality with my own (arguably more interpretive)
work on marital equality (Harris 2006b), thereby extrapolating from the
discussion in the preceding chapter. First, I distill the main points of these
publications. Next, I explore the different ways that each deals with the
issues of locating inequality, discerning its forms, documenting examples,
and identifying causes.

My goal is to demonstrate that Collins, Chang, and Schwalbe et al.
do not make a significant departure from the first assumption of the conventional wisdom; that is, they all presume that it is the sociologists' job
to find and explain inequality as an objective phenomenon. By carefully
summarizing and critiquing these authors' work, I hope to demonstrate
the implications that a more interpretive social constructionist approach
has for the study of equality and inequality in all areas of social life, not
just marital relations. A rigorously interpretive approach challenges the
conventional wisdom because it focuses squarely on the meanings that
"inequality" has *for people,* as well as how those meanings are achieved
in everyday life.[2]

Summarizing Collins, Chang, and Schwalbe et al.

Collins on Situational Stratification

Randall Collins is a prolific author who has an encyclopedic knowledge of sociological theory and research (see Collins 1988, 1994). While he is familiar with interactionist work, it would probably be more accurate to describe him as a Weberian conflict scholar who draws eclectically from interactionist-related sources, such as Goffman (1967). His message in "Situational Stratification," however, does echo many interactionist themes. In short, Collins calls for more ethnographic research on people's actual experiences of inequality by systematically observing the interaction that takes place in a wide range of diverse "subjective worlds." Collins couches this argument within his longstanding view of micro-macro linkages and within a historical tale about a fundamental shift in the nature of stratification.

For Collins, macrostructures are not so much self-subsistent entities as they are aggregated chains of interaction (Collins 1981). The "state," the "economy," and the "culture" are shorthand ways of referring to patterns of interaction. Large social structures and aggregate statistics are nothing without the ritualistic behaviors that constitute them. Collins argues that "microsituational data"—the kind of data interactionists are usually interested in—take priority over macrodata because "nothing has reality unless it is manifested in a situation somewhere" (Collins 2000, p. 18). Accordingly, the best way to ground theories is through detailed observation and analysis of people's thoughts, words, and actions as they occur in concrete situations. At the same time, though, Collins does not dismiss macrosociologies. Those approaches provide crude but helpful approximations of social life. However, statistical charts and related macrorealities must be "microtranslated" by studying the repetitive everyday events that comprise those realities (Collins 1983, p. 187).

While microevents have always formed the basis of macrorealities, Collins asserts, there was a closer relationship between the two realms in the past than in recent times. In previous centuries, what sociologists think of as macroinequalities (such as differences in class or power) were highly institutionalized and public. For example, members of the nobility and other status groups not only had more prestige and economic clout; their reputations preceded them. Everybody knew who deserved deference, and it was frequently and ceremoniously expressed in daily encounters. Persons were treated more as manifestations of social categories (e.g., servant or head of the household) than as individuals with individual reputations. The present state of affairs stands in distinct contrast, Collins (2000, p. 38) argues: "Contemporary social structure generates a life experience in which most individuals have at least intermittent, and sometimes quite extensive, situational distance from macrostructured relationships."

Since approximately the beginning of the twentieth century, stratification experiences have increasingly been tied to particularized networks. The micro events that constitute stratification operate differently in different "circuits" of interaction.[3] As a result, Collins suggests (2000, pp. 17, 27), individuals may rank one way on an abstract occupational prestige survey but the opposite way when evaluated by their companions at certain social gatherings. For example, imagine an awkward, overweight surgeon at various kinds of parties. Or, consider how influential scholars may be completely unknown or even disrespected outside of the particular circle of academics who appreciate their work.

Thus, very much in interactionist fashion, Collins doubts that the statistics and graphs so common in sociological textbooks can adequately convey the reality of inequality. In order to better understand people's experiences with inequality, he believes sociologists need to make systematic ethnographic observations of how and whether people incorporate and act upon it. Instead of asking "Who has what?" sociologists should investigate how people may use or fail to use their status (or wealth or power) in everyday life. "We need to undertake a series of studies looking at the conversion of abstract macrodistributions . . . into the actual distribution of advantages in situational practice" (Collins 2000, p. 18).

Chang on Class Transformation

While Collins is interested in the social shaping of diverse stratification experiences in everyday situations, Chang focuses on the role of meaning in the creation of large-scale social classes. Chang's article presents an intricate historical account of the structural changes that have occurred in China over the past several decades. He hopes his article will help elevate symbolic interactionism "to the status of a significant competitor and contributor in the club of macro sociology" (Chang 2000, p. 223). Although Marxists and Weberians incorporate some analysis of "meaning" in their research, Chang argues, they have not done so to the degree that interactionism can (pp. 224, 247–248). To demonstrate the contribution interactionism can make, he delineates three kinds of meaning—

"motivation-oriented meaning," "action course–oriented meaning," and "justification-oriented meaning" (p. 228)—and explains the role they played in China's transition from a five-class system to a seven-class system. His analysis specifies many interest groups in China, but centers around the interpretations of the Chinese Communist Party (CCP) and how they provoked, guided, and justified the economic reforms that began in 1978. Chang examined news reports and government documents, but also interviewed 125 Chinese individuals who had undergone a change in their class stratification.

The foil for Chang's article is the Marxist argument that economic changes are generated when the current economic system has depleted (or nearly so) its ability to develop productivity (Chang 2000, p. 228). Chang is not convinced that objective structural strains are what provoke reform. He proposes a trademark interactionist explanation that focuses on actors' cognition—what he calls *perceived relative strain:* "[The] perceived comparative inferiority of an economic structure is more relevant for understanding the basic change of a structure. . . . This perceived inferiority derives from comparing the given economic structure with one or more alternatives, real or imagined, that are believed to be more capable of promoting productivity" (p. 229). Chang argues that some Chinese began making such comparisons in the years just before the reforms began. Statements made by leading reformers (Deng and Hu) show that they were aware that capitalist countries appeared to be doing better than China, and that semicapitalist farming was proving more productive than collective farming within China itself. Chang believes that these perceptions, not an objective structural strain, are ultimately what drove reformers to act.

To enact changes, reformers needed to get their message to the majority of the Chinese people. It took four or five years to accomplish this. Deng and his followers first needed to acquire positions of power in the CCP; they did so by winning a publicized philosophical debate with entrenched communists about the necessity to test political beliefs against reality. Once in control, reformers publicized the successes of privatized farms and encouraged peasants to follow suit. Subsequent successes, Chang asserts, persuaded the masses that basic economic changes were needed in cities as well.

As reforms were being made, additional meanings were generated. Deng and other leaders defined the economic changes as "ideology-free" experiments rather than as explicit moves toward capitalism. To illustrate, Chang (2000, p. 233) cites Deng's well-known slogan "A cat is a good cat, be it black or white, as long as it captures rats." Still, Chang argues, this "action course–oriented meaning" could not suffice on its own. The changes being made in China conflicted with years of socialization in China. The Chinese people had come to believe deeply in the superiority of socialist economies.

Consequently, reformers used three justifications to promote the legitimacy of the new agenda in order to augment the stated objective of increasing productivity. The first justification argued that new business practices actually adhered to the overarching framework of socialism because (a) they were being conducted on collectively owned land and (b) "the nature of an economic system was determined by the ownership of the means of production, not by how it was used" (Chang 2000, p. 234). The second justification claimed that an economy that included private businesses could still be classified as a socialist system if the majority of the means of production were collectively or state owned. The third justification argued that it was necessary for private businesses to promote economic development until their productivity ran its course and a purer form of socialism resulted.

Although different segments of the population responded differently to these three justifications, most Chinese adopted and acted on the interpretations promoted by the leading reformers. Many intended and unintended consequences resulted. In particular, two new classes—the bourgeoisie and the petty bourgeoisie—have arisen. Also, there has been some shift between (and within) the relative positions of the remaining five classes—the bureaucratic/managerial class, the professional class, the clerical class, the working class, and the farming class.

Chang's conclusion is that mechanistic analyses of social change must be replaced by nonmechanistic ones, and interactionists can best accomplish this task. Economic situations can be interpreted in different ways. The manner in which powerful leaders act and the way the masses respond depend on the meanings they give things. Thus, Chang argues, meaning is a "world-constituting force" that must be taken into account when scholars study macrolevel phenomena such as the class structure of a nation. Although Chang provides no explicit methodological directives, the implication from his study is that these meanings are accessible by examining public statements and by interviewing representative members of the population in question.

Schwalbe et al. on the Reproduction of Inequality

Like Collins, Schwalbe et al. (2000) are critical of the vast literature that summarizes inequalities in statistical tables and graphs. However, their criticism is centered less around the diverse experiences that quantitative data gloss. Their main argument is that scholars have not paid enough attention to the question, "How are these inequalities created and reproduced?" (p. 419). While some scholars might respond that there are innumerable causal arguments made in the pages of quantitative books and articles on inequality, Schwalbe et al. are seeking a somewhat different kind of answer than that provided by variable analysis. Through careful ethnographic work, the authors argue, researchers can directly observe the recurrent patterns of behavior that create and reproduce inequality. Because these generic social processes (Prus 1996) may operate in similar ways across innumerable diverse contexts, Schwalbe et al. believe this sort of inquiry can contribute much to understanding how various forms of inequality arise and remain stable.

Actually, they argue (Schwalbe et al. 2000, pp. 421–422), a large amount of this kind of qualitative work has already been done on inequality. In preparing their article, the authors read scores of such studies in order to conceptualize and extract the processes most central to the creation and maintenance of oppressive situations. By treating the previous ethnographic research as data and subjecting it to analytic induction, the authors arrived at the following four concepts: othering, subordinate adaptation, boundary maintenance, and emotion management. These four processes, they argue, are "essential and generative" in that any situation of inequality will inevitably depend on them for its existence.

Schwalbe et al. (2000, p. 422; cf. Fine 1994) refer to othering as "the process whereby a dominant group defines into existence an inferior group." This process underlies race and gender relations, but also myriad other inequalities, such as how temporary workers may be depicted by their employers as unskilled and unmotivated (Schwalbe et al. 2000, p. 423). While othering can be direct and blatant, it can also be subtle. Those in positions of power (e.g., CEOs and politicians) can use their resources to present superior self-images that by implication create and denigrate supposedly inferior others.

Subordinate adaptation refers to the tactics that oppressed persons may employ to deal with the inequalities they face. For example, subordinates may adapt by "hustling," using illegal and or dishonest means to exploit others for financial gain. Because targets are usually the weak, this adaptation helps reinforce inequality. Or, in order to salvage a sense of self, subordinate groups may create alternative subcultures with distinctive systems for attaining prestige. These beliefs and practices, however, can be "debilitating and risky, and diminish chances for mainstream success" (Schwalbe et al. 2000, p. 428).

With the term "boundary maintenance" Schwalbe et al. make the point that the differences between groups, in terms of resources and privileges, are not self-sustaining even after they are in place. It takes interactional work to secure the borders. Boundaries between the haves and have-nots are maintained by (1) the transmission of cultural capital; (2) the operation of networks; and (3) the use (or threat) of interpersonal violence. Thus, men's advantage over women may be reproduced as parents and teachers inculcate different skills and predilections into boys and girls, as gatekeepers exclude potential network members based on gendered criteria, and as husbands physically dominate their wives.

The last inequality-producing process that Schwalbe et al. identify is emotion management. Inequality, though beneficial to some, frequently generates uncomfortable feelings of shame, anger, resentment, and hopelessness in others. These emotions can be destabilizing to the system, and so must be dealt with. One strategy is to regulate the discourse that could arouse emotions and mobilize action. The careful use of metaphors by elites can desensitize subordinates from their negative feelings and encourage them to act to maintain inequality. This is reflected in the way employees are taught methods of emotion work ("think of the customer as a guest in your home") that will earn the most money for their employers, regardless of the long-term effects on workers' sense of self (Hochschild 1983).

In their conclusion, Schwalbe et al. encourage researchers to jettison reifying notions of structure that obscure the way people *do* things together in ways that reproduce inequality. With the four concepts of othering, subordinate adaptation, boundary maintenance, and emotion management, they hope to provide a theoretical framework for subsequent qualitative studies of inequality. Future research, they suggest, could "directly examine" the operation and nuances of these generic social processes through careful ethnographic inquiry. They parallel Collins (2000) by arguing that "the key analytic question is not about resources or their distribution, but about how resources are used, in any given time and place, to create and reproduce patterns of action and experience" (Schwalbe et al. 2000, p. 440).

Harris on Marital Equality

My own research (Harris 2001, 2006b), like the articles by Collins, Chang, and Schwalbe et al., also highlights the common interactionist themes of meaning and interaction. However, in my opinion, my approach differs from that found in the other three publications in ways that again underscore the difference between objective and interpretive constructionism. First, I began with the assumption that inequality is an interpretation rather than an objective condition. Second, I have proposed that scholars should bracket the concept, turn it into a topic rather than a resource, and study how people tell stories that transform ambiguous experiences into coherent narratives about inequality. In so doing, I have attempted to combine Blumer's (1969) formulation of interactionism with compatible constructionist concepts from phenomenology (Schutz 1964), ethnomethodology (Garfinkel 1967; Pollner 1987), and narrative analysis (Gubrium and Holstein 1995, 1997; Maines 1993; Riessman 1993). In short, I used some similar theoretical resources to those used by Collins, Chang, and Schwalbe et al., but attempted to conduct my research in a more rigorously interpretive fashion.

Taking marital equality as my point of departure, I have critiqued previous research in order to open a space for an interpretive construc-tionist agenda. In the past four decades, quantitative and qualitative researchers alike have studied the costs, benefits, prerequisites, and impediments of marital equality. They have done so by adopting (implic-itly or explicitly) particular definitions of what qualifies as an equal or unequal marriage. There are two big problems, I argued. First, marital scholars do not agree with each other on how to define and measure inequality. Consequently, the same couple may be categorized as equal or unequal depending on which approach is used. Second, it is likely that many of the scholarly meanings and measurement devices do not res-onate with the diverse ways that respondents may perceive equalities and inequalities in their marriages—if and when the issue is relevant to them.

With this critique in mind, I have tried to investigate and demon-strate how the issue of equality/inequality might enter the experiences of married people. I did so by soliciting interviews with thirty individuals who defined their own marriages as equal or unequal. Unlike previous scholars who developed interview guides that reflected a preconceived meaning of equality (Deutsch 1999), I asked more open-ended questions that were intended to promote respondents' storytelling. I wanted to encourage respondents to construct narrative accounts about the issues that concerned them, while recognizing that the research setting shaped the production of those accounts (see also Atkinson and Silverman 1997; Holstein and Gubrium 1995a). I then analyzed and presented the stories I heard through Schutz's (1964) notions of "domains of relevance" and "typifications." These concepts suggest that forms of inequality can be seen as socially acquired interpretive constructs that people use to make sense of the world. No object has inherent meaning (Blumer 1969).

People typify indeterminate things as this or that depending on the purposes they pursue and the perspectives they take as they interact within particular discursive environments (Gubrium and Holstein 2000). These typifications do not break out randomly, but tend to reflect culturally constructed categories and concerns. Thus, I considered the various examples and themes that previous researchers have focused on—such as instances of "power" or "the division of labor"—to be socially acquired typifications and domains of relevance. I then used these Schutzian concepts to compare scholarly research with lay accounts.

In my book *The Meanings of Marital Equality* (Harris 2006b), I presented lengthy excerpts from nine of my respondents' narratives, five of which I portrayed as somewhat "familiar" or similar to scholarly domains of relevance, and four I cast as "unfamiliar." Of the two "familiar" tales, Deborah's was perhaps most memorable. Deborah depicted her relationship as very unequal due to an imbalance of power. She described her husband Bill as a traditional male who liked to be "the man of the house." As examples of "power trips" that her husband went on, she recounted her husband's habit of yelling at her for invading his privacy in the bathroom and for failing to anticipate which tool he needed when they worked together in the yard. She also claimed that Bill second-guessed her purchases and had even prevented her from going back to college.

Though Deborah's story resembled the common scholarly theme of "power," I noted that the indicators she relied upon were not the same as might be found in many quantitative scales and observational checklists. Moreover, I suggested that her narrative did not merely convey information about objective states of affairs but actively constituted a sense of reality. The experiential particulars she used as examples could each be typified in many different ways. Deborah (and the rest of my respondents) would likely, if questioned in a different context, recast the same biographical events into different narrative patterns. For example, I believe that if my interview had centered on "dysfunctional marriages" or "rude behavior," Deborah might have typified some of the same instances of her marital past as elements within those domains, rather than power inequality.

For the "unfamiliar" tale, the case of Matthew stands out for me. This respondent drew creatively on the Bible as an interpretive resource in order to craft a portrait of his marriage as thoroughly egalitarian. With the concepts of "submitting," "relinquishing," and "elevating," Matthew presented his own analysis of the generic processes that purportedly created and reproduced the equality that existed in his marriage (and the inequality that existed in others' relationships). His religious conception of marital equality is foreign to the secular viewpoints presented in most mainstream scholarly accounts. Nevertheless, I deemed it worthy of consideration for the way it could sensitize researchers to (a) the diverse meanings equality can have and (b) the interpretive practices (e.g., demarcating domains of relevance and typifying examples) that produce those meanings.

The point of my research, then, is that marital researchers have tended to heavy-handedly transform their subjects' experiences into typified elements of *scholarly* tales about inequality. Moreover, I am claiming that stratification research in general tends to overlook the stories of inequality that everyday people live by, as well as the methods through which (and settings within which) people construct those narratives. To remedy this neglect, I have called for more research that attempts to salvage the meanings, however shifting and transitory, that the equality/inequality dichotomy has for people.

Comparison and Critique

So far this chapter has summarized the main points of four recent proposals (including my own) for the development of a more interpretive, interactionist approach to inequality. I argue that each proposal is interesting and worth considering. Many crisscrossing similarities and differences can be found between these agenda-setting works, depending on readers' purposes and perspectives. My goal is to distinguish between traditional and more interpretive constructionist approaches to studying equality and inequality in social life. In what follows, then, I highlight those elements in Collins, Chang, and Schwalbe et al. that—despite the authors' differences—reflect their shared commitment to the conventional wisdom about inequality. In contrast to the approach taken in this book, the authors of the other three publications all assume that it is primarily the *sociologist's* prerogative to find and explain the inequality that exists, objectively, in society. This assumption is apparent in their treatment of four central issues: locating inequality; discerning its forms; documenting its manifestations; and tracing its causes and effects.

Locating Inequality

For Collins, Chang, and Schwalbe et al., inequality clearly does exist in society. "It" is a thing out there, waiting for sociologists to find. For example, at one point Collins (2000, p. 17) cites a reputable source and states authoritatively, "The distribution of income and wealth has become increasingly unequal since 1970." Similarly, Chang (2000, pp. 242–243) makes statements such as "New dimensions of stratification have emerged within the working class" and "Cross-region inequality has also increased significantly." Meanwhile, in their introduction, Schwalbe et al. (2000, p. 421) make their position abundantly clear: "We take inequality to be endemic to and pervasive in late capitalist societies."

However, these authors also assert that though inequality does exist, sometimes it does not present itself clearly. Correctly identifying inequality is difficult. Much of the uncertainty hinges on the idea that inequality, while thing-like, also depends (to an unexplored degree) on the way sociologists and laypersons choose to look at it. The tension between analysts' and members' depictions of inequality, however, is not converted into a full-blown research topic (as it would be for a more interpretive constructionist). Rather, it is either glossed over or dismissed as priority is given to the researcher's perspective.

Consider Collins's (2000) critique of quantitative studies of occupational prestige. He argues that some sociologists treat the statistics produced by these studies as if they captured the realities of stratification when they actually may distort those realities. On page 18 he asks, "What is the real-life standing of construction workers when they display a style of outdoor muscular activity that receives respect . . . [and] when the prestigious style of automobile is the big, trucklike 'sports utility vehicle'?" But as Collins develops his argument that quantitative surveys neglect subjective diversity, he simultaneously highlights and minimizes the importance of people's perceptions: "Occupational prestige can only be realistically understood if *we* can survey situations of occupational encounters and judge the actual situational stratification that takes place" (p. 18; emphasis added). Thus, while Collins describes inequality as difficult to measure and contingent on members' perspectives, he still characterizes it as a factual, observable phenomenon. He assumes that there is one real version of inequality—"the actual stratification" that is out there. Moreover, it is up to sociologists to observe and decode "it."

I find a similar pattern in Chang's article. Like Collins, Chang also presumes that inequality exists factually. He does acknowledge, though, that the nature of the inequality that is "there" is shaped both by people's perceptions and by the way *he* defines it:

> I define "class stratification" as a system of class hierarchy in which the relative position of each class is determined by its location in the power relations between classes, by the direct or indirect returns to the exercise of its power, and by the way it is *perceived* by its own members as well as by the members of the other classes. *Based on this definition,* two distinctive patterns of class stratification *may be identified* on the Chinese mainland. (Chang 2000, p. 237; emphasis added)

Thus, the importance of people's perceptions is built right into Chang's definition. However, it is extremely unclear how these perceptions factor into the "two distinctive patterns" of inequality that "may be identified." Let me also point out Chang's use of the passive tense here. Exactly who is identifying the patterns? That murky issue is what an interpretive constructionist approach would focus on, along with other questions related to the representation of reality.[4]

Schwalbe et al., though they take a somewhat more interpretive slant than either Collins or Chang, also tend to confound lay and analytical treatments of inequality. For example, recall their description of othering as "the process whereby a dominant group defines into existence a subordinate group" (Schwalbe et al. 2000, p. 422). That is a very curious sentence: Is the phrase "defines into existence" being used in a primarily objective or interpretive manner? If Schwalbe et al. were conducting a rigorously interpretive analysis, wouldn't there be quote marks around "dominant" and "subordinate"? Exactly who decided that the dominant group is dominant, and that the subordinate group is subordinate? Where do researchers' definitions begin and members' definitions end?

In contrast to these authors, in my research I attempted to treat inequality as entirely dependent on people's interpretive practices. I tried to remain acutely sensitive to the question, "Who is doing the 'stratifying,' people or the sociologist?" While not denying human suffering and exploitation, I have claimed that experiencing a troubling state of affairs as "unequal" is first and foremost an interpretive accomplishment. From an interpretive constructionist perspective, equal and unequal states of affairs only exist when members of a setting describe or understand situations in those terms. My goal was thus to demonstrate how my respondents "defined into existence" equal and unequal states of affairs through their storytelling practices.

Discerning Inequality's Forms

If inequality is presumed to exist, then what shapes does it take? Collins, Chang, and Schwalbe et al. have confident ideas about the various forms of inequality that exist out there. Collins (2000, p. 20), following Weber, devotes much attention to the concepts of class, status, and power. He also sets aside a special section devoted to deference, and delineates two power subtypes—deference power and efficacy power (p. 33). Chang, as I mentioned earlier, is concerned mostly with class (and China's putative transformation from a five-tier to a seven-tier system), but he also writes much about power. The subtypes he coins are not precisely the same as

Collins's, though. He posits three components of "position based power": "power locus," "power sweep," and "power use" (Chang 2000, p. 246). Schwalbe et al., meanwhile, depict the inequalities they discuss as falling under the domains of race, class, gender, and sexuality. They believe each form is crucial, and they chastise previous researchers for not examining all four of these inequalities in the course of their studies: "Even when one form of inequality (e.g., gender) is brought into an analysis, it is not uncommon to see other forms (e.g., race and class) left out or barely mentioned" (Schwalbe et al. 2000, p. 443).

Collins, Chang, and Schwalbe et al. thus make reasonable and intelligent attempts to specify various kinds of inequalities amenable to sociological research. But their efforts lead more to objective than interpretive analyses. From an interpretive constructionist perspective, it would not make sense to cite a famous sociologist (e.g., Weber) in order to justify why one is focusing on a particular form or forms of inequality. Nor would one assume that there is one, or three, or four forms of inequality, with a predetermined number of subtypes, that merit attention. Rather, the issue of discerning the forms of inequality and ranking their importance would be the *members'* practical task. For an interpretive constructionist, what merits attention are the forms of inequality that people themselves are concerned with. Thus, the only reason to incorporate Weber's tripartite conceptualization into one's study would be if it were actually used as a meaning-making resource by the participants of an interaction that the researcher was investigating. An interpretive constructionist scholar would not assume that a particular form of inequality was in play at a certain place and time, or even that the issue of inequality was relevant at all.

This is the approach I attempted to take in my study. First I tried to investigate, instead of presuming, what forms of inequality mattered to my respondents. Then I used my data to show that not all of these forms coincided with the venerable and ready-made concepts of classical sociology, as in the case of Matthew's religious account or Alicin's story about her husband's intellectual inferiority. Moreover, I argued, those persons who do employ familiar sociological concepts may do so in a highly selective or idiosyncratic fashion, as in my respondents' narratives about power and the division of labor.

Documenting Examples

If inequality is presumed to exist and to take particular forms—which are reasonable though objectivist assumptions—then it also makes sense to seek out examples of the inequalities. And that is exactly what Collins, Chang, and Schwalbe et al. do. Recall that Collins was very interested in power and deference. To document instances of these phenomena, he presents a number of examples drawn from his personal experiences. At the beginning of his article, for instance, he asks readers to consider some "typical scenes," one of which involves "a muscular black youth, wearing baggy pants and hat turned backwards and carrying a boom box" who "dominates the sidewalk space . . . while middle-class whites palpably shrink back in deference" (Collins 2000, p. 17). Later, Collins depicts the nature of contemporary highway driving in order to bolster his point that macroinequalities (such as class) may be only partially microtranslated into actual experiences in everyday situations.

> [Situational dominance] may be mildly correlated with sheer physical property: an expensive, fast car lords it over ordinary cars by passing them; overt *deference* is displayed as a car captures the dominant trajectory of motion . . . so that other cars get out of the way when they see it coming. . . . Here *we* see that economic power translates into situational dominance to some extent. (Collins 2000, p. 40; emphasis added)

An interpretive constructionist scholar would note that Collins's characterization of these instances as examples of deference and dominance is potentially problematic. In this sort of analysis there is "the danger of the observer substituting his view of the field of action for the view held by the actor[s]" (Blumer 1969, p. 74). These situations could be characterized in many different ways. The documentary method of interpretation is very much in operation as Collins's themes and examples acquire their sense through mutual elaboration (Garfinkel 1967; see also Prus 1999, p. 153; Watson and Goulet 1998).

While Collins draws primarily on personal observations to cast doubt on the veracity of many quantitative measures, Chang makes extensive use of statistics as evidence of China's class transformation. He cites without hesitation the *Statistical Yearbook of China* (*SYC*) and other sources. Notice also Chang's use of the passive voice as he describes the changes that "have stratified" the Chinese people:

> Reform policies have significantly affected the life chances of peasants. In 1997 China's population was 1.24 billion. About 70 percent of the population lived in the countryside (*SYC* 1998:105). But 18.5 percent of the rural labor force actually worked in village and township enterprises (*SYC* 1998:127); 40 million to 80 million people migrated to cities, taking temporary jobs as *peasant workers* . . . ; 6 million were employed in rural private enterprises (*SYC* 1998:152); and a signifi-

cant proportion were engaged in self-employed businesses. Only the remaining rural population constituted the farming class (or rural working class).

These changes have stratified the formerly homogenous peasants into three broad categories: the rural petty bourgeois, the marginal stratum of peasant workers, and the farming class. The emergence of the first two categories suggests that the rigid divide between *nongye renkou* (rural residents) and *fei nongye renkou* (nonrural residents) has blurred. (Chang 2000, p. 241; emphasis in original)

Here Chang's evidence for the existence of the Chinese class system is derived from members' systems and procedures for counting and classifying people. While interpretive constructionist scholars often treat statistics as products of and flexible resources for people's agendas (Heritage 1984, pp. 168–176; Kitsuse and Cicourel 1963; Zimmerman and Pollner 1970, p. 83), Chang incorporates them confidently into his account, ignoring all of the hidden interpretive work that goes into producing and employing official statistics. An interpretive constructionist would wonder: "Do Chinese people use these concepts (e.g., 'peasant workers') to characterize their situations as manifestations of class stratification? How, when, and where do they articulate these terms with the messy details of their everyday experiences?"

In the article by Schwalbe et al., the authors provide mostly implicit examples of inequality, as they are interested primarily in the four processes that sustain it. Their data is neither personal observations nor statistics, but the findings (or "makings") of previous ethnographic research. Still, in passages like the one below, authors subtly frame as unequal those situations where some persons have less money than others and/or are victimized for having less money.

From classic studies of gangs . . . Gypsies . . . fortune tellers . . . and drug dealers . . . qualitative research has shown how members of subordinate groups, rather than challenge the system or push their way into the mainstream, organize to exploit it from the edge. Usually this means exploiting those who are vulnerable—the jobless, the elderly, the uneducated, the addicted. This kind of hustling exploits the human fallout from extra-local inequalities, and in turn helps to reproduce those inequalities by further debilitating the weak. (Schwalbe et al. 2000, p. 429)

When hustlers take advantage of people with minimal financial resources, Schwalbe et al. argue, they are reinforcing already existing inequalities by making the poor even poorer.

As difficult as it may be to contemplate from within mundane reason (Pollner 1987), examples of economic disparities are not inherent indicators of inequality. They must be typified as such, rather than being ignored, noticed but considered irrelevant (e.g., compared to spiritual concerns), or taken as indicators of some other problem. It certainly may be demonstrable that some person or group possesses more wealth than another. Nevertheless, affixing the label "unequal" to that state of affairs is an interpretive act. There is nothing in the situation that absolutely necessitates that particular characterization, rather than other possible characterizations. Once applied, though, the label of inequality helps create the meaning of the situation, while the situation gives some sense to the term "unequal."[5] Thus, though it may be difficult for some readers to recognize, in the passage above, Schwalbe et al. are themselves reproducing inequality on a deeper level. By juxtaposing the theme of inequality with examples of the poor getting poorer, they are implicitly reproducing a *sense* of inequality with which many sociologists are familiar.

In contrast, an interpretive constructionist agenda would make the creation of inequality meanings the explicit focus of research. What are examples of inequalities that members of a setting perceive? How do speakers select and transform a set of indeterminate examples in order to accomplish certain interactional objectives? Do people make interpretive connections between "inequalities" in one place/time and another? If so, how? In short, what is missing from traditional scholarly research on inequality is an appreciation of people as interpretive ethnographers of their own lives (see also Gubrium and Holstein 1995). This kind of agenda is much different than those proposed by Chang, Collins, and Schwalbe et al., who assume that it is ultimately the sociologist's prerogative to identify and assemble examples of inequality. This assumption is reasonable and justifiable, but it leads to analyses that are more objectivist than interpretive.

Causality and Motive Talk

Once inequality is presumed to exist, to take certain forms, and to manifest itself in concrete examples, conventional scholars can then attempt to trace the cause-and-effect linkages between the precursors and consequences of inequality, including the motivations that drive people to act as they do in relation to inequality. Thus, a fourth major difference between Collins's, Chang's, and Schwalbe et al.'s relatively conventional accounts and a more interpretive constructionist account has to do with whether or not the researcher tends to treat causality as a topic or a resource.

Consider Collins. He argues that, in modern times, macroinequalities are not always directly microtranslated into everyday experiences. As a result, one's wealth may or may not manifest itself in consumption ability. For the super rich, he claims, the appeal of money may not be its usefulness for buying things.

> The main attraction of having extremely large amounts of money may be the emotional energies and symbolic membership markers of being on the phone at all hours of night and day, engaging in exciting transactions. In terms of sheer consumption power, the extremely wealthy have attained the maximum of what they can get as material benefits; yet most of them continue to work, sometimes obsessively lengthy hours, until advanced ages. . . . It appears the value of money at this level is all in the microexperience, the activity of wielding money in highly prestigious circuits of exchange. Money here translates into situational power and into nothing else. (Collins 2000, p. 21)

In this extract Collins assigns motives—both "thoughts" and "feelings"—to elites (see Chapters 2 and 3 in this volume). Emotional energies, symbolic membership, excitement, and situational power are offered as reasons why the ultra wealthy continue to work hard even when they appear to have no need for additional funds. Certainly, other parties (including wealthy persons themselves) might attribute this behavior to different motives—such as greed, habit, drive, self-fulfillment, duty, neurosis, altruism, or ego—depending in part on the audiences and interactional objectives at hand.

While Collins does not use the term "motivation," Chang does so explicitly. As I summarized earlier, one of Chang's arguments was that China's class transformation should be traced not to the mechanical operation of an objective social structure. Chang treats meaning—the "perceived relative strain" discussed above—as the main causal factor behind the reform movement:

> "Motivation" here refers to the driving force that pushed Chinese society toward a presumably better alternative to its prereform system. The dominant social actors (the top reformers, the ruling party, and the majority of the public who support the change) share this motivation to various degrees as a potent societal impulse. (Chang 2000, p. 228)

Again, an interpretive constructionist scholar might ask: "What other reasons and motives could be offered for this behavior? By whom? In what contexts?"

Schwalbe et al. also confidently posit connections between various causes and effects of inequality. Recall that they defined emotion management as an essential feature of the reproduction of inequality. In their view, inequality causes certain destabilizing emotions (e.g., anger), and this leads dominant groups to regulate societal discourse so those feelings can be muted. The authors further argue that people may actively organize the mundane aspects of public gatherings so that inequality-reinforcing emotions are generated. They cite a previous study to explain:

> Scripted events . . . reproduce inequality by *encouraging* subordinates to ignore inequality and embrace the dominant regime. . . . For example, Schwalbe shows how the leaders of men's movement gatherings artfully combine simple acts—decorating a room with totemic objects, burning incense, playing ethereal music, drumming, chanting, invoking spirits, and excluding women—to *induce* a feeling of emotional communion that *compelled* men to ignore political conflicts, social class differences, and sexist behavior by other men. (Schwalbe et al. 2000, p. 438; emphasis added)

While they carefully skirt the issue of whether people are purposefully inducing feelings in others, Schwalbe et al. nonetheless construct a causal chain of events that characterizes—from an omniscient viewpoint—the putative emotions, behaviors, and settings of the gatherings. A more interpretive scholar might wonder whether it is the participants or the authors who have assigned the parts, chosen the props, and set the scene within which all the participants are portrayed as acting.

In contrast to Collins's, Chang's, and Schwalbe et al.'s approaches, an interpretive constructionist approach would convert motivations into motive talk and would then proceed to study competing vocabularies of motive and the interactional dynamics of their use (Mills 1940; Potter and Wetherell 1987, chap. 4). The researcher would refrain (as much as possible) from assigning motives and causes in order to study how reasons are proffered, accepted, contested, revised, and so on.[6]

In my research, I tried to stay more in line with this latter approach. I did not search respondents' speech and behavior for clues to their real motivations. Instead, I focused on the ways spouses assigned motives (to themselves and others) and identified the causes and effects of inequality. Recall my respondent Deborah, for example. She offered an explanation for her husband's "power trips" that bolstered her larger story about the inequality in her marriage. She suggested that because she "came into the relationship with nothing" and he "put a roof over

[her] head," her husband felt justified in not treating her as an equal (Harris 2006b, p. 80). Another one of my respondents, however, mobilized a similar but inverted rags-to-riches plot line in order to explain his wife's reportedly bossy demeanor. Remember that Wayne attributed the source of his wife's personality to a status change that went to her head: When his wife, Tonya, became his comanager at a prominent hotel in a small town, her newfound power and prestige slowly turned her into a domineering person (Harris 2006b, pp. 77–78).

What I have attempted to demonstrate with this interview data is a basic point: just as scholars impute motives and make causal linkages that support their larger narratives, so too do people. Their accounts also interpretively constitute conditions of inequality, the reasons behind them, and the victims and villains involved (see also Best 1999; Holstein and Miller 1990; Loseke 2003). Their tales may be as informative and interesting as scholarly versions and merit close attention.

Conclusion

Is it the sociologist's prerogative to identify and explain inequality? I have argued that, to date, that has been the usual assumption among sociologists. The conventional wisdom in sociology is that inequality is "one of the most significant and decisive facts of human societies" (Maines 2000, p. 257) and that it is sociology's charter to document its extent, causes, and consequences. This premise unifies a wide array of competing approaches within the general rubrics of conflict theory and functionalism alike.

Recently, symbolic interactionists and other (semi-)interpretive scholars have attempted to demonstrate the contribution they can make to understanding situations that fall on the "unequal" side of the equal/unequal dichotomy. However, as I have tried to show in this chapter, these scholars have also tended to replicate the conventional wisdom.[7] In order to develop a more distinctive approach to inequality, perhaps a different premise is needed: Nothing is inherently unequal. This *un*conventional wisdom may provide a useful starting point for studying how individuals and groups construct versions of inequality by *interpretively* documenting (in Garfinkel's [1967] sense) its extent, precursors, and consequences.

The idea that "nothing is inherently unequal" may strike some readers as outrageous, if not silly. However, much interactionist research in the field of deviance has grown out of a similar premise—that no act is inherently deviant. Recall from Chapter 1 Becker's influential statement that "deviance is *not* a quality of the act the person commits. . . . The deviant is one to whom that label has successfully been applied" (Becker 1973, p. 9; but also see Holstein 1993; Pollner 1987). Similarly, the rich tradition of research on the interpretive construction of social problems can be traced, among other sources, to Blumer's statement that "social problems are fundamentally products of a process of collective definition instead of existing independently as a set of objective social arrangements with an intrinsic makeup" (Blumer 1971, p. 298; see also Loseke 1999; Holstein and Miller 2003). To say that nothing is inherently unequal seems no more bizarre than to claim that nothing is inherently deviant or problematic. Perhaps this unconventional premise will prove no less useful for researchers than earlier premises have.

But what does it mean to say that inequality is "not inherent"? Upon what is it "contingent"? Through what processes is it "constructed"? As I have argued in this book, much ambiguity pervades the ideas of contingency and construction. Consequently, scholars have used the same concepts to convey very different points. Researchers who presume the world is "built up" in the daily interactions of people may not necessarily be taking the viewpoint that it is people's *interpretive* practices that bring a recognizable world into being. For example, Collins (2000, p. 18) asserts that macroinequalities must be "microtranslated" into everyday experience in order to have any real existence; Chang (2000, p. 246) describes meaning as a "world-constituting force, a major factor that has contributed to China's . . . change of class structure"; and Schwalbe et al. (2000, p. 440) encourage studies of how people actively use resources "to create and reproduce patterns of action and experience."

The trouble is that an interpretive social constructionist approach would use nearly the exact same language to say something quite different. Like Collins, an ISC approach would study how people "microtranslate" inequalities, but it would do so by examining how people employ inequality-related concepts from the larger culture (e.g., class or marital power) as they give meaning to the indeterminate complexities of their everyday lives (see Holstein and Miller 2003; Loseke 1999, 2001). Like Chang, an ISC approach would consider interpretation to be a "world-constituting force," but in a less realist sense. For an interpretive constructionist "the world" is constituted by the way people think or talk it into being (Heritage 1984, p. 290; Pollner 1987, p. 7), not by the way a few meanings here or there contribute to the creation of objective social structures.[8] And, like Schwalbe et al., an ISC approach would be interested in how people "create patterns of action and experience," but *create* in the sense of selectively linking and transforming ambiguous incidents into comprehensible narrative patterns (Gubrium and Holstein 1997, pp. 146–147).

I don't want to overstate the difference between conventional and interpretive constructionist approaches. No matter how strictly constructionist an interactionist attempts to be, some assumptions must be made about the world out there (Best 2003). At the very least, the constructionist scholar assumes that the interpretive practices that constitute the world are demonstrably real. Beyond that, some constructionists have found it helpful to self-consciously incorporate somewhat "realist" observations of the social context in order to explain the differing contents and consequences of interpretations that are made in different settings (e.g., Loseke 1999; Weinberg 2001). However, these observations are limited and cautious, and made with the recognition that they could be subjected to constructionist analysis at any time (Gubrium and Holstein 1997, p. 120; Gubrium and Holstein 1999).

Also, I do not want to give the impression that all claims about inequality, because they are "social constructions," are erroneous. To say that a story about inequality is an interpretation doesn't mean it is necessarily false, just that it is not the only potentially useful account that might be given. And to say that inequality is an interpretation is not to argue that the concept or issue should be set aside in favor of more objective concerns. If all the meanings we take to be real are socially constructed, then there is no need to search desperately for rock-solid footing. I am not arguing that sociologists should give up on inequality as an overarching theme for their research and advocacy. A large number of people (me included) have found scholarly narratives about inequality to be particularly applicable and compelling. Undoubtedly they will continue to do so. Ideally, interpretive constructionist research on inequality can simply add a dose of clarity and humility (rather than despair) to the study and amelioration of injustice, by explicating the ways in which inequalities (like all social problems) are reflexively constituted by those who think and talk about them (see also Blumer 1971; Loseke 1999; Holstein and Miller 2003; Spector and Kitsuse 1977).

What I *am* arguing is that among the emerging agendas reviewed in this chapter, not all of them make a significant departure from the conventional sociological wisdom on inequality. There is another option besides treating inequality as a more or less factual condition that arises out of exploitive relations between groups, the functional requirements of a self-organizing system, or any other scenario. Researchers can treat inequality as a conceptual tool that people use to create a sense of social order. Not all interactionists need to treat inequality in this way; certainly not all sociologists should do so. Nevertheless, I think it is important that some scholars try to understand the generic *interpretive* processes that make inequality a recognizable, experienced feature of the world. These processes are arguably as generative and essential as the generic processes Schwalbe et al. and others are interested in.

Notes

An earlier version of this chapter appeared previously as "Challenging the Conventional Wisdom: Recent Proposals for the Interpretive Study of Inequality," *Human Studies* 27 (2004): 113–136.

1. For example, see Blumer (1969), Denzin (1989), Prus (1996), Psathas (1980), and Reynolds (1993).

2. Despite the textbook formulations that ignore interactionism, there are interactionist-related publications (current and classic) that deal with inequality in some way—though not, I argue (Harris 2006a), in a thoroughly interpretive or constructionist fashion (e.g., see Anderson and Snow 2001; Horowitz 1997; Maines and McCallion 2000; Mehan 1992; Shibutani and Kwan 1965; Whyte 1943). In this chapter I have chosen to limit my focus to recent programmatic works that move the study of inequality in interpretive directions. I do this principally to facilitate a detailed comparison of ongoing research agendas that are attempting to build on past traditions and conceptualize new paths for future inquiry. My choice of articles is also justified by the reactions the papers have received. Chang's article has been characterized as "a very ambitious analysis, even awesome in scope . . . [that] well deserves our careful and considered attention" (Maines 2000, p. 253). Schwalbe et al.'s article has been described as a "milestone essay" (Anderson 2001, pp. 392–393). Regarding Collins's (2000) paper, I feel confident that a programmatic article by this influential and well-known scholar is worthy of my attention here.

3. Here Collins cites Zelizer (1994) for the concept of interactional circuits, but the point being made sounds somewhat reminiscent of Shibutani's (1961) interactionist treatment of status ladders and social worlds.

4. In his commentary on Chang's article, Maines (2000, p. 255) asserts that stratification in China is actually much more messy and complicated than Chang lets on and that more research would be needed to get it right. A constructionist approach, in contrast, would set aside the goal of getting it right. Instead, the goal would be to study the interpretive processes involved with assembling a coherent story about class stratification, as well as the different meanings that competing stories convey.

5. The ethnomethodological notions of indexicality and the etcetera principle (Heritage 1984) suggest that an unresolved swarm of potential meanings will always remain around the concept of inequality, and readers or listeners will need to search the context in order to comprehend (but never fully) the

practical implications of the term. For example, is the inequality just a mathe-
matical difference? Is it a problem? Is it a fixable problem? Is it immoral? Who
is to blame? What is to be done? What is the person's reason for telling me
about this? (See Garfinkel 1967, pp. 38–41.)

6. There is tension between Blumer's first premise of interactionism and the
interactionist approach to motive talk that can be difficult to resolve. When
researchers use the notion that "human beings act toward things on the basis of
the meanings that the things have for them" (Blumer 1969, p. 2) as an explanatory resource, it can conflict with another interactionist idea—that the avowal and
imputation of motives creates order out of chaos (Hopper 1993). In my view, the
constructionist approach would accept Blumer's premise as largely true, but still
would be extremely cautious about relying on that principle as a warrant to
impute motives at will—as Collins, Chang, and Schwalbe et al. appear to do.
Here it is worth noting that Chang refers repeatedly to "justifications" without
acknowledging Scott and Lyman's (1968) special use of that term.

7. By invoking this premise, I do not intend to imply that large disparities
in wealth are "really" no big deal, or that slavery is "really" equal after all, or
anything of the sort. However, what I am suggesting is that social actors have
considerable interpretive latitude when identifying equalities and inequalities in
their social relationships and everyday lives. Interactionists and social constructionists have long argued that people can define problematic situations in many
ways and that different definitions can have a large impact on how they act
(Blumer 1971; Spector and Kitsuse 1977; Holstein and Miller 2003; Loseke
1999). For an interactionist, the point of invoking the idea that "meaning is not
inherent" is not to argue with the claims made by laypersons, activists, or mainstream sociologists—for example, claims that there are (or are not) real inequalities with real effects. Rather, the main purpose is to encourage researchers *to
investigate* (a) the different inequality objects that may exist in diverse social
worlds, as well as (b) the contingent interpretive processes that bring those
experienced objects into existence.

8. I believe my critique would also apply to scholars such as Lamont and
Fournier (1992, pp. 6–7) and Roy (2001, p. 183), who combine an interest in
culture and inequality while still confidently making statements such as "social
inequality is growing rapidly" and "classes are groups of people . . . who are
differentially rewarded for their efforts." For positions similar to the one I have
adopted in this chapter, see Berard (2006) and Berbrier (2008). Berbrier (2008,
p. 585) critiques many avowedly constructionist publications on race/ethnicity,
arguing that their main focus is actually on "uncovering how racial constructs
serve the dominant group or its ideology, rather than uncovering social processes more broadly involved in reality construction."

7
Conclusion

A s the past six chapters show, theory and research on the social construction of reality is extensive and proliferating. Everything these
days is said to be constructed, but for different reasons and in different
ways. Sometimes the diversity of constructionism can be a strength, as
different insights emanate from contrasting perspectives. However, the
various meanings and forms of social constructionism can also create
confusion and ambiguity. Various authors and readers can talk past one
another. The same terminology—achieve, create, produce, work, and so
on—can be used in arguments that are simultaneously parallel, overlapping, and contradictory. This state of affairs may lead some to give up
on constructionism or doubt its efficacy. Some question whether the
label "constructionism" indicates anything meaningful at all, since all
sociologists (if not all social scientists) might be described as constructionist to some degree (Maines 2001, 2003).

In this book, I have attempted to make the conceptual waters a bit
less muddy by clarifying the differences and similarities between two
forms of analysis: objective social constructionism (OSC) and interpretive social constructionism (ISC). By focusing on five topics—mind,
emotions, family diversity, marital equality, and social inequality—I
have highlighted the contrasting assumptions, choices, strategies, and
arguments that are made by those working primarily within one or the
other orientation. At the same time, I have shown that the difference
between the two camps is often one of degree and nuance.

I contend that across many areas of social inquiry, constructionism
has been and will continue to be used in relatively objective and interpretive fashion by different authors (and by the same authors on different occasions). I hope some readers will be tempted to apply the

131

OSC/ISC distinction to the literature in their own diverse areas of interest, as Mitch Berbrier (2008) has done with race. I believe that readers will find that constructionist research—whether on education, health, economic markets, the military, or other topics—will often be complicated by the tension between OSC and ISC.

In what follows, I further explain and defend the position I have taken by answering nine frequently asked questions (FAQs). This list of questions is based on past comments received from peer reviewers, colleagues, students, and friends who were subjected to ideas from particular chapters or the whole book. These questions also occurred to me as I imagined the potential responses and interests that future readers may have. I intend these FAQs to provide a concise summary and conclusion to my book.

FAQs About Objective and Interpretive Constructionism

What, Succinctly, Is the Difference between OSC and ISC?

Objective social constructionism is the argument that *real states of affairs*—such as actual thoughts, emotions, families, or inequalities—are not automatic but are contingent on social factors. Interpretive social constructionism is the argument that *meanings*—such as understandings or claims about putative thoughts, emotions, families, or inequalities—are not automatic but are contingent on social factors.

How Do OSC and ISC Scholars Tend to Study the Construction of "X" (the Phenomenon of Interest)?

Objective and interpretive researchers both study how some phenomenon—or "X"—is socially constructed. But there are some standard differences in how they do so. Below are four points of contrast that tend to recur across a variety of constructionist subfields. Please note that this list is illustrative, not comprehensive, and that it refers to examples discussed in greater detail in earlier chapters.

Defining X. Objective constructionists tend to define X, the "constructed" phenomenon in question. They assume that X exists and has discernible properties, even though they may express qualms about prior definitions or suggest that the concept should be used in a more careful or sensitive fashion than it previously has been.

Some objective constructionist researchers suggest that mind is an inner dialogue (Blumer 1969); that emotion is a biological sense and a clue to one's perspective (Hochschild 1983); that a family consists of people who live together, support each other, and are committed to each other (Schwartz and Scott, 2007, p. 3); that an equal marriage involves sharing responsibility for earning money, doing housework, caring for children, and making decisions (Schwartz 1994); that the study of social inequality can be aided if analysts make key distinctions between "deference power" and "efficacy power" (Collins 2000) or between "power locus," "power sweep," and "power use" (Chang 2000).

Interpretive constructionists tend to bracket X. They refrain from making assumptions about X's existence or properties, or at least attempt to minimize such assumptions, in order to study the meanings that other people give to X. If interpretive researchers define X, they tend to do so simply by referring to it as an idea or claim.

As for examples among interpretive constructionists, mind (Edwards 1997), emotions (Staske 1996), family (Gubrium and Holstein 1990), marital equality, and social inequality (Harris 2006b) have all been studied as understandings or attributions that people create and apply in everyday life. These scholars try to refrain from explicitly or implicitly adopting traditional definitions of the constructed phenomena in question.

Collecting and measuring occurrences of X. Objective constructionists tend to develop and employ systems for measuring X and/or finding examples of it. Some OSC researchers have documented the rigidity or flexibility of mind-sets (Zerubavel 1997), the strategies people use to perform emotional labor (Hochschild 1983), and the work it takes to feed a family (Devault 1991) by listening to people's statements and observing their actions. They have gathered qualitative and quantitative evidence in order to gauge the extent to which marriages are egalitarian or social classes are stratified (Chang 2000; Hochschild 1989).

In contrast, interpretive constructionists tend to study other people's strategies for measuring X and/or invoking examples of it. ISC researchers have studied the meanings that may be made and the purposes that may be served by making claims about what someone knows or feels (Edwards 1997; Whalen and Zimmerman 1998) or about how close or functional a family relationship is (Gubrium and Holstein 1990). Concepts such as "submitting" or "being accepted for who you are" have been studied as laypersons' resources for assembling and interpreting evidence of the egalitarian or inegalitarian nature of their marriages (Harris 2006b).

Explaining the causes of X. Objective constructionists attempt to delineate the various factors and forces that produce, maintain, inhibit, or change actual states of affairs. These factors and forces can be generally categorized as external social constraints, internal social constraints, and human discretion or free will (see Berger 1963).

Some OSC scholars have suggested that cultural norms shape the development of the human mind (Blumer 1969), the experience and display of emotions (Clark 1997), the structure of kinship (Stockard 2002), spouses' sense of fairness (Deutsch 1999), and the risky economic strategies that subordinate groups sometimes pursue (Schwalbe et al. 2000).

Interpretive constructionists, in contrast, study causal claimsmaking as a meaning-making process. They tend to set aside any interest in the "real" reasons for the existence of "objective" states of affairs, as they prefer to analyze such explanations as "motive talk." However, interpretive constructionists do tend to posit explanations for how and why understandings or claims are made, by focusing on external social constraints, internal social constraints, and individual discretion.

The stated intentions and reasons that purportedly cause or guide conduct have been studied by ISC scholars as culturally learned vocabularies that actors creatively use to manage the impressions of critical audiences (Benoit 1997; Scott and Lyman 1968); similarly, emotion categories (such as "hysterical") have also been studied as culturally acquired resources that people strategically use to explain conduct to others (Whalen and Zimmerman 1998). When individuals claim that they are retiring in order to spend time with their families or that a spouse is domineering due to his or her childhood, ISC scholars treat these sorts of assertions as causal attributions that give meaning to actors, their conduct, and the larger situation (Gubrium and Holstein 1990; Harris 2006b).

Advocating for policies, remedies, or social reforms related to X. Objective constructionists tend (implicitly or explicitly) to propose solutions to social problems that are related to X. For example, Zerubavel (1991) suggests that suicide could be reduced if more individuals were encouraged to adopt flexible rather than rigid or fuzzy mind-sets. OSC scholars have argued that laborers would be less alienated from their feelings, fewer families would be dysfunctional, more marriages would be egalitarian, and less unlawful behavior would occur if workplaces were structured differently (Erera 2002; Hochschild 1983, 1989; Schwalbe et al. 2000).

Interpretive constructionists tend to study "remedies" as claims that give meaning both to X and to purportedly related social problems. For example, ISC scholars have studied (as meaning-making assertions) claims such as "changing criminal mind-sets will lower recidivism" (Fox 2001), "road rage could be reduced by improving mass transit" (Best and Furedi 2001), "family dysfunctions are ameliorated by the presence of strong fathers and husbands" (Gubrium 1992), and "mutual submission makes for egalitarian and happy couples" (Harris 2006b).

What Are Some of the Recurring Tensions and Overlaps That Complicate the Distinction Between Objective and Interpretive Constructionism?

The difference between OSC and ISC can be difficult to spot. Objectivist and interpretive scholars may make divergent arguments even while they use identical terminology, espouse identical theoretical memberships, and employ similar methods to collect similar kinds of data. Moreover, the two camps do genuinely share some analytical interests and proclivities—in meaning, objective reality, and progressive social reforms, for example—which makes the OSC/ISC distinction a matter of degree or emphasis rather than a strict dichotomy.

Overlapping vocabularies and theoretical allegiances. Constructionists tend to highlight "contingency," "indeterminacy," and interactional "work" while arguing against "essentialism," "reification," and "taken for granted realities." They study how X is "achieved," "created," "formed," "made," "produced," "transformed," and "undermined." But all of these concepts may be given a relatively objective or interpretive spin. Similarly, constructionist scholars may announce that they are adopting or incorporating "interactionist," "ethnomethodological," or "phenomenological" perspectives while pursuing relatively objective or interpretive analyses. For example, Schwalbe et al. (2000) draw on interactionism and ethnomethodology to study how inequality, as an objective reality, is dependent on the emotional and adaptive work performed by individuals and groups. Harris (2006b) draws on interactionism and ethnomethodology to study how equality and inequality, as interpreted realities, are worked up in the narratives people tell about their own and others' lives.

Overlapping methods. Constructionists are often associated with qualitative more than quantitative inquiry. In-depth interviews, participant observation, textual analyses, and other methodologies may be considered constructionist because they can be sensitive to what people *do* and *think* in their everyday lives (as compared to, say, closed-ended survey questions). However, qualitative methods can be used in a relatively objective or interpretive fashion. What matters is not necessarily the technique but the specific theoretical assumptions that scholars bring to the methods they use (Gubrium and Holstein 1997; Harris 2003). For example, data from in-depth interviews and from observed conversations have been used to study "emotion work" in an objective and interpretive sense—that is, as work that creates or modifies actual feelings (Hochschild 1983) and as work that creates or modifies depictions of emotions (Staske 1996; see also Frith and Kitzinger 1998). Harris (2003) re-analyzed Kimball's (1983) interview data in order to argue that marital equality could be seen as an interpretive rather than objective production.

Overlapping interests in meaning. Like interpretive constructionists, objective constructionists may set out to study (in part) meaningmaking. They may even acknowledge the general principle that "meaning is not inherent." But their interest in these matters is not as thoroughgoing as that of interpretive constructionists. The latter focus more persistently on the production of meaning—especially (but not only) the meaning of the main phenomenon being investigated, or X. For example, "mind" has been studied as the (objectively real) ability to think and guide one's conduct (Blumer 1969); in contrast, "mind" and its purported traits have been studied as meanings that people attribute to themselves and others (Edwards 1997). Objectivist scholars may admit the arbitrary nature of any definition of family but then they proceed (unlike rigorously interpretive scholars) to authoritatively describe and explain the actual properties of real familial relationships (Erera 2002). Objectivist scholars suggest that real emotions may be shaped by the meanings people give to situations via cognitive emotion work (Hochschild 1983), whereas interpretive scholars focus more deeply on the perceived or claimed ontological status of emotions (Gubrium 1989).

Overlapping interests in objective reality. Like objective constructionists, interpretive constructionists make assumptions and assertions about objective reality, even if only implicitly. They assume that there is a world out there that can be studied, that it contains human beings, meanings, practices, and so on. Interpretive constructionists sometimes posit the existence of cultural resources (categories, norms, etc.), interactional objectives (justifying, teasing, complaining, praising, etc.), and other social phenomena. Try though they might, it seems impossible even for the strictest interpretive constructionists to refrain from making at least some objectivist assumptions or assertions about the world (Best 2003). However, interpretive scholars are usually more self-conscious and humble about the knowledge claims they make, and readily admit that anything that they or others assert can be deconstructed (Holstein and Gubrium 2008).

For example, interpretive constructionists have suggested that descriptions of emotion and family are shaped by the settings in which they are produced, and that these settings can be identified, compared, and analyzed by the researcher in ways that go beyond what the participants themselves may know or say (Gubrium 1992; Gubrium and Holstein 1990, 1999). Sanders (2005) suggests that interpretive scholars may engage implicitly in the kind of "motive talk" they eschew when they attempt to discern the interactional purposes that may be served when people invoke mental states such as "surprise" or "concern."

Overlapping interests in the practical implications of research. Objective constructionists are more likely to make explicit statements about the practical usefulness of their research. A focus on explaining the real causes of real social problems lends itself more easily to advocacy (e.g., policy recommendations). However, interpretive constructionists also try to conduct research that will make a positive impact on the world. They are not always on the periphery, but sometimes take sides, or else they suggest that others who take sides could benefit from reading their work (cf. Gusfield 1984). Gergen and Gergen (2006), as an example, describe how interpretive principles can inform practical work in therapy and organizations. Interpretive scholars sometimes challenge the "naturalness" of the knowledge claims of the powerful— for example, about proper family functioning (e.g., Gubrium and Holstein 1990; Haney and March 2003). Implicit in constructionism is the assumption that it is good to be tolerant and inquisitive of the meanings that other people live by, and that information about such meanings (and how they are produced) can help individuals and groups make more effective choices (Barber 1991; Gubrium and Holstein 2005; Harris 2006b, pp. 159–163).

Do Objective and Interpretive Social Constructionists Really Constitute Distinct and Coherent Camps?

This is a legitimate question, given the nuances and overlaps I have just described. I agree that OSC and ISC should not be treated as though they were separated by a stark or impenetrable divide. But I suggest that the distinction I draw does have merit, even though the contrast is not always clear-cut. I intend the terms "objective constructionism" and "interpretive constructionism" to be heuristic concepts that readers can use to make sense of their own and others' research. This chapter and book provide guidelines for detecting when an author switches from one form of argument to the other. But it is important to acknowledge that the ways in which theoretical perspectives get divided up will always be somewhat arbitrary; the boundaries between alternate "theories" and "subfields" are usually more permeable than insular (Zerubavel 1995).

OSC/ISC thus refers to a continuum and not a dichotomy. Strictly speaking, it is somewhat problematic even to refer to an "interpretive constructionist study" or an "objective constructionist scholar." Any report and any scholar will almost certainly exhibit both objective and interpretive tendencies, so such descriptions must be seen as approximate and comparative. Moreover, a scholar's research program may become more or less interpretive over time or a single report may come to be viewed differently as readers' perspectives change.[1] OSC and ISC are forms of arguments or analyses, and scholars can alternate between them without consciously realizing or explicitly indicating that they are doing so.

Isn't the Phrase "Objective Constructionism" Self-Contradictory?

I have been asked this question on multiple occasions by interpretive scholars who would prefer to draw a brighter line between themselves and their more objectivist counterparts. One commentator told me that "those who study social life without understanding that 'meaning is not inherent' don't deserve to be called objective social constructionists. They aren't constructionists at all." A different commentator suggested that the phrase "objective constructionism" was simply too "charitable" to objectivists. To these readers, studying the social construction of reality means studying the creation of meaning; consequently, the phrase "objective constructionism" appears oxymoronic.

I can sympathize with that point of view, but it seems less sensible to me the more I recognize two apparent facts about the constructionist literature: first, a great many sociologists are conducting (and will continue to conduct) self-proclaimed "constructionist" analyses in fairly objectivist fashion; second, virtually all constructionist studies contain both objective and interpretive aspects, in varying proportions. In light of this state of affairs, it seems futile to try to tell particular scholars that they really are *not* constructionists and that they should stop using key terms (such as create, produce, work) as if they were engaging in constructionist analyses. The better response, in my opinion, is to carefully specify the differences and similarities between OSC and ISC in order to clarify what is going on, and will likely continue to go on, in various manifestations of constructionist research.

Are You Arguing That One Type of Constructionism Is Better Than the Other?

It does not seem useful to proclaim that one form of constructionist analysis is, in general, superior to another. Relatively objective and interpretive constructionists are usually able to offer reasonable arguments for the legitimacy or plausibility of their approaches. Both OSC and ISC research have made and should continue to make important contributions to our understanding of social life.

However, my personal preference is for analyses that are more interpretive rather than objective, and this bias has shaped this book. Rigorously interpretive scholarship is more interesting to me, even though it seems less likely to be funded generously, published in top journals, or received warmly by lay audiences. Many audiences appear to find relatively objective analyses more compelling than thoroughly interpretive analyses.[2] That is perhaps why there tends to be less constructionist research—on mind, emotions, family diversity, marital equality, social inequality, and other social phenomena—that takes a highly interpretive approach. In my view, interpretive research tends to be underappreciated.

How Do OSC and ISC Relate to Distinctions Made by Previous Scholars?

The contrast between objective and interpretive constructionism seems roughly analogous to distinctions that some scholars have already invoked—sometimes briefly—such as performative and constitutive constructionism (Gubrium and Holstein 1997, pp. 215–216, n. 3), ontological and epistemic constructionism (Edwards 1997, pp. 47–48), and the construction of "objects" versus "ideas" (Hacking 1999, p. 14). In this book, I have tried to clarify and extend these prior discussions. Specifically, I have shown in greater detail how OSC and ISC arguments can be simultaneously *divergent* (e.g., focusing on different kinds of "realities"), *overlapping* (e.g., using similar methods and vocabularies), and *parallel* (e.g., relating the issues of freedom and constraint to the construction process).

While explaining the differences and similarities between OSC and ISC, I have also tried to summarize and illuminate diverse strands of research on a broad range of interesting social phenomena.

The OSC/ISC distinction is also somewhat related, but certainly not identical, to other taxonomies of constructionism.[3] Commentators have most commonly asked me to compare OSC/ISC with Best's (2003) notion of "contextual" and "strict" constructionism. Best uses those terms to distinguish two relatively interpretive forms of constructionism within the literature on social problems. Both contextual and strict constructionists examine claimsmaking about "troublesome" behavior or conditions. The focus of their analyses is on how social problems are viewed or characterized by different individuals and groups. Thus, both contextual and strict constructionists tend to understand the phrase "social problems are human products" to mean that "problems are defined into being through the claims people make about them" (see Blumer 1971; Loseke 1999; Schneider 1985). More objectivist scholars, in contrast, would understand the phrase "social problems are human products" to mean that "real problems are generated by human activity."

However, there is some loose affinity between OSC/ISC and contextual/ strict constructionism. If OSC/ISC is a spectrum, then strict constructionists would be placed further toward the interpretive pole. Scholars such as Ibarra and Kitsuse (2003) seek to minimize or eliminate any explicit or implicit references to objective reality. For example, they worry when contextual constructionists try to assess the validity of actors' claims about problems, since that practice contradicts the premises (i.e., meaning is not inherent) and focus (i.e., meaningmaking) of interpretive social constructionism. Best (2003) argues that even the most thoroughly interpretive scholars cannot help but make some assumptions about objective reality, and he suggests that contextual constructionists can reasonably divide their attention between both objective and interpretive concerns.

In the interests of brevity, I will not rehash these debates in full (see also Holstein and Gubrium 2003; Ibarra 2008). My point is simply that the contrast between contextual and strict constructionism is relevant but by no means equivalent to the distinction between OSC and ISC.

Can You Provide a More Complete Overview of Constructionism's History and Varieties?

Fortunately or unfortunately, the literature on constructionism is too vast for any single person to read and summarize concisely. My focus has been on distinguishing between two predominant forms of constructionist analysis that tend to recur across diverse subfields. I have applied the OSC/ISC distinction to large swaths of theory and research, but I admittedly have not attempted to provide a fully comprehensive discussion of constructionism's origination and development. For more on those topics, readers should see other sources.

Constructionism's roots can be traced to—or at least similar ideas can be found within—many earlier sources, from specific thinkers such as Aristotle, Kant, and Nietzsche to philosophical traditions such as Buddhism, Marxism, nominalism, phenomenology, and pragmatism.[4] Constructionism has been nurtured in many disciplines, such as sociology, psychology, anthropology, communication, and education.[5] It has been applied to many diverse topics, including science and technology, health and medicine, race and ethnicity, sexualities, and globalization.[6]

I suspect that the tension between OSC and ISC complicates most if not all types of constructionist scholarship, and I invite readers to investigate the degree to which this hypothesis is true.

Why Is the OSC/ISC Distinction Important?

Given the vastness of the constructionist literature, the speed with which it is currently being produced, and its continued relevance for understanding and intervening in social life, it is important to take stock of how the perspective is being used. Currently, many researchers are offering up superficially identical but analytically divergent studies of "the social construction of X." Constructionist authors often adopt objective and interpretive orientations without being aware (or explicitly indicating to their readers) that they are doing so. To make the best use of constructionist research, I believe it would be helpful if more of us recognized when and how OSC arguments differ from ISC arguments. My own application of this distinction has shown that there is still much room and need for rigorously interpretive studies of social phenomena—from the most micro and benign to the most macro and political.

Notes

1. For example, see Holstein and Gubrium (2007, pp. 342–343) on the evolving scholarship produced by constructionist Ralph LaRossa, as well as Fine and Kleinman (1986) on conflicting readings of G. H. Mead's work.
2. See also Spector and Kitsuse (1977, pp. 63–72) and Pollner (1991) for discussions of some reasons why objective arguments are pursued more than rigorously interpretive arguments.

3. For example, Gergen (1999, pp. 59–60, n. 30) contrasts "social constructionism" with "constructivism," "radical constructivism," "social constructivism," and "sociological constructionism." All of these forms of constructionism seem fairly interpretive; they each focus on the factors that shape the production of meanings, understandings, or claims.

4. See Aspers (2007); Hacking (1999); Moore (1995); Prus (2003); Reynolds (2003); Schutz (1970); Weinberg (2008).

5. See Best (2008a); Faubion and Marcus (2008); Foster and Bochner (2008); Gergen and Gergen (2008); Wortham and Jackson (2008).

6. See Alasuutari (2008); Atkinson and Gregory (2008); Berbrier (2008); Crawley and Broad (2008); Restivo and Croissant (2008).

Bibliography

Agger, B. 2000. *Public Sociology: From Social Facts to Literary Acts.* Lanham, MD: Rowman and Littlefield.

Agnew, R. 2001. "Building on the Foundation of General Strain Theory: Specifying the Types of Strain Most Likely to Lead to Crime and Delinquency." *Journal of Research in Crime and Delinquency* 38:319–361.

Ahlander, N. R., and K. S. Bahr. 1995. "Beyond Drudgery, Power, and Equity: Toward an Expanded Discourse on the Moral Dimensions of Housework in Families." *Journal of Marriage and the Family* 57:54–68.

Alasuutari, P. 2008. "Constructionist Research and Globalization." In *Handbook of Constructionist Research,* edited by J. A. Holstein and J. F. Gubrium, pp. 767–783. New York: Guilford.

Albas, C., and D. Albas. 1988. "Emotion Work and Emotion Rules: The Case of Exams." *Qualitative Sociology* 11:259–274.

Alger, J., and S. Alger. 1997. "Beyond Mead: Symbolic Interaction Between Humans and Felines." *Society and Animals* 5:65–81.

Amato, P. R. 2000. "Diversity Within Single-Parent Families." In *Handbook of Family Diversity,* edited by D. H. Demo, K. R. Allen, and M. A. Fine, pp. 149–172. New York: Oxford.

Anderson, L. 2001. "Editor's Introduction." *Symbolic Interaction* 24:391–394.

Anderson, L., and D. A. Snow. 2001. "Inequality and the Self: Exploring Connections from an Interactionist Perspective." *Symbolic Interaction* 24:395–406.

Anderson, M. L., and H. F. Taylor. 2001. *Sociology: The Essentials.* Belmont, CA: Wadsworth.

Antaki, C. 2004. "Reading Minds or Dealing with Interactional Implications?" *Theory & Psychology* 14:667–683.

Arluke, A. 1998. "Managing Emotions in an Animal Shelter." In *Inside Social Life,* 2nd ed., edited by S. Cahill, pp. 254–266. Los Angeles: Roxbury.

Arrighi, B. A. 2001. *Understanding Inequality: The Intersection of Race/ Ethnicity, Class, and Gender.* Lanham, MD: Rowman and Littlefield.

Aspers, P. 2007. "Nietzsche's Sociology." *Sociological Forum* 22:474–499.

Athens, L. H. 1993. "Blumer's Advanced Course on Social Psychology."
    Studies in Symbolic Interaction 14:163–193.
———. 1994. "The Self as Soliloquy." *Sociological Quarterly* 35:521–532.
Atkinson, P., and M. Gregory. 2008. "Constructions of Medical Knowledge." In
    Handbook of Constructionist Research, edited by J. A. Holstein and J. F.
    Gubrium, pp. 593–608. New York: Guilford.
Atkinson, P., and W. Housley. 2003. *Interactionism: An Essay in Sociological
    Amnesia.* London: Sage.
Atkinson, P., and D. Silverman. 1997. "Kundera's Immortality: The Interview
    Society and the Invention of the Self." *Qualitative Inquiry* 3:304–325.
Averill, J. 1994. "In the Eyes of the Beholder." In *The Nature of Emotion:
    Fundamental Questions,* edited by P. Ekman and R. J. Davidson, pp. 7–14.
    New York: Oxford.
Babbie, E. 1986. *Observing Ourselves: Essays in Social Research.* Prospect
    Heights, IL: Waveland.
Baca Zinn, M., and D. S. Eitzen. 2005. *Diversity in Families,* 7th ed. Boston,
    MA: Allyn and Bacon.
Baca Zinn, M., and B. Wells. 2000. "Diversity Within Latino Families: New
    Lessons for Family Social Science." Pp. 252–273 in *Handbook of Family
    Diversity,* edited by D. H. Demo, K. R. Allen, and M. A. Fine. New York:
    Oxford.
Baker, C. D. 1984. "The 'Search for Adultness': Membership Work in
    Adolescent-Adult Talk." *Human Studies* 7:301–323.
———. 2002. "Ethnomethodological Analyses of Interviews." In *Handbook of
    Interview Research: Context and Method,* edited by J. F. Gubrium and J. A.
    Holstein, pp. 777–795. Thousand Oaks, CA: Sage.
Bakker, J. I., and T. R. A. Bakker. 2006. "The Club DJ: A Semiotic and
    Interactionist Analysis." *Symbolic Interaction* 29:71–82.
Barber, M. 1991. "The Ethics Behind the Absence of Ethics in Alfred Schutz's
    Thought." *Human Studies* 14:129–140.
Barrett, L. F. 2006. "Solving the Emotion Paradox: Categorization and the
    Experience of Emotion." *Personality and Social Psychology Review*
    10:20–46.
Bartkowski, J. P., and J. G. Read. 2003. "Veiled Submission: Gender, Power,
    and Identity Among Evangelical and Muslim Women." *Qualitative
    Sociology* 26:71–92.
Baxter, J. 1997. "Gender Equality and Participation in Housework: A Cross-
    National Perspective." *Journal of Comparative Family Studies* 28:220–247.
Baxter, J., and M. Western. 1998. "Satisfaction with Housework: Examining the
    Paradox." *Sociology* 32:101–120.
Becker, H. 1953. "Becoming a Marihuana User." *American Journal of
    Sociology* 59:235–242.
Becker, H. 1973 [1963]. *Outsiders: Studies in the Sociology of Deviance.* New
    York: Free Press.
Bellas, M. L. 1999. "Emotional Labor in Academia: The Case of Professors."
    Annals of the American Academy of Political and Social Science
    561:96–110.

———. 2001. "The Gendered Nature of Emotional Labor in the Workplace." In *Gender Mosaics,* edited by D. Vannoy, pp. 269–278. Los Angeles: Roxbury.

Benin, M. H., and J. Agostinelli. 1988. "Husbands' and Wives' Satisfaction with the Division of Labor." *Journal of Marriage and the Family* 50:349–361.

Benoit, P. J. 1997. *Telling the Success Story: Acclaiming and Disclaiming Discourse.* Albany, NY: SUNY.

Benokraitis, N. V. 2000. *Feuds About Families: Conservative, Centrist, Liberal, and Feminist Perspectives.* Upper Saddle River, NJ: Prentice-Hall.

Benson, J. K. 1977. "Organizations: A Dialectical View." *Administrative Science Quarterly* 22:1–21.

Berard, T. J. 2003. "Ethnomethodology as Radical Sociology: An Expansive Appreciation of Melvin Pollner's 'Constitutive and Mundane Versions of Labeling Theory.'" *Human Studies* 26:431–448.

———. 2006. "From Concepts to Methods: On the Observability of Inequality." *Journal of Contemporary Ethnography* 35:236–256.

Berbrier, M. 2000. "Ethnicity in the Making: Ethnicity Work, the Ethnicity Industry, and a Constructionist Framework for Research." In *Perspectives on Social Problems,* Vol. 12, edited by J. A. Holstein and G. Miller, pp. 69–88. Stamford, CT: JAI.

———. 2008. "The Diverse Construction of Race and Ethnicity." In *Handbook of Constructionist Research,* edited by J. A. Holstein and J. F. Gubrium, pp. 567–591. New York: Guilford.

Berger, B. 1981. *The Survival of a Counterculture: Ideological Work and Everyday Life Among Rural Communards.* Berkeley: University of California Press.

Berger, B., and P. L. Berger. 1983. *The War over the Family: Capturing the Middle Ground.* Garden City, NY: Anchor.

Berger, P. 1963. *Invitation to Sociology.* Garden City, NY: Anchor.

Berger, P. L., and T. Luckmann. 1966. *The Social Construction of Reality: A Treatise in the Sociology of Knowledge.* Garden City, NY: Doubleday.

Besen, Y. 2006. "Exploitation or Fun? The Lived Experience of Teenage Employment in Suburban America." *Journal of Contemporary Ethnography* 35:319–340.

Best, J. 1999. *Random Violence: How We Talk About New Crimes and New Victims.* Berkeley: University of California Press.

———. 2000. "The Apparently Innocuous 'Just,' the Law of Levity, and the Social Problems of Social Construction." In *Perspectives on Social Problems,* Vol. 12, edited by J. A. Holstein and G. Miller, pp. 3–14. Stamford, CT: JAI.

———. 2003. "But Seriously Folks: The Limitations of the Strict Constructionist Interpretation of Social Problems." In *Challenges and Choices: Constructionist Perspectives on Social Problems,* edited by J. A. Holstein and G. Miller, pp. 51–69. New York: Aldine de Gruyter.

———. 2008. "Historical Development and Defining Issues of Constructionist Inquiry." In *Handbook of Constructionist Research,* edited by J. A. Holstein and J. F. Gubrium, pp. 41–64. New York: Guilford.

Best, J., and F. Furedi. 2001. "The Evolution of Road Rage in Britain and the United States." In *How Claims Spread: Cross-National Diffusion of Social Problems,* edited by J. Best, pp. 107–127. New York: Aldine de Gruyter.

Bittman, M., P. England, N. Folbre, L. Sayer, and G. Matheson. 2003. "When Does Gender Trump Money? Bargaining and Time in Household Work." *American Journal of Sociology* 109:186–214.

Blair, S. L., and M. P. Johnson. 1992. "Wives' Perceptions of the Fairness of the Division of Household Labor: The Intersection of Housework and Ideology." *Journal of Marriage and the Family* 54:570–581.

Blair, S. L., and D. T. Lichter. 1991. "Measuring the Division of Household Labor: Gender Segregation of Housework Among American Couples." *Journal of Family Issues* 12:91–113.

Blaisure, K. R., and K. R. Allen. 1995. "Feminists and the Ideology and Practice of Marital Equality." *Journal of Marriage and the Family* 57:5–19.

Blood, R. O., and D. M. Wolfe. 1960. *Husbands and Wives.* Glencoe, IL: Free Press.

Blumer, H. 1969. *Symbolic Interactionism: Perspective and Method.* Englewood Cliffs, NJ: Prentice-Hall.

———. 1971. "Social Problems as Collective Behavior." *Social Problems* 18:298–306.

———. 1972. "Action vs. Interaction." *Society* 9:50–53.

———. 1981. "George Herbert Mead." In *The Future of the Sociological Classics,* edited by B. Rhea, pp. 136–169. London: Allen and Unwin.

Bogdan, R., and S. Taylor. 1989. "Relationships with Severely Disabled People: The Social Construction of Humanness." *Social Problems* 36:135–148.

Bolton, S. C. 2001. "Changing Faces: Nurses as Emotional Jugglers." *Sociology of Health & Illness* 23:85–100.

———. 2005. *Emotion Management in the Workplace.* New York: Palgrave Macmillan.

Brekhus, W. H. 2003. *Peacocks, Chameleons, Centaurs: Gay Suburbia and the Grammar of Social Identity.* Chicago: University of Chicago Press.

———. 2007. "The Rutgers School: A Zerubavelian Culturalist Cognitive Sociology." *European Journal of Social Theory* 10:453–470.

Brines, J. 1993. "The Exchange Value of Housework." *Rationality and Society* 5:302–340.

Broad, K. L., S. L. Crawley, and S. Foley. 2004. "Doing Real Family Values: The Interpretive Practice of Families in the GLBT Movement." *Sociological Quarterly* 45:509–527.

Bruner, J. 1987. "Life as Narrative." *Social Research* 54:11–32.

Cahill, S. E. 2004. *Inside Social Life: Readings in Sociological Psychology and Microsociology,* 4th ed. Los Angeles: Roxbury.

Cahill, S. E., and R. Eggleston. 1994. "Managing Emotions in Public: The Case of Wheelchair Users." *Social Psychology Quarterly* 57:300–312.

Callero, P. L. 1991. "Toward a Sociology of Cognition." In *The Self-Society Dynamic: Cognition, Emotion, and Action,* edited by J. A. Howard and P. L. Callero, pp. 43–54. New York: Cambridge.

Cancian, F. 1995. "Truth and Goodness: Does the Sociology of Inequality Promote Social Betterment?" *Sociological Perspectives* 38:339–356.

Carrington, C. 2004. "The Political Economy of Constructing Family." In *Families and Society,* edited by S. Coltrane, pp. 303–308. Belmont, CA: Wadsworth/Thompson.

Cerulo, K. A. 2002. "Establishing a Sociology of Culture and Cognition." In *Culture in Mind: Toward a Sociology of Culture and Cognition,* edited by K. A. Cerulo, pp. 1–12. New York: Routledge.

Chambliss, D. F. 1989. "The Mundanity of Excellence: An Ethnographic Report on Stratification and Olympic Swimmers." *Sociological Theory* 7:70–86.

Chang, J. H-Y. 2000. "Symbolic Interaction and Transformation of Class Structure: The Case of China." *Symbolic Interaction* 23:223–251.

Charon, J. M. 2007. *Symbolic Interactionism: An Introduction, an Interpretation, an Integration,* 9th ed. Upper Saddle River, NJ: Pearson.

Chayko, M. 2002. *Connecting: How We Form Social Bonds and Communities in the Internet Age.* Albany, NY: SUNY.

Cherlin, A. J. 2003. "Should the Government Promote Marriage?" *Contexts* 2:22–29.

Clanton, G. 1989. "Jealousy in American Culture, 1945–1985: Reflections from Popular Literature." In *The Sociology of Emotions: Original Essays and Research Papers,* edited by D. D. Franks and E. D. McCarthy, pp. 179–193. Greenwich, CT: JAI.

Clark, C. 1997. *Misery and Company: Sympathy in Everyday Life.* Chicago: University of Chicago Press.

Cohen, P. N., and L. M. Casper. 2002. "In Whose Home? Multigenerational Families in the United States, 1998–2000." *Sociological Perspectives* 45:1–20.

Coleman, M. T. 1988. "The Division of Household Labor: Suggestions for Future Empirical Consideration and Theoretical Development." *Journal of Family Issues* 9:132–148.

Coleman, M., and L. H. Ganong, eds. 2004. *Handbook of Contemporary Families: Considering the Past, Contemplating the Future.* Thousand Oaks, CA: Sage.

Coles, R. L. 2006. *Race and Family: A Structural Approach.* Thousand Oaks, CA: Sage.

Collins, R. 1981. "On the Micro-Foundations of Macro-Sociology." *American Journal of Sociology* 86:964–1014.

———. 1983. "Micromethods as a Basis for Macrosociology." *Urban Life* 12:84–202.

———. 1988. *Theoretical Sociology.* San Diego, CA: Harcourt Brace Jovanovich.

———. 1994. *Four Sociological Traditions.* New York: Oxford.

———. 2000. "Situational Stratification: A Micro-Macro Theory of Inequality." *Sociological Theory* 18:17–43.

———. 2004. "Internalized Symbols and the Internal Process of Thinking." In *Interaction Ritual Chains,* by R. Collins, pp. 183–220. Princeton: Princeton University Press.

Coltrane, S. 1998. *Gender and Families.* Thousand Oaks, CA: Pine Forge.

Condit, C. M., and J. L. Lucaites. 1993. *Crafting Equality: America's Anglo-African Word.* Chicago: University of Chicago Press.

Conrad, P., and J. W. Schneider. 1992. *Deviance and Medicalization: From Badness to Sickness.* Philadelphia: Temple.

Coontz, S. 1992. *The Way We Never Were: American Families and the Nostalgia Trap.* New York: Basic Books.

———. 2000. "Historical Perspectives on Family Diversity." In *Handbook of Family Diversity,* edited by D. H. Demo, K. R. Allen, and M. A. Fine, pp. 15–31. New York: Oxford.

Coontz, S., M. Parson, and G. Raley, eds. 1999. *American Families: A Multicultural Reader.* New York: Routledge.

Copp, M. 1998. "When Emotion Work Is Doomed to Fail: Ideological and Structural Constraints on Emotion Management." *Symbolic Interaction* 21:299–328.

Cosmides, L., and J. Tooby. 2000. "Evolutionary Psychology and the Emotions." In *Handbook of Emotions,* edited by M. Lewis and J. M. Haviland-Jones, pp. 91–115. New York: Guilford.

Coulon, A. 1995. *Ethnomethodology.* Thousand Oaks, CA: Sage.

Coulter, J. 1979. *The Social Construction of Mind.* Totowa, NJ: Rowman and Littlefield.

———. 1989. *Mind in Action.* Atlantic Highlands, NJ: Humanities Press International.

Crawley, S. L., and K. L. Broad. 2008. "The Construction of Sex and Sexualities." In *Handbook of Constructionist Research,* edited by J. A. Holstein and J. F. Gubrium, pp. 545–566. New York: Guilford.

Crompton, R., and C. Lyonette. 2005. "The New Gender Essentialism: Domestic and Family 'Choices' and Their Relation to Attitudes." *British Journal of Sociology* 56:601–620.

Daniels, A. K. 1987. "Invisible Work." *Social Problems* 34:403–415.

Davis, K. 2006 [1947]. "Final Note on a Case of Extreme Isolation." In *The Production of Reality,* 4th ed., edited by J. O'Brien, pp. 89–95. Thousand Oaks, CA: Pine Forge.

Davis, K., and W. Moore. 1945. "Some Principles of Stratification." *American Sociological Review* 10:242–249.

Demo, D. H., K. R. Allen, and M. A. Fine, eds. 2000. *Handbook of Family Diversity.* New York: Oxford.

Denzin, N. K. 1989. *Interpretive Interactionism.* Newbury Park, CA: Sage.

Derné, S. 1994. "Structural Realities, Persistent Dilemmas, and the Construction of Emotional Paradigms: Love in Three Cultures." In *Social Perspectives on Emotion,* edited by W. M. Wentworth and J. Ryan, pp. 281–308. Greenwich, CT: JAI.

Deutsch, F. M. 1999. *Halving It All: How Equally Shared Parenting Works.* Cambridge, MA: Harvard University Press.

Devault, M. 1991. *Feeding the Family.* Chicago: University of Chicago Press.

Dewey, J. 1989 [1932]. *Ethics.* In *The Later Works,* Vol. 7, edited by Jo Ann Boydston. Carbondale: Southern Illinois University Press.

Dobson, J. C. 2006. "Media Provides Cover for Assault on Traditional Marriage." Available at www.cnn.com/2006/US/06/28/dobson.gaymarriage/index.html (accessed July 24, 2007).

Dolgin, J. L. 1997. *Defining the Family: Law, Technology, and Reproduction in an Uneasy Age.* New York: New York University Press.

Dollahite, D. C., L. D. Marks, and M. A. Goodman. 2004. "Families and Religious Beliefs, Practices, and Communities: Linkages in a Diverse and Dynamic Cultural Context." In *Handbook of Contemporary Families: Considering the Past, Contemplating the Future,* edited by M. Coleman and L. H. Ganong, pp. 411–431. Thousand Oaks, CA: Sage.

Duncombe, J., and D. Marsden. 1998. "'Stepford Wives' and 'Hollow Men'? Doing Emotion Work, Doing Gender and 'Authenticity' in Intimate Heterosexual Relationships." In *Emotions in Social Life,* edited by G. Bendelow and S. J. Williams, pp. 211–227. New York: Routledge.

Dunn, J. L. 2005. "'Victims' and 'Survivors': Emerging Vocabularies of Motive for Battered Women Who Stay." *Sociological Inquiry* 75:1–30.

Durkheim, E. 1984 [1933]. *The Division of Labor in Society.* New York: Free Press.

Edwards, D. 1997. *Discourse and Cognition.* Thousand Oaks, CA: Sage.

———. 1999. "Emotion Discourse." *Culture and Psychology* 5:271–291.

Edwards, D., and A. Fasulo. 2006. "'To Be Honest': Sequential Uses of Honesty Phrases in Talk-in-Interaction." *Research on Language and Social Interaction* 39:343–376.

Edwards, D., M. Ashmore, and J. Potter. 1995. "Death and Furniture: The Rhetoric, Politics, and Theology of Bottom Line Arguments Against Relativism." *History of the Human Sciences* 8:25–49.

Edwards, D., and J. Potter. 2005. "Discursive Psychology, Mental States and Descriptions." In *Conversation and Cognition,* edited by H. te Molder and J. Potter, pp. 241–259. New York: Cambridge.

Ekman, P. 1994. "All Emotions Are Basic." In *The Nature of Emotion: Fundamental Questions,* edited by P. Ekman and R. J. Davidson, pp. 15–19. New York: Oxford.

Emerson, R. M., and S. L. Messinger. 1977. "The Micro-Politics of Trouble." *Social Problems* 25:121–134.

Enarson, E. 1993. "Emotion Workers on the Production Line: The Feminizing of Casino Card Dealing." *NWSA Journal* 5:218–232.

Erera, P. I. 2002. *Family Diversity: Continuity and Change in the Contemporary Family.* Thousand Oaks, CA: Sage.

Erickson, R. J., and W. J. C. Grove. 2008. "Emotional Labor and Health Care." *Sociology Compass* 2:704–733.

Faubion, J. D., and G. E. Marcus. 2008. "Constructionism in Anthropology." In *Handbook of Constructionist Research,* edited by J. A. Holstein and J. F. Gubrium, pp. 67–84. New York: Guilford.

Fernandez-Kelly, M. P. 1990. "Delicate Transactions: Gender, Home, and Employment Among Hispanic Women." In *Uncertain Terms: Negotiating Gender in American Culture,* edited by G. Ginsberg and A. L. Tsing, pp. 183–195. Boston: Beacon.

Ferris, K. 2004. "Seeing and Being Seen: The Moral Order of Celebrity Sightings." *Journal of Contemporary Ethnography* 33:236–264.

Figert, A. E. 2003. "Science Constructs PMS." In *Social Problems: Constructionist Readings,* edited by D. R. Loseke and J. Best, pp. 127–134. Hawthorne, NY: Aldine de Gruyter.

Fine, G. A. 1997. "Naturework and the Taming of the Wild: The Problem of 'Overpick' in the Culture of Mushroomers." *Social Problems* 44:68–88.

Fine, G. A., and S. Kleinman. 1986. "Interpreting the Sociological Classics: Can There Be a 'True' Meaning of Mead?" *Symbolic Interaction* 9:129–146.

Fine, M. 1994. "Working the Hyphens: Reinventing Self and Other in Qualitative Research." In *Handbook of Qualitative Research,* edited by N. K. Denzin and Y. Lincoln, pp. 70–82. Thousand Oaks, CA: Sage.

Fine, M. A., D. H. Demo, and K. R. Allen. 2000. "Family Diversity in the 21st Century: Implications for Research, Theory, and Practice." In *Handbook of Family Diversity,* edited by D. H. Demo, K. R. Allen, and M. A. Fine, pp. 440–448. New York: Oxford.

Fishman, P. M. 1978. "Interaction: The Work Women Do." *Social Problems* 25:397–406.

Flaherty, M. G. 1984. "A Formal Approach to the Study of Amusement in Social Interaction." *Studies in Symbolic Interaction* 5:71–82.

———. 2003. "Time Work: Customizing Temporal Experience." *Social Psychology Quarterly* 66:17–33.

Foley, L. 2005. "Midwives, Marginality, and Public Identity Work." *Symbolic Interaction* 28:183–203.

Foley, L., and C. Faircloth. 2000. "The Parenting Self: Narrative Resources and Identity Work in Parents' Stories." In *Perspectives on Social Problems,* Vol. 12, edited by J. A. Holstein and G. Miller, pp. 235–254. Stamford, CT: JAI.

Fontana, A. 2002. "Postmodern Trends in Interviewing." In *Handbook of Interview Research: Context and Method,* edited by J. F. Gubrium and J. A. Holstein, pp. 161–175. Thousand Oaks, CA: Sage.

Forsberg, H., and A. Vagli. 2006. "The Social Construction of Emotions in Child Protection Case-Talk." *Qualitative Social Work* 5:9–31.

Foster, E., and A. P. Bochner. 2008. "Social Constructionist Perspectives in Communication Research." In *Handbook of Constructionist Research,* edited by J. A. Holstein and J. F. Gubrium, pp. 85–106. New York: Guilford.

Fox, K. J. 2001. "Self-Change and Resistance in Prison." In *Institutional Selves: Troubled Identities in a Postmodern World,* edited by J. F. Gubrium and J. A. Holstein, pp. 176–192. New York: Oxford.

Freedman, J., and G. Combs. 1996. *Narrative Therapy: The Social Construction of Preferred Realities.* New York: W. W. Norton.

Frith, H., and C. Kitzinger. 1998. "'Emotion Work' as a Participant Resource: A Feminist Analysis of Young Women's Talk-in-Interaction." *Sociology* 32:299–320.

Garfinkel, H. 1967. *Studies in Ethnomethodology.* Englewood Cliffs, NJ: Prentice-Hall.

Gergen, K. J. 1999. *An Invitation to Social Construction.* London: Sage.

Gergen, K. J., and M. M. Gergen. 2008. "Social Construction and Psychological Inquiry." In *Handbook of Constructionist Research,* edited by J. A. Holstein and J. F. Gubrium, pp. 171–188. New York: Guilford.

Gergen, M. M., and K. J. Gergen. 2006. "Narratives in Action." *Narrative Inquiry* 16:112–121.

Gimlin, D. L. 2002. *Body Work: Beauty and Self-Image in American Culture.* Berkeley: University of California Press.

Glenn, N. D., S. Nock, and L. J. Waite, et al. 2002. "Why Marriage Matters: Twenty-One Conclusions from the Social Sciences." *American Experiment Quarterly* 5:34–44.

Goffman, E. 1959. *The Presentation of Self in Everyday Life.* New York: Doubleday.

———. 1963. *Behavior in Public Places.* New York: Free Press.

———. 1967. *Interaction Ritual.* New York: Doubleday.

———. 1971. *Relations in Public.* New York: Basic Books.

Goode, E. 1994. *Deviant Behavior,* 4th ed. Englewood Cliffs, NJ: Prentice-Hall.

Gordon, S. L. 1990. "The Sociology of Sentiments and Emotion." In *Social Psychology: Sociological Perspectives,* edited by M. Rosenberg and R. H. Turner, pp. 562–592. New Brunswick, NJ: Transaction.

Greder, K. A., and W. D. Allen. 2007. "Parenting in Color: Culturally Diverse Perspectives on Parenting." In *Cultural Diversity and Families: Expanding Perspectives,* edited by B. S. Trask and R. R. Hamon, pp. 118–135. Thousand Oaks, CA: Sage.

Greer, K. 2002. "Walking an Emotional Tightrope: Managing Emotions in a Women's Prison." *Symbolic Interaction* 25:117–139.

Gubrium, J. F. 1988. *Analyzing Field Reality.* Newbury Park, CA: Sage.

———. 1989. "Emotion Work and Emotive Discourse in the Alzheimer's Disease Experience." *Current Perspectives on Aging and the Life Cycle* 5:243–268.

———. 1992. *Out of Control: Family Therapy and Domestic Disorder.* Newbury Park, CA: Sage.

———. 1993. *Speaking of Life: Horizons of Meaning for Nursing Home Residents.* New York: Aldine de Gruyter.

———. 2003 [1986]. "The Social Preservation of Mind: The Alzheimer's Disease Experience." In *Inner Lives and Social Worlds: Readings in Social Psychology,* edited by J. A. Holstein and J. F. Gubrium, pp. 180–190. New York: Oxford.

Gubrium, J. F., and J. A. Holstein. 1990. *What Is Family?* Mountain View, CA: Mayfield.

———. 1993. "Phenomenology, Ethnomethodology, and Family Discourse." In *Sourcebook of Family Theories and Methods: A Contextual Approach,* edited by P. G. Boss, W. J. Doherty, R. LaRossa, W. R. Schumm, and S. K. Steinmetz, pp. 651–672. New York: Plenum.

———. 1995. "Biographical Work and New Ethnography." In *The Narrative Study of Lives,* Vol. 3, edited by R. Josselson and A. Lieblich, pp. 45–58. Thousand Oaks, CA: Sage.

———. 1997. *The New Language of Qualitative Method.* New York: Oxford.

———. 1999. "At the Border of Narrative and Ethnography." *Journal of Contemporary Ethnography* 28:561–573.

———. 2000. "The Self in a World of Going Concerns." *Symbolic Interaction* 23:95–115.

———, eds. 2001. *Institutional Selves: Troubled Identities in a Postmodern World.* New York: Oxford.

———. 2005. "Interpretive Practice and Social Action." In *The Sage Handbook of Qualitative Research,* 3rd ed., edited by N. K. Denzin and Y. S. Lincoln, pp. 483–505. Thousand Oaks, CA: Sage.

———. 2008. "The Constructionist Mosaic." In *Handbook of Constructionist Research,* edited by J. A. Holstein and J. F. Gubrium, pp. 3–10. New York: Guilford.

———. 2009a. *Analyzing Narrative Reality.* Thousand Oaks, CA: Sage.

———. 2009b. "The Everyday Work and Auspices of Authenticity." In *Authenticity in Culture, Self, and Society,* edited by P. Vannini and J. P. Williams, pp. 121–138. United Kingdom: Ashgate.

Gubrium, J. F., and R. J. Lynott. 1987. "Measurement and the Interpretation of Burden in the Alzheimer's Disease Experience." *Journal of Aging Studies* 1:265–285.

Gusfield, J. R. 1984. "On the Side: Practical Action and Social Constructivism in Social Problems Theory." In *Studies in the Sociology of Social Problems,* edited by J. W. Schneider and J. I. Kitsuse, pp. 31–51. Noorwood, NJ: Ablex.

Haas, L. 1980. "Role-Sharing Couples: A Study of Egalitarian Marriages." *Family Relations* 29:289–296.

———. 1982. "Determinants of Role-Sharing Behavior: A Study of Egalitarian Couples." *Sex Roles* 8:747–760.

Hacking, I. 1999. *The Social Construction of What?* Cambridge, MA: Harvard University Press.

Hall, P. M. 1987. "Interactionism and the Study of Social Organization." *Sociological Quarterly* 28:1–22.

Haney, L., and M. March. 2003. "Married Fathers and Caring Daddies: Welfare Reform and the Discursive Politics of Paternity." *Social Problems* 50:461–481.

Hank, K., and H. Jürges. 2007. "Gender and the Division of Household Labor in Older Couples: A European Perspective." *Journal of Family Issues* 28:399–421.

Harris, S. R. 2000a. "Meanings and Measurements of Equality in Marriage: A Study of the Social Construction of Equality." In *Perspectives on Social Problems,* Vol. 12, edited by J. A. Holstein and G. Miller, pp. 111–145. Stamford, CT: JAI.

———. 2000b. "The Social Construction of Equality in Everyday Life." *Human Studies* 23:371–393.

———. 2001. "What Can Interactionism Contribute to the Study of Inequality? The Case of Marriage and Beyond." *Symbolic Interaction* 24:455–480.

———. 2003. "Studying Equality/Inequality: Naturalist and Constructionist Approaches to Equality in Marriage." *Journal of Contemporary Ethnography* 32:200–232.

———. 2006a. "Social Constructionism and Social Inequality: An Introduction to a Special Issue of *JCE.*" *Journal of Contemporary Ethnography* 35:223–235.

———. 2006b. *The Meanings of Marital Equality.* Albany, NY: SUNY.

———. 2008. "Constructionism in Sociology." In *Handbook of Constructionist Research,* edited by J. A. Holstein and J. F. Gubrium, pp. 231–247. New York: Guilford.

Hawkins, A. J., C. M. Marshall, and K. M. Meiners. 1995. "Exploring Wives' Sense of Fairness About Family Work." *Journal of Family Issues* 16:693–721.

Hawkins, A. J., T. A. Roberts, S. L. Christiansen, and C. M. Marshall. 1994. "An Evaluation of a Program to Help Dual-Earner Couples Share the Second Shift." *Family Relations* 43:213–220.

Heiner, R. 2002. *Social Problems: An Introduction to Critical Constructionism.* New York: Oxford.

Hendrick, S. S., and C. Hendrick. 2006. "Measuring Respect in Close Relationships." *Journal of Social and Personal Relationships* 23:881–899.

Hendrix, L. 1994. "What Is Sexual Inequality? On the Definition and Range of Variation." *Cross-Cultural Research* 28:287–307.

Herd, P., and M. H. Meyer. 2002. "Care Work: Invisible Civic Engagement." *Gender and Society* 16:665–688.

Heritage, J. 1984. *Garfinkel and Ethnomethodology.* Cambridge: Polity.

———. 2005. "Cognition in Discourse." In *Conversation and Cognition,* edited by H. te Molder and J. Potter, pp. 184–202. New York: Cambridge.

Herman-Kinney, N. J. 2003. "Deviance." In *Handbook of Symbolic Interactionism,* edited by L. T. Reynolds and N. J. Herman-Kinney, pp. 695–720. Walnut Creek, CA: AltaMira.

Hewitt, J. P. 1997. *Self and Society: A Symbolic Interactionist Social Psychology.* Needham Heights, MA: Allyn and Bacon.

Higginson, J. G. 1999. "Defining, Excusing, and Justifying Deviance: Teen Mothers' Accounts for Statutory Rape." *Symbolic Interaction* 22:25–44.

Himsel, A. J., and W. A. Goldberg. 2003. "Social Comparisons and Satisfaction with the Division of Housework: Implications for Men's and Women's Role Strain." *Journal of Family Issues* 24:843–866.

Hochschild, A. R. 1979. "Emotion Work, Feeling Rules, and Social Structure." *American Journal of Sociology* 85:551–575.

———. 1983. *The Managed Heart: Commercialization of Human Feeling.* Berkeley: University of California Press.

———. 1997. *The Time Bind: When Work Becomes Home and Home Becomes Work.* New York: Henry Holt.

Hochschild, A., with A. Machung. 1989. *The Second Shift.* New York: Avon Books.

Hollander, J., and H. R. Gordon. 2006. "The Processes of Social Construction in Talk." *Symbolic Interaction* 29:183–212.

Holstein, J. A. 1993. *Court-Ordered Insanity: Interpretive Practice and Involuntary Commitment.* New York: Aldine de Gruyter.

Holstein, J. A., and J. F. Gubrium. 1995a. *The Active Interview.* Thousand Oaks, CA: Sage.

———. 1995b. "Deprivatization and the Construction of Domestic Life." *Journal of Marriage and the Family* 57:894–908.

———. 1999. "What Is Family? Further Thoughts on a Social Constructionist Approach." *Marriage and Family Review* 28:3–20.

———. 2000. *Constructing the Life Course,* 2nd ed. Walnut Creek, CA: AltaMira.

———. 2003. "A Constructionist Analytics for Social Problems." In *Challenges and Choices: Constructionist Perspectives on Social Problems,* edited by J. A. Holstein and G. Miller, pp. 187–208. New York: Aldine de Gruyter.

———. 2007. "Constructionist Perspectives on the Life Course." *Sociology Compass* 1:335–352.

———. 2008. "Constructionist Impulses in Ethnographic Fieldwork." In *Handbook of Constructionist Research,* edited by J. A. Holstein and J. F. Gubrium, pp. 373–395. New York: Guilford.

Holstein, J. A., and G. Miller. 1990. "Rethinking Victimization: An Interactional Approach to Victimology." *Symbolic Interaction* 13:103–122.

————. 2003. "Social Constructionism and Social Problems Work." In *Challenges and Choices: Constructionist Perspectives on Social Problems,* edited by J. A. Holstein and G. Miller, pp. 70–91. New York: Aldine de Gruyter.

Holyfield, L., and G. A. Fine. 1997. "Adventure as Character Work: The Collective Taming of Fear." *Symbolic Interaction* 20:343–363.

Homans, G. C. 1958. "Social Behavior as Exchange." *American Journal of Sociology* 63:597–606.

Hopper, J. 1993. "The Rhetoric of Motives in Divorce." *Journal of Marriage and the Family* 55:801–813.

Horlick-Jones, T. 2005. "Risk-Work: Professional Discourse, Accountability, and Everyday Action." *Health, Risk, and Society* 7:293–307.

Horowitz, R. 1997. "Barriers and Bridges to Class Mobility and Formation: Ethnographies of Stratification." *Sociological Methods and Research* 25:495–538.

Hunter, C. H. 1984. "Aligning Actions: Types and Social Distribution." *Symbolic Interaction* 7:155–174.

Ibarra, P. R. 2008. "Strict and Contextual Constructionism in the Sociology of Deviance and Social Problems." In *Handbook of Constructionist Research,* edited by J. A. Holstein and J. F. Gubrium, pp. 355–369. New York: Guilford.

Ibarra, P. R., and J. I. Kitsuse. 2003. "Claims-Making Discourse and Vernacular Resources." In *Challenges and Choices: Constructionist Perspectives on Social Problems,* edited by J. A. Holstein and G. Miller, pp. 17–50. New York: Aldine de Gruyter.

Jankowiak, W. R., ed. 2008. *Intimacies: Love and Sex Across Cultures.* New York: Columbia University Press.

John, D., B. A. Shelton, and K. Luschen. 1995. "Race, Ethnicity, Gender, and Perceptions of Fairness." *Journal of Family Issues* 16:357–379.

Kamo, Y. 1988. "Determinants of Household Division of Labor: Resources, Power, and Ideology." *Journal of Family Issues* 9:177–200.

Kemper, T. D. 1989. "Themes and Variations in the Sociology of Emotions." In *Research Agendas in the Sociology of Emotions,* edited by T. D. Kemper, pp. 3–23. Albany, NY: SUNY.

————. 2000. "Social Models in the Explanation of Emotions." In *Handbook of Emotions,* edited by M. Lewis and J. M. Haviland-Jones, pp. 45–58. New York: Guilford.

Kerbo, H. R. 2009. *Social Stratification and Inequality: Class Conflict in Historical, Comparative, and Global Perspective,* 7th ed. New York: McGraw-Hill.

Kimball, G. 1983. *The 50/50 Marriage.* Boston: Beacon.

Kitsuse, J. I., and A. V. Cicourel. 1963. "A Note on the Uses of Official Statistics." *Social Problems* 11:131–139.

Knapp, S. J. 1999. "Analyzing Narratives of Expertise: Toward the Development of a Burkeian Pentadic Scheme." *Sociological Quarterly* 40:587–612.

————. 2002. "Authorizing Family Science: An Analysis of the Objectifying Practices of Family Science Discourse." *Journal of Marriage and Family* 64:1038–1048.

Knudson-Martin, C., and A. R. Mahoney. 2005. "Moving Beyond Gender: Processes That Create Relationship Equality." *Journal of Marital and Family Therapy* 31:235–246.

Koro-Ljunberg, M. 2008. "A Social Constructionist Framing of the Research Interview." In the *Handbook of Constructionist Research,* edited by J. A. Holstein and J. F. Gubrium, pp. 429–444. New York: Guilford.

Kurdek, L. A. 2004. "Gay Men and Lesbians: The Family Context." In *Handbook of Contemporary Families: Considering the Past, Contemplating the Future,* edited by M. Coleman and L. H. Ganong, pp. 96–115. Thousand Oaks, CA: Sage.

Kwan, S., and M. N. Trautner. 2009. "Beauty Work: Individual and Institutional Rewards, the Reproduction of Gender, and Questions of Agency." *Sociology Compass* 3:49–71.

Laird, J. 2000. "Culture and Narrative as Central Metaphors for Clinical Practice with Families." In *Handbook of Family Diversity,* edited by D. H. Demo, K. R. Allen, and M. A. Fine, pp. 338–358. New York: Oxford.

Lamanna, M. A., and A. Riedmann. 2006. *Marriages and Families: Making Choices in a Diverse Society,* 9th ed. Belmont, CA: Wadsworth/Thomson.

Lamont, M., and M. Fournier. 1992. "Introduction." In *Cultivating Differences: Symbolic Boundaries and the Making of Inequality,* edited by M. Lamont and M. Fournier, pp. 1–17. Chicago: University of Chicago Press.

Lamont, M., and V. Molnár. 2002. "The Study of Boundaries in the Social Sciences." *Annual Review of Sociology* 28:167–195.

Lennon, M. C., and S. Rosenfield. 1994. "Relative Fairness and the Division of Housework: The Importance of Options." *American Journal of Sociology* 100:506–531.

Lerman, R. 1996. *In the Company of Newfies: A Shared Life.* New York: Henry Holt.

Lillard, A. S. 1998. "Ethnopsychologies: Cultural Variations in Theories of Mind." *Psychological Bulletin* 123:3–32.

Lindesmith, A. R., A. L. Strauss, and N. K. Denzin. 1999. *Social Psychology,* 8th ed. Thousand Oaks, CA: Sage.

Lively, K. J. 2006. "Emotions in the Workplace." In *Handbook of the Sociology of Emotions,* edited by J. H. Turner and J. E. Stets, pp. 569–590. New York: Springer.

Locke, A. 2003. "'If I'm Not Worried, I'm Nervous, Does That Make Sense?': The Use of Emotion Concepts by Athletes in Accounts of Performance." *Forum: Qualitative Social Research* 4(1). Online journal, available at www.qualitative-research.net/fqs-texte/1-03/1-03locke-e.htm.

Lofland, J. 1976. *Doing Social Life: The Qualitative Study of Human Interaction in Natural Settings.* New York: Wiley.

Lofland, L. H. 1985. "The Social Shaping of Emotion: The Case of Grief." *Symbolic Interaction* 8:171–190.

Lois, J. 2001. "Managing Emotions, Intimacy, and Relationships in a Volunteer Search and Rescue Group." *Journal of Contemporary Ethnography* 30:131–179.

Loseke, D. R. 1987. "Lived Realities and the Construction of Social Problems: The Case of Wife Abuse." *Symbolic Interaction* 10:229–243.

———. 1999. *Thinking About Social Problems: An Introduction to Constructionist Perspectives.* New York: Aldine de Gruyter.

———. 2001. "Lived Realities and Formula Stories of 'Battered Women.'" In *Institutional Selves: Troubled Identities in a Postmodern World,* edited by J. F. Gubrium and J. A. Holstein, pp. 107–126. New York: Oxford.

————. 2003. "Conditions, People, Morality, Emotion: Expanding the Agenda of Constructionism." In *Challenges and Choices: Constructionist Perspectives on Social Problems,* edited by J. A. Holstein and G. Miller, pp. 120–129. New York: Aldine de Gruyter.

Loseke, D. R., and S. E. Cahill. 1984. "The Social Construction of Deviance: Experts on Battered Women." *Social Problems* 31:296–310.

Loseke, D. R., and M. Kusenbach. 2008. "The Social Construction of Emotion." In *Handbook of Constructionist Research,* edited by J. A. Holstein and J. F. Gubrium, pp. 511–529. New York: Guilford.

Low, J. 2008. "Structure, Agency, and Social Reality in Blumerian Symbolic Interactionism: The Influence of Georg Simmel." *Symbolic Interaction* 31:325–343.

Lutz, C. A. 1988. *Unnatural Emotions: Everyday Sentiments on a Micronesian Atoll and Their Challenges to Western Theory.* Chicago: University of Chicago Press.

Lynch, M., and D. Bogen. 2005. "'My Memory Has Been Shredded': A Non-Cognitivist Investigation of 'Mental' Phenomena." In *Conversation and Cognition,* edited by H. te Molder and J. Potter, pp. 226–240. New York: Cambridge.

Lyng, S. 1990. "Edgework: A Social Psychological Account of Voluntary Risk Taking." *American Journal of Sociology* 95:851–886.

Maines, D. R. 1993. "Narrative's Moment and Sociology's Phenomena: Toward a Narrative Sociology." *Sociological Quarterly* 34:17–38.

————. 2000. "Some Thoughts on the Interactionist Analysis of Class Stratification: A Commentary." *Symbolic Interaction* 23:253–258.

————. 2001. *The Faultline of Consciousness: A View of Interactionism in Sociology.* New York: Aldine de Gruyter.

————. 2003. "Interactionism's Place." *Symbolic Interaction* 26:5–18.

Maines, D. R., and M. J. McCallion. 2000. "Urban Inequality and the Possibilities of Church-Based Intervention." In *Studies in Symbolic Interaction,* Vol. 3, edited by N. K. Denzin, pp. 43–53. Greenwich, CT: JAI.

Major, B. 1993. "Gender, Entitlement, and the Distribution of Family Labor." *Journal of Social Issues* 49:141–159.

Mannheim, K. 1952. *Essays on the Sociology of Knowledge.* London: Routledge and Kegan Paul.

Manning, P. K. 2001. "Semiotics, Semantics and Ethnography." In *Handbook of Ethnography,* edited by P. Atkinson, A. Coffey, S. Delamont, J. Lofland, and L. Lofland, pp. 145–159. Thousand Oaks, CA: Sage.

Marger, M. N. 1999. *Social Inequality: Patterns and Processes.* Mountain View, CA: Mayfield.

Martin, P. Y. 2005. *Rape Work: Victims, Gender, and Emotions in Organizational and Community Context.* New York: Routledge.

Marvasti, A. 2008. "Interactional Constructionism." In *Handbook of Constructionist Research,* edited by J. A. Holstein and J. F. Gubrium, pp. 315–330. New York: Guilford.

Maynard, D. W. 2006. "Cognition on the Ground." *Discourse Studies* 8:105–115.

McDonald, G. W. 1980. "Family Power: The Assessment of a Decade of Theory and Research, 1970–1979." *Journal of Marriage and the Family* 42:841–854.

Mead, G. H. 1934. *Mind, Self, and Society.* Chicago: University of Chicago Press.

Mehan, H. 1992. "Understanding Inequality in Schools: The Contribution of Interpretive Studies." *Sociology of Education* 65:1–20.

Meltzer, B. N. 2003. "Mind." In *Handbook of Symbolic Interactionism,* edited by L. T. Reynolds and N. J. Herman-Kinney, pp. 253–266. Lanham, MD: Rowman and Littlefield.

Miller, G. 1991. "Family as Excuse and Extenuating Circumstance: Social Organization and Use of Family Rhetoric in a Work Incentive Program." *Journal of Marriage and the Family* 53:609–621.

———. 2001. "Changing the Subject: Self-Construction in Brief Therapy." In *Institutional Selves: Troubled Identities in a Postmodern World,* edited by J. F. Gubrium and J. A. Holstein, pp. 64–83. New York: Oxford.

———. 2003. "Getting Serious About an Applied Constructionism of Social Problems." In *Challenges and Choices: Constructionist Perspectives on Social Problems,* edited by J. A. Holstein and G. Miller, pp. 236–254. New York: Aldine de Gruyter.

Mills, C. W. 1940. "Situated Actions and Vocabularies of Motive." *American Sociological Review* 6:904–913.

———. 1959. *The Sociological Imagination.* New York: Oxford.

Mizan, A. N. 1994. "Family Power Studies: Some Major Methodological Issues." *International Journal of Sociology of the Family* 24:85–91.

Model, S. 1981. "Housework by Husbands: Determinants and Implications." *Journal of Family Issues* 2:225–237.

Moore, R. J. 1995. "Dereification in Zen Buddhism." *Sociological Quarterly* 36:699–723.

Mullaney, J. L. 2006. *Everyone Is Not Doing It: Abstinence and Personal Identity.* Chicago: University of Chicago Press.

Musolf, G. H. 2003. *Structure and Agency in Everyday Life: An Introduction to Social Psychology,* 2nd ed. Lanham, MD: Rowman and Littlefield.

Nelson, E. D. 2001. "The Things That Dreams Are Made On: Dreamwork and the Socialization of 'Stage Mothers.'" *Qualitative Sociology* 24:439–458.

O'Brien, J., ed. 2006. *The Production of Reality,* 4th ed. Thousand Oaks, CA: Pine Forge.

Ore, T. E., ed. 2003. *The Social Construction of Difference and Inequality,* 2nd ed. New York: McGraw-Hill.

Ortiz, S. M. 2006. "Using Power: An Exploration of Control Work in the Sport Marriage." *Sociological Perspectives* 49:527–557.

Owens, E. 2007. "Nonbiologic Objects as Actors." *Symbolic Interaction* 30:567–584.

Pasternak, B., C. R. Ember, and M. Ember. 1997. *Sex, Gender, and Kinship: A Cross-Cultural Perspective.* Upper Saddle River, NJ: Prentice-Hall.

Peterson, G. 2006. "Cultural Theory and Emotions." In *Handbook of the Sociology of Emotions,* edited by J. H. Turner and J. E. Stets, pp. 114–134. New York: Springer.

Peterson, R. A. 2005. "In Search of Authenticity." *Journal of Management Studies.*

Pierce, J. 1995. *Gender Trials: Emotional Lives in Contemporary Law Firms.* Berkeley: University of California Press.

Piña, D. L., and V. L. Bengtson. 1993. "The Division of Labor and Wives' Happiness: Ideology, Employment, and Perceptions of Support." *Journal of Marriage and the Family* 55:901–912.

Pleck, J. H. 1985. *Working Wives/Working Husbands.* Beverly Hills, CA: Sage.

Plummer, K. 2006. "Rights Work: Constructing Lesbian, Gay and Sexual Rights in Modern Times." In *Rights: Sociological Perspectives,* edited by Lydia Morris, pp. 152–167. New York: Routledge.

Pollner, M. 1987. *Mundane Reason: Reality in Everyday and Sociological Discourse.* New York: Cambridge.

———. 1991. "Left of Ethnomethodology." *American Sociological Review* 56:370–380.

Pollner, M., and L. McDonald-Wikler. 2003 [1985]. "The Social Construction of Unreality: A Case of a Family's Attribution of Competence to a Severely Retarded Child." In *Inner Lives and Social Worlds: Readings in Social Psychology,* edited by J. A. Holstein and J. F. Gubrium, pp. 290–301. New York: Oxford.

Pollner, M., and J. Stein. 2001. "Doubled Over in Laughter: Humor and the Construction of Selves in Alcoholics Anonymous." In *Institutional Selves: Troubled Identities in a Postmodern World,* edited by J. F. Gubrium and J. A. Holstein, pp. 46–63. New York: Oxford.

Pope, C. 2002. "Contingency in Everyday Surgical Work." *Sociology of Health and Illness* 24:369–384.

Potter, J. 2006. "Cognition and Conversation." *Discourse Studies* 8:131–140.

Potter, J., and M. Mulkay. 1985. "Scientists, Interview Talk: Interviews as a Technique for Revealing Participants' Interpretive Practices." In *The Research Interview: Uses and Approaches,* edited by M. Brenner, J. Brown, and D. Canter, pp. 247–271. London: Academic Press.

Potter, J., and M. Wetherell. 1987. *Discourse and Social Psychology: Beyond Attitudes and Behaviour.* London: Sage.

Prus, R. 1996. *Symbolic Interaction and Ethnographic Research: Inter- subjectivity and the Study of Human Lived Experience.* Albany, NY: SUNY.

———. 1997. *Subcultural Mosaics and Intersubjective Realities: An Ethno- graphic Research Agenda for Pragmatizing the Social Sciences.* Albany, NY: SUNY.

———. 1999. *Beyond the Power Mystique: Power as Intersubjective Accom- plishment.* Albany, NY: SUNY.

———. 2003. "Ancient Forerunners." In *Handbook of Symbolic Interactionism,* edited by L. T. Reynolds and N. J. Herman-Kinney, pp. 19–38. Lanham, MD: Rowman and Littlefield.

Psathas, G. 1980. "Approaches to the Study of the World of Everyday Life." *Human Studies* 3:3–17.

Puchta, C., and J. Potter. 2002. "Manufacturing Individual Opinions: Market Research Focus Groups and the Discursive Psychology of Evaluation." *British Journal of Social Psychology* 41:345–363.

Rank, M. R. 2000. "Poverty and Economic Hardship in Families." In *Handbook of Family Diversity,* edited by D. H. Demo, K. R. Allen, and M. A. Fine, pp. 293–315. New York: Oxford.

Rapley, T. J. 2001. "The Art(fullness) of Open-Ended Interviewing: Some Considerations on Analysing Interviews." *Qualitative Research* 1:303–323.

Reinarman, C. 2005. "Addiction as Accomplishment: The Discursive Construction of Disease." *Addiction Research and Theory* 13:307–320.

Restivo, S., and J. Croissant. 2008. "Social Constructionism in Science and Technology Studies." In *Handbook of Constructionist Research,* edited by J. A. Holstein and J. F. Gubrium, pp. 213–229. New York: Guilford.

Reynolds, L. T. 1993. *Interactionism: Exposition and Critique,* 3rd ed. Dix Hills, NY: General Hall.

———. 2003. "Intellectual Precursors." In *Handbook of Symbolic Interactionism,* edited by L. T. Reynolds and N. J. Herman-Kinney, pp. 39–58. Lanham, MD: Rowman and Littlefield.

Reynolds, L. T., and N. J. Herman-Kinney, eds. 2003. *Handbook of Symbolic Interactionism.* Lanham, MD: Rowman and Littlefield.

Riesman, D., with N. Glazer and R. Denney. 1950. *The Lonely Crowd.* New Haven, CT: Yale.

Riessman, C. K. 1990. *Divorce Talk: Women and Men Make Sense of Personal Relationships.* New Brunswick, NJ: Rutgers.

———. 1993. *Narrative Analysis.* Newbury Park, CA: Sage.

———. 2002. "Analysis of Personal Narratives." In *Handbook of Interview Research: Context and Method,* edited by J. F. Gubrium and J. A. Holstein, pp. 695–710. Thousand Oaks, CA: Sage.

Risman, B. J., and D. Johnson-Sumerford. 1998. "Doing It Fairly: A Study of Postgender Marriages." *Journal of Marriage and Family* 60:23–40.

Roopnarine, J. L., and U. P. Gielen, eds. 2005. *Families in Global Perspective.* Boston: Pearson.

Rosenberg, M. 1990. "Reflexivity and Emotions." *Social Psychology Quarterly* 53:3–12.

Rosenblatt, P. C. 1994. *Metaphors of Family Systems Theory: Toward New Constructions.* New York: Guilford.

Rosenbluth, S. C., J. M. Steil, and J. H. Whitcomb. 1998. "Marital Equality: What Does It Mean?" *Journal of Family Issues* 19:227–244.

Roy, W. G. 2001. *Making Societies: The Historical Construction of Our World.* Thousand Oaks, CA: Pine Forge.

Russell, J. A. 1991. "Culture and the Categorization of Emotions." *Psychological Bulletin* 110:426–450.

Ryen, A., and D. Silverman. 2000. "Marking Boundaries: Culture as Category Work." *Qualitative Inquiry* 6:107–128.

Sanders, C. R. 2003a. "Actions Speak Louder Than Words: Close Relationships Between Humans and Nonhuman Animals." *Symbolic Interaction* 26:405–426.

———. 2003b. "Understanding Dogs: Caretakers' Attributions of Mindedness in Canine-Human Relationships." In *Inner Lives and Social Worlds: Readings in Social Psychology,* edited by J. A. Holstein and J. F. Gubrium, pp. 191–201. New York: Oxford.

Sanders, C. R., and A. Arluke. 1993. "If Lions Could Speak: Investigating the Animal-Human Relationship and the Perspectives of Nonhuman Others." *Sociological Quarterly* 34:377–390.

Sanders, R. E. 2005. "Validating 'Observations' in Discourse Studies: A Methodological Reason for Attention to Cognition." In *Conversation and Cognition,* edited by H. te Molder and J. Potter, pp. 57–78. New York: Cambridge.

Sandstrom, K. L., D. D. Martin, and G. A. Fine. 2003. *Symbols, Selves, and Social Reality: A Symbolic Interactionist Approach to Social Psychology and Sociology.* Los Angeles: Roxbury.

Sarat, A., and W. L. F. Felstiner. 1988. "Law and Social Relations: Vocabularies of Motive in Lawyer/Client Interaction." *Law and Society Review* 22:737–769.

Schachter, S., and J. E. Singer. 1962. "Cognitive, Social, and Physiological Determinants of Emotional State." *Psychological Review* 69:379–399.

Scheff, T. J. 1993. "Toward a Social Psychological Theory of Mind and Consciousness." *Social Research* 60:171–195.

———. 2006. "A Theory of Genius." In *The Production of Reality,* 4th ed., edited by J. O'Brien, pp. 296–308. Thousand Oaks, CA: Pine Forge.

Schieman, S. 2006. "Anger." In *Handbook of the Sociology of Emotions,* edited by J. H. Turner and J. E. Stets, pp. 493–515. New York: Springer.

Schneider, D. M. 1980. *American Kinship: A Cultural Account,* 2nd ed. Chicago: University of Chicago Press.

Schneider, J. W. 1985. "Social Problems Theory: The Constructionist View." *Annual Review of Sociology* 11:209–229.

Schutz, A. 1964. "Equality and the Meaning Structure of the Social World." In *Collected Papers,* Vol. 2, edited by A. Brodersen, pp. 226–273. The Hague, Netherlands: Martinus Nijhoff.

———. 1970. *On Phenomenology and Social Relations.* Chicago: University of Chicago Press.

Schwalbe, M., S. Godwin, D. Holden, D. Schrock, S. Thompson, and M. Wolkomir. 2000. "Generic Processes in the Reproduction of Inequality: An Interactionist Analysis." *Social Forces* 79:419–452.

Schwartz, M. A., and B. M. Scott. 2007. *Marriages and Families: Diversity and Change,* 5th ed. Upper Saddle River, NJ: Prentice-Hall.

Schwartz, P. 1994. *Peer Marriage: How Love Between Equals Really Works.* New York: Free Press.

Schweingruber, D., and N. Berns. 2003. "Doing Money Work in a Door-to-Door Sales Organization." *Symbolic Interaction* 26:447–471.

———. 2005. "Shaping the Selves of Young Salespeople Through Emotion Management." *Journal of Contemporary Ethnography* 34:679–706.

Scott, M. B., and S. M. Lyman. 1968. "Accounts." *American Sociological Review* 33:46–62.

Seccombe, K., and R. L. Warner. 2004. *Marriages and Families: Relationships in Social Context.* Belmont, CA: Wadsworth/Thomson.

Seidman, S. 2003. *The Social Construction of Sexuality.* New York: Norton.

Shapiro, T. M. 1998. *Great Divides: Readings in Social Inequality in the United States.* Mountain View, CA: Mayfield.

Shaw, S. M. 1988. "Gender Differences in the Definition and Perception of Household Labor." *Family Relations* 37:333–337.

Shelton, B. A., and D. John. 1996. "The Division of Household Labor." *Annual Review of Sociology* 22:299–322.

Shibutani, T. 1955. "Reference Groups as Perspectives." *American Journal of Sociology* 60:562–569.

———. 1961. *Society and Personality: An Interactionist Approach to Social Psychology.* Englewood Cliffs, NJ: Prentice-Hall.

Shibutani, T., and K. M. Kwan. 1965. *Ethnic Stratification: A Comparative Approach.* New York: Macmillan.

Smith, A. C., III, and S. Kleinman. 1989. "Managing Emotions in Medical School." *Social Psychology Quarterly* 52:56–69.

Smith, A. D., and W. J. Reid. 1986. *Role-Sharing Marriage.* New York: Columbia University Press.

Smith, C. W. 1982. "On the Sociology of Mind." In *Explaining Human Behavior,* edited by P. Secord, pp. 211–228. Beverly Hills, CA: Sage.

Smith, D. 1993. "The Standard North American Family: SNAF as an Ideological Code." *Journal of Family Issues* 14:50–65.

Smith, R. T. 2008. "Passion Work: The Joint Production of Emotional Labor in Professional Wrestling." *Social Psychology Quarterly* 71:157–176.

Smith-Lovin, L. 1995. "The Sociology of Affect and Emotion." In *Sociological Perspectives on Social Psychology,* edited by K. S. Cook, G. A. Fine, and J. S. House, pp. 118–148. Boston: Allyn and Bacon.

Snow, D., and L. Anderson. 1987. "Identity Work Among the Homeless: The Verbal Construction and Avowal of Personal Identities." *American Journal of Sociology* 92:1336–1371.

Snyder, E. E. 1990. "Emotion and Sport: A Case Study of Collegiate Women Gymnasts." *Sociology of Sport Journal* 7:254–270.

Snyder, E. E., and R. Ammons. 1993. "Baseball's Emotion Work: Getting Psyched to Play." *Qualitative Sociology* 16:111–132.

Spector, M., and J. I. Kitsuse. 1977. *Constructing Social Problems.* Menlo Park, CA: Cummings.

Spencer, J. W. 1992. "Negotiating Role Definitions and the Working Consensus in Self-Work." *Sociological Inquiry* 62:291–307.

Stacey, J. 2004. "Marital Suitors Court Social Science Spin-Sters: The Unwittingly Conservative Effects of Public Sociology." *Social Problems* 51:131–145.

Stack, C. B. 1974. *All Our Kin: Strategies for Survival in a Black Community.* New York: Harper and Row.

Stack, C. B., and L. Burton. 1993. "Kinscripts." *Journal of Comparative Family Studies* 24:157–170.

Stapleton, J., and R. Bright. 1976. *Equal Marriage.* Nashville, TN: Abingdon.

Staske, S. A. 1996. "Talking Feelings: The Collaborative Construction of Emotion in Talk Between Close Relational Partners." *Symbolic Interaction* 19:111–135.

———. 1998. "The Normalization of Problematic Emotion in Conversations Between Close Relational Partners: Interpersonal Emotion Work." *Symbolic Interaction* 21:58–86.

———. 1999. "Creating Relational Ties in Talk: The Collaborative Construction of Relational Jealousy." *Symbolic Interaction* 22:213–246.

Stebbins, L. F. 2001. *Work and Family: A Reference Handbook.* Santa Barbara: ABC-CLIO.

Steinberg, R. J., and D. M. Figart. 1999. "Emotional Labor Since *The Managed Heart.*" *Annals of the American Academy of Political and Social Science* 561:8–26.

Stenross, B., and S. Kleinman. 1989. "The Highs and Lows of Emotional Labor: Detectives, Encounters with Criminals and Victims." *Journal of Contemporary Ethnography* 17:435–452.

Sternberg, R. J. 1990. *Metaphors of Mind: Conceptions of the Nature of Human Intelligence.* New York: Cambridge.

Sterponi, L. 2003. "Account Episodes in Family Discourse: The Making of Morality in Everyday Interaction." *Discourse Studies* 5:79–100.

Stets, J., and J. Turner, eds. 2006. *Handbook of the Sociology of Emotions.* New York: Springer.

Stevens, D., G. Kiger, and P. J. Riley. 2001. "Working Hard and Hardly Working: Domestic Labor and Marital Satisfaction Among Dual-Earner Couples." *Journal of Marriage and Family* 63:514–526.

Stockard, J. 2002. *Marriage in Culture: Practice and Meaning Across Diverse Societies.* New York: Harcourt.

Stone, L. 2000. *Kinship and Gender: An Introduction,* 2nd ed. Boulder, CO: Westview.

Straus, M. A., and C. L. Yodanis. 1995. "Marital Power." In *Encyclopedia of Marriage and the Family,* Vol. 2, edited by D. Levinson, pp. 437–442. New York: Macmillan.

Strauss, A., S. Fagerhaugh, B. Suczek, and C. Wiener. 1982. "Sentimental Work in the Technologized Hospital." *Sociology of Health and Illness* 4:254–278.

Strydom, P. 2007. "A Cartography of Contemporary Cognitive Social Theory." *European Journal of Social Theory* 10:339–356.

Thoits, P. A. 1989. "The Sociology of Emotions." *Annual Review of Sociology* 15:317–342.

———. 1996. "Managing the Emotions of Others." *Symbolic Interaction* 19:85–109.

Thompson, L. 1991. "Family Work: Women's Sense of Fairness." *Journal of Family Issues* 12:181–196.

Thorne, B. 1993. *Gender Play: Girls and Boys in School.* New Brunswick, NJ: Rutgers.

Tichenor, V. J. 2005. *Earning More and Getting Less: Why Successful Wives Can't Buy Equality.* New Brunswick, NJ: Rutgers.

Turner, J., and J. Stets. 2005. *The Sociology of Emotions.* New York: Cambridge.

Twiggs, J., E. J. McQuillan, and M. M. Ferree. 1998. "Meaning and Measurement: Reconceptualizing Measures of the Division of Household Labor." *Journal of Marriage and the Family* 61:712–724.

Ulmer, J. T., and J. W. Spencer. 1999. "The Contribution of an Interactionist Approach to Research and Theory on Criminal Careers." *Theoretical Criminology* 3:95–124.

Valsiner, J., and R. van der Veer. 2000. *The Social Mind: Construction of the Idea.* New York: Cambridge.

van Brakel, J. 1994. "Emotions: A Cross-Cultural Perspective on Forms of Life." *Social Perspectives on Emotion* 2:179–237.

Vryan, K. D., P. A. Adler, and P. Adler. 2003. "Identity." In *Handbook of Symbolic Interactionism,* edited by L. T. Reynolds and N. J. Herman-Kinney, pp. 367–390. Walnut Creek, CA: AltaMira.

Walzer, S. 2006. "Children's Stories of Divorce." In *Couples, Kids, and Family Life,* edited by J. F. Gubrium and J. A. Holstein, pp. 162–177. New York: Oxford.

Wanderer, J. J. 1987. "Simmel's Forms of Experiencing: The Adventure as Symbolic Work." *Symbolic Interaction* 10:21–28.

Warner, R. L. 1986. "Alternative Strategies for Measuring Household Division of Labor." *Journal of Family Issues* 7:79–95.

Waskul, D., and P. Vannini. 2008. "Smell, Odor, and Somatic Work: Sense-Making and Sensory Management." *Social Psychology Quarterly* 71:53–71.

Watson, G., and J. G. Goulet. 1998. "What Can Ethnomethodology Say About Power?" *Qualitative Inquiry* 4:96–113.

Watzlawick, P. 2006. "Self-Fulfilling Prophecies." In *The Production of Reality,* 4th ed., edited by J. O'Brien, pp. 382–394. Thousand Oaks, CA: Pine Forge.

Weinberg, D. 1997. "The Social Construction of Non-Human Agency: The Case of Mental Disorder." *Social Problems* 44:217–234.

———. 2001. "Self-Empowerment in Two Therapeutic Communities." In *Institutional Selves: Troubled Identities in a Postmodern World,* edited by J. F. Gubrium and J. A. Holstein, pp. 84–104. New York: Oxford.

———. 2008. "The Philosophical Foundations of Constructionist Research." In *Handbook of Constructionist Research,* edited by J. A. Holstein and J. F. Gubrium, pp. 13–39. New York: Guilford.

Whalen, J., and D. H. Zimmerman. 1998. "Observations on the Display and Management of Emotion in Naturally Occurring Activities: The Case of 'Hysteria' in Calls to 9-1-1." *Social Psychology Quarterly* 61:141–159.

Wharton, A. S. 1999. "The Psychosocial Consequences of Emotional Labor." *Annals of the American Academy of Political and Social Science* 561:158–176.

White, G. M. 2000. "Representing Emotional Meaning: Category, Metaphor, Schema, Discourse." In *Handbook of Emotions,* edited by M. Lewis and J. M. Haviland-Jones, pp. 30–44. New York: Guilford.

Whyte, W. F. 1943. *Street Corner Society.* Chicago: University of Chicago Press.

Wierzbicka, A. 1999. *Emotions Across Languages and Cultures: Diversity and Universals.* Cambridge: Cambridge.

Wilcox, W. B., and S. L. Nock. 2006. "What's Love Got to Do with It? Equality, Equity, Commitment, and Women's Marital Quality." *Social Forces* 84:1321–1345.

Wiley, N. 2006. "Pragmatism and the Dialogical Self." *International Journal for Dialogical Science* 1:5–21.

Wolkomir, M. 2001. "Emotion Work, Commitment, and the Authentication of the Self: The Case of Gay and Ex-Gay Christian Support Groups." *Journal of Contemporary Ethnography* 30:305–334.

Wolkomir, M., and J. Powers. 2007. "Helping Women and Protecting the Self: The Challenge of Emotional Labor in an Abortion Clinic." *Qualitative Sociology* 30:153–169.

Woolgar, S., and D. Pawluch. 1985. "Ontological Gerrymandering: The Anatomy of Social Problems Explanations." *Social Problems* 32:214–227.

Wortham, S., and K. Jackson. 2008. "Educational Constructionisms." In *Handbook of Constructionist Research,* edited by J. A. Holstein and J. F. Gubrium, pp. 107–127. New York: Guilford.

Zelizer, V. 1994. *The Social Meaning of Money.* New York: Basic Books.

Zerubavel, E. 1991. *The Fine Line: Making Distinctions in Everyday Life.* New York: Free Press.

———. 1995. "The Rigid, the Fuzzy, and the Flexible: Notes on the Mental Sculpting of Academic Identity." *Social Research* 62:1093–1106.

———. 1997. *Social Mindscapes: An Invitation to Cognitive Sociology.* Cambridge, MA: Harvard University Press.

———. 2007. "Generally Speaking: The Logic and Mechanics of Social Pattern Analysis." *Sociological Forum* 22:131–145.

Zimmerman, D. H., and M. Pollner. 1970. "The Everyday World as a Phenomenon." In *Understanding Everyday Life,* edited by J. D. Douglas, pp. 80–103. Chicago: Aldine.

Zurcher, L. A. 1982. "The Staging of Emotion: A Dramaturgical Analysis." *Symbolic Interaction* 5:1–22.

Index

Agency, 1, 3, 13, 28, 31, 44, 46n11, 48–49, 51, 61, 76, 91–92, 96, 98, 134
Antaki, Charles, 42
Atkinson, Paul, 17
Authenticity, 46n7, 54, 63–65, 85

Baca Zinn, Maxine, 77
Benson, Kenneth, 13–14
Berard, Timothy, 24n8
Berbrier, Mitch, 130n8, 132
Berger, Peter, 1, 3, 7, 13–14, 19, 91
Biographical work, 17, 96–98
Blood, Robert, 90
Blumer, Herbert, 2–3, 7, 29–33, 38, 42, 43, 45n2
Boundary work, 15, 33–34, 114
Bracketing, 5, 7, 16, 18, 38, 46n8, 55, 59, 65, 78–79, 92, 115, 140
Brekhus, Wayne, 36
Bright, Richard, 88–89

Causality, 6–7, 10–12, 24n4, 24n6, 28, 90–92, 123–126, 134
Chair (as an example), viii, 3, 16
Chang, Johannes Han-Yin, 110–112, 117–124, 127
Clanton, Gordon, 49
Class, 13–14, 110–112, 118, 121–122
Cognitive Self Change (CSC), 39–40

Collins, Randall, 32, 108–110, 117–121, 123–124, 127
Conflict theory, 107–108, 126, 128
Constructionist synonyms, 1, 4, 6–7, 13, 38, 68, 127, 135, 142n3
Contextual constructionism, 140
Contingency, viii, 8–10, 12, 14, 24n4, 24n5, 31, 33, 48–49, 102
Conventional wisdom about equality and inequality, 107–108, 117, 126
Conversational work, 16
Coulter, Jeff, 44
CSC. See Cognitive Self Change

Defining concepts (difficulty of), 2, 49–50, 57, 69n2, 69n5, 73–74, 88–89, 99, 115, 118–119
Deutsch, Francine, 89, 91–92
Devault, Marjorie, 16, 24n9
Deviance, 1, 4, 11–13, 127
Dewey, John, 104
Dichotomies, 19, 20, 33–34
Documentary method of interpretation, 35–37, 45n4, 121, 126
Domains of relevance, 93–94, 115–117
Durkheim, Emile, 36

Edwards, Derek, 44

Equality and inequality, 107–108, 117, 126
Essentialism, 10–12, 77
Etcetera principle, 129n5. *See also* Defining concepts
Ethnomethodology, 2, 3, 43, 135

Fernandez-Kelley, Patricia, 77
Fishman, Pamela, 16, 24n9
Fox, Kathryn, 39–40
Frith, Hannah, 68
Functionalism, 107–108, 126, 128
Furedi, Frank, 65–66

Garfinkel, Harold, 37, 45n4
Gender, 16, 24n9, 52, 100
Generic social processes, 1, 38, 113–114, 129
Gergen, Kenneth, 137, 142n3
Gergen, Mary, 137
Goffman, Erving, 31, 51
Gordon, Steven, 49
Gubrium, Jaber, 9–10, 18, 38–40, 44, 45n6, 80, 98

Hacking, Ian, vii, 8, 139
Hochschild, Arlie, 21, 47, 49–55, 63–68, 89, 91
Holstein, James, 9–10, 18, 80
Houseley, William, 17

IEM. *See* Interpretive emotion management
IFD. *See* Interpretive family diversity
Indexicality, 3, 42, 129n5
Inequality, 10, 13, 18, 19, 23, 93; and equality, 107–108, 117, 126
Interpretive emotion management (IEM), 55–68, 124; ambiguity of bodily states, 57–59; defining emotions, 55–57; employment, 62–63; interpersonal management, 62; neglect of, 68; norms, 56, 61–62; social problems, 65–66; upgrading and downgrading emotional labels, 59–61, 66
Interpretive family diversity (IFD), 4, 9–10, 17, 22, 72, 77–86; constructionist analyses, 81–84; defining family, 78–79; implications for policy, 84–85; kinds of diversity, 79–81; neglect of, 84
Interpretive social constructionism (ISC): as a continuum with OSC, viii, 17–18, 20, 44, 137–138; definition of, vii, 2–5, 132; differences from ISC, 132–135; emotions, 55–68, 124; family diversity, 77–86; marital equality, 92–104; mind, 36–45; overlaps with ISC, viii, 28, 85, 128, 135–138; social inequality, 13–14, 18, 107ff; theoretical roots of, 2, 12, 19, 115, 135, 140–141

Kimball, Gayle, 88–89
Kitzinger, Celia, 68
Kleinman, Sherryl, 54
Knudson-Martin, Carmen, 89

Luckmann, Thomas, 1, 3, 7, 13–14, 19

Mahoney, Anne, 89
Maines, David, 1–2, 6–7, 17, 129n4
Mannheim, Karl, 35
Marital equality, 14, 22–23, 87, 114–117; constructionist analyses, 90–92, 96–98, 100–101; defining equality, 88–89, 92–94; division of labor, 89–91, 93–96, 99–102; equality as an interpretation or claim, 92–98; equality as an objective condition, 87–92; measuring equality, 89–90, 94–96; "perceptions of fairness" literature, 99–100
Marx, Karl, 110–111
Mead, George Herbert, 29–32, 37–38, 141n1
Metaphors, 80–81
Miller, Gale, 83–84
Mills, C. Wright, 66
Mind, 20–21, 25n10, 27, 124; in animals, 30, 37–38; cognitive socialization, 33; criminal mind-sets, 39–40; flexible mind-sets, 35;

fuzzy mind-sets, 34–35, 40; as an interpretation or claim, 36–43; mind work, 37; as an objective entity or ability, 27–36; rigid mind-sets, 34–36
Motive talk, 7, 11, 31, 39–40, 42–43, 46n11, 46n12, 78, 83–84, 123–126, 130n6, 137
Myth versus reality, 5, 11, 18, 31, 38–39, 44, 46n8, 85, 99, 128. *See also* Authenticity; Bracketing

Obama, Barack, 62
Objective emotion management (OEM), 47–55, 66–68, 114; defining emotions, 49–50; in employment, 47, 52–55; interpersonal management, 52; norms of, 51–52, 56; and social problems, 53–55; surface and deep acting, 50–54, 64, 66
Objective family diversity, 73–77, 84–86; constructionist analyses, 76–77; defining family, 73–74; kinds of diversity, 74–75; policy implications, 84–85
Objective social constructionism (OSC): as a continuum with ISC, viii, 17–18, 20, 44, 137–138; definition of, vii, 5–7, 132; differences from ISC, 132–135; and emotions, 47–55, 66–68, 114; and family diversity, 73–77, 84–86; and marital equality, 87–92, 98–104; and mind, 16, 27–36; overlaps with ISC, viii, 85, 128, 135–138; and social inequality, 13–14, 18, 107; theoretical roots of, 5, 12, 19, 135, 140–141
O'Brien, Jodi, 8–10, 24n5
OEM. *See* Objective emotion management
OFD. *See* Objective family diversity
Ore, Tracy, 10–12
Organizations, 13–14
Othering, 114, 119
OSC. *See* Objective social constructionism

Parallel arguments, 8, 28, 48, 73, 131, 139
Pollner, Melvin, 13–14
Potter, Jonathan, 44
Power, 14, 93, 96–98, 116, 120–121, 133
Purposes, viii, 3, 4, 19, 41–43, 79, 98

Qualitative methods, 5, 31–32, 35–36, 38, 43, 68, 100–102, 125–126, 135–136; studying expert informants, 101; studying expert practitioners, 101
Quantitative methods, 36, 90, 94–95, 99–100, 109, 112–113, 121–122

Reflexivity, 3, 42, 93, 128
Reification, 12, 14, 19, 24n8
Religion, 28, 116–117
Riesman, David, 36
Romney, Mitt, 42, 46n9
Rosenberg, Morris, 58–59
Rosenblatt, Paul, 80–81

Sanders, Clinton, 37–38, 40, 44, 45n6
Schachter, Stanley, 57–58
Scheff, Thomas, 32
Schutz, Alfred, 3, 93, 115–116
Schwalbe, Michael, 13–14, 24n7, 112–114, 119–120, 122–123, 125, 127
Schwartz, Pepper, 88–89, 99
Self-fulfilling prophecies, 5–6, 69n7
Singer, Jerome, 57–58
Smith, Allen, 54
Smith, Dorothy, 71
SNAF. *See* Standard North American Family
Social constraints, 3, 28, 31, 51–53, 61–62, 67, 76–77, 82–83, 91–92
Social problems, 3–4, 17–18, 31, 40, 65–66, 127; social problems work, 17
Social reform, 23, 84–85, 102–104, 134–135, 137
Standard North American Family (SNAF), 21–22
Stapleton, Jean, 88–89

Staske, Shirley, 60–62
Status, 52–53, 109–110
Stets, Jan, 68
Stockard, Janice, 75–77
Stratification. *See* Inequality
Strict constructionism, 18, 140
Symbolic interaction, 2–3, 29–37

Thomas theorem, 7
Thought work, 16
Tichenor, Veronica, 100–101
Turner, Jonathan, 68

Typification, 115–117, 123

van Brakel, Jaap, 50

Wells, Barbara, 77
Whalen, Jack, 62–63
Wiley, Norbert, 32
Wolfe, Donald, 90
Work, 14–17, 100–101

Zerubavel, Eviatar, 32–37, 42–44, 45n2
Zimmerman, Don, 62–63

About the Book

Has constructionism become a victim of its own success? Scott Harris argues that, as more scholars adopt the approach, its key concepts are being used in differing and even contradictory ways—thus undercutting the vitality of its application as a research tool. To help clear the waters, he critically examines current debates and delivers a powerful call to launch a renewed constructionism.

Harris traces how constructionism has evolved into two distinct perspectives—interpretive and objective—as he delves into timely topics such as social inequality, marital equality, and family diversity. He also evaluates each perspective's strengths, as well as its unique contributions. Sharpened definitions of the goals and vocabulary of both schools of thought, he demonstrates, give us a more lucid understanding of the pressing social issues of our time.

Scott R. Harris is associate professor of sociology at Saint Louis University and author of *The Meanings of Marital Equality*.

.